Twayne's United States Authors Series

Sylvia E. Bowman, *Editor*

INDIANA UNIVERSITY

Richard Wilbur

RICHARD WILBUR

By DONALD L. HILL

University of Michigan

 117

Twayne Publishers, Inc.   ::   New York

FOR HELEN

Preface

THIS BOOK about Richard Wilbur is not an impartial study. Ever since I first read some of Wilbur's early poems about fifteen years ago, I have been convinced that he is one of the most accomplished and rewarding poets writing today. I am sure that many other readers not yet well acquainted with his work might come to feel as I do about it, and I hope that my commentary may be of some use to them. I think it may be, because much of Wilbur, without being at all forbidding or hermetic, is not easy to read well. But I should say immediately that I have not attempted to write a free-standing book. Instead, I have assumed a reader who is ready to provide himself with copies of Wilbur's books, to read them carefully, and to keep them open as he compares his impressions with mine.

In discussing the poems I have relied largely on that disputed device, the paraphrase. Whatever the success of my own efforts, I do not doubt that the paraphrase may have its value. I am conscious that this value will vary for different readers, and I hope it will be taken for granted that the paraphrase never says what the poem says in its immeasurably richer way. A paraphrase is only a study aid, like a dictionary, or even more like a talkative companion who keeps pointing to certain passages, raising questions of interpretation, and then supplying his own answers. Something, after all, can be learned about poems from taking this long way around.

In the first four chapters I have discussed Wilbur's four collections of poems in the order of their publication. Within the chapters I have grouped the poems into loose subject categories of my own devising: war, nature, art, and so on. Many of the poems might equally well be considered in other categories. Although I have not discussed all the poems of any of the books, I have had something to say about all those that mean much to me, and I do not think I have passed over any poems of major importance.

The reader will see that I am sometimes doubtful about the meaning of a passage or of some larger aspect of a poem, and he will probably think that I should have been doubtful in some places where I am not. In addition to the interpretations, which are the most important feature of the study, I have often traced interconnections among poems, pointed out major themes and technical achievements, attempted to meet certain attacks on the poems, and offered my own critical opinions. The final chapter is an effort to characterize Wilbur's general position, ideologically and technically, and to locate him with reference to some of his contemporaries.

In a study of this kind, it would always be useful, to say the least, to have the author's answers to one's questions. I have never met Mr. Wilbur, nor have I written to consult him about anything in this book except the biographical facts, which he kindly consented to verify. I have refrained not from lack of curiosity but from two articles of belief: first, that this kind of study can have a certain usefulness without the aid of the poet; and, second, that a man who has taken the trouble to write and publish poems ought not to be asked to interpret them. Mr. Wilbur is, therefore, in no way responsible for anything I have said here.

I do wish to acknowledge with gratitude a debt to my friend and colleague Donald Hall, from whom I have learned a great deal, not only about Wilbur's work but about contemporary poetry generally. Mr. Hall generously read the manuscript at two different stages and made many valuable suggestions. To Wilbur's publishers, Harcourt, Brace and World, I owe thanks for permission to quote from his books of poems; to the University of Michigan for a sabbatical leave which I spent working on the book; and finally to my wife Helen for sympathetic interest, advice, and labor beyond thanks.

DONALD L. HILL

Ann Arbor, Michigan, 1964

Acknowledgments

Permission has kindly been granted by Harcourt, Brace and World, Inc., to quote from Wilbur's collections of poems: *The Beautiful Changes, Ceremony, Things of This World,* and *Advice to a Prophet*; by Twayne Publishers, Inc., to quote from Wilbur's article "The Genie in the Bottle," in *Mid-Century American Poets,* edited by John Ciardi; and by *The New Yorker* to quote the poem "Seed Leaves."

Contents

Chronology

1921   March 1, Richard Wilbur was born in New York City, the son of Lawrence Wilbur, an artist; his mother's father and grandfather had been newspaper editors.

1923   Family moved to a farm in New Jersey.

1938   Entered Amherst College, where he edited the college newspaper and thought of journalism as a career. In the summers he was a vagrant and "toured most of the forty-eight states by freight-car."[1] Poetry was not his primary interest then, he says, and adds that "it was not until World War II took me to Cassino, Anzio, and the Siegfried Line that I began to versify in earnest."[2]

1942   Graduated from Amherst and married Charlotte Ward. Served with the 36th Infantry Division in Europe.

1947   *The Beautiful Changes* published. Received the M.A. at Harvard and was elected a member of the Society of Fellows.

1950   *Ceremony* published. Appointed Assistant Professor at Harvard.

1951   John Ciardi has recorded this grateful memory: "In 1951 when I was teaching at Harvard, a number of friends—all of them valued poets—organized a small group that met irregularly to talk about the poems each brought with him. The group continued to meet for two years or so through a number of memorable evenings. The regular core of that group consisted of Richard Eberhart, John Holmes, Archibald MacLeish, Richard Wilbur, and myself. I am indebted to those meetings for some of the happiest and best poet's talk I have ever heard."[3]

1952   Began year's leave in New Mexico as a Guggenheim Fellow.

1954   Won a Prix de Rome Fellowship and spent 1954-55 in Italy.

1955   *A Bestiary* published, a book of quotations about beasts selected from various authors by Wilbur and illustrated by Alexander Calder. Wilbur's verse translation of Molière's *Le Misanthrope* published in book form and produced at The Poets' Theatre in Cambridge. Appointed to a professorship at Wellesley College.

1956 *Things of This World* published. In December the operetta *Candide,* with music by Leonard Bernstein, book by Lillian Hellman, and most of the lyrics by Wilbur, appeared at the Martin Beck Theatre in New York.

1957 Won the Pulitzer Prize, the National Book Award, and the Edna St. Vincent Millay Memorial Award for *Things of This World.*

1958 Became General Editor of the Dell Laurel Poetry Series.

1959 Moved to Wesleyan University as Professor of English.

1961 *Advice to a Prophet* published.

1963 Awarded a second Guggenheim Fellowship. Verse translation of Molière's *Tartuffe* published. *Loudmouse,* a children's book, published.

1964 *Tartuffe* co-recipient of the Bollingen Prize for translation.

Richard Wilbur

CHAPTER 1

The Beautiful Changes (1947)

I *Wilbur's Early Style*

ONE CONSPICUOUS FEATURE of Richard Wilbur's first collection of poems, *The Beautiful Changes,* is its meditative, speculative disposition, evident both in the choice and in the treatment of subjects. It is a poetry of ideas, moderately learned and allusive, strict in its logic as in its phrasing, given to weighing alternative attitudes, fond of arguments and of their consequences. Wilbur often begins by describing a scene or an object and concludes by making a moral, epistemological, or metaphysical point about it. The speaker is observant and reflective but not detached; often a poem will proceed by drawing him into an emotional relationship with what has caught his attention. He enjoys an extended definition, as in "Grace" or in "Lightness," and everywhere shows his pleasure in the multiple meanings of words. He develops a poem with a rigor and coherence that recall John Donne, and with some of the same delight in clever turns of logic and in the sudden vistas of paradox.

Intellectuality is common enough in modern poetry. In itself it has no merit at all, and in clumsy hands it may prove to be a blight. It is best to keep back judgment for particular poems and note only that Wilbur is one of those poets who build their poems on a logical framework. This characteristic begins to be remarkable or distinctive only when we notice, as we must, that in some ways Wilbur is an unusually sensuous poet. In his early poems this sensuousness expresses itself partly in the constant appeal of his lines to the ear and partly in the sharpness, justice, and fullness of the descriptive detail. His penchant for seeing scenes and objects (or hearing sounds, or touching things) in the light of general ideas does not prevent his giving close attention to the things observed, and his inferences are well-rooted in his objects. He respects the individuality of objects and tries, like any modern describer, to see them freshly—that is, without preconceptions—and to break through to a sense of their uniqueness:

> A bell diphthonging in an atmosphere
> Of shying night air summons some to prayer
> Down in the town, two deep lone miles from here,
>
> Yet wallows faint or sudden everywhere,
> In every ear, as if the twist wind wrung
> Some ten years' tangled echoes from the air.
>
> . . . .
>
> ("A Dubious Night")

or

> Sycamore, trawled by the tilt sun,
> Still scrawl your trunk with tattered lights, and keep
> The spotted toad upon your patchy bark, . . .
>
> . . . .
>
> ("Poplar, Sycamore")

A surprising energy and boldness, without loss of accuracy, animate his verbs and adjectives, and their precision often depends not only on their visual suggestiveness but also on their sounds, which are delicately enlisted to aid in the description.

The interest of Wilbur's description thus depends partly on his capacity for close disinterested observation and partly on his linguistic ingenuity—or, more broadly, on his technical skill. This skill, which even in his first book deserves to be called brilliant, naturally extends far beyond description into every aspect of his work—into the whole organization and movement or pace of his poems and into all their intricate inner relationships. No one has ever denied his technical mastery; the only question is whether it amounts too often to mere virtuosity. The virtuosity is the more apparent because he writes almost always in strict forms, some conventional and some original, with rhyme, regular stanza forms, and traditional meters. When a poet accepts a clear set of rules, his technical success is easier to judge than when he takes a broader freedom. Even in his first poems Wilbur shows an astonishing ease and vigor within the most confining forms. His skills include the ability to achieve a poise and self-assurance beautiful in themselves—what earned his work the ambiguous epithet "elegant"; an almost unfailingly telling adjustment of thought to the sentence structure; and a constant word-play that is exciting because it requires a constant revaluation of familiar things.

[18]

The Beautiful Changes (1947)

Another characteristic of the early poems is a pervasive good humor, a sweetness of spirit, unusual among the major poets of the century. There is no despair here, no prophetic warning, no denunciation, no fanaticism, no sourness or disgust, little satire, and not much violence. In the war poems and in a few others some of the ugliest aspects of life are faced or touched on; some poems conceive of sad truths or moods; but the dominant tone of the book is one of humor and high spirits. Can a major poet be good-humored in our time? Wilbur's work presents the question, and I must return to it.

I have named four qualities—admittedly overlapping—that seem to me apparent in *The Beautiful Changes*: a speculative and logical temper, sharp and true observation, technical virtuosity, and a kind of amused good humor. Most of this chapter is devoted to giving them some degree of illustration or demonstration. Still other qualities, less prominent perhaps, but no less pervasive, are discernible to the reader as he studies Wilbur's style in particular poems.

Meanwhile, his technique and especially his attachment to strict forms deserve to be considered in some detail. Almost all of the forty-two poems in *The Beautiful Changes* are highly organized. All but five, for example, are rhymed, a high proportion nowadays. The rhyme schemes are sometimes simple and conventional, occasionally complex and conventional (as in the two sonnets "O" and "Praise in Summer"), often complex and unconventional. Sometimes when the rhyme scheme itself is familiar, the number of feet in the lines varies in unfamiliar patterns, as in "My Father Paints the Summer" (*ababcc*, but *552632*) or "Lightness" (*aabbcc*, but *455445*, etc.). Almost always the first stanza serves as an exactly followed model for the others. There are several poems in which short stanzas have corresponding rhymes (*abxc, abxc;* or *xaxb, xaxb*), and a few other linking devices appear, such as terza rima (both *444* and *555*). Some poems are built on extremely elaborate stanzas, as is "Sunlight Is Imagination" (*4a 4b 4b 5a 4a 2c 2a 1c 5d*); each of the five stanzas after the first is introduced by a one-stress line rhyming with the final line of the preceding stanza. As for meters, Wilbur confines himself as a rule to iambics, usually strict. Only a few poems are in what might be called loose or "strong-stress" rhythms ("Mined Country," "Potato," "The Beautiful Changes"). One poem ("Lightness") is chiefly anapestic. But the aural impression of these strict stanzas is often modified, indeed sometimes annihilated, by a very free and characteristic use of enjambment. He gets some of his happiest effects by ticking off his rhymes quietly and casually, all in their places, while running the often elaborate sentences of a connected argument through the line-ends and stanza divisions. A good example is "A Dutch Courtyard":

> What wholly blameless fun
> To stand and look at pictures. Ah, they are
> Immune to us. This courtyard may appear
> To be consumed with sun,
>
> Most mortally to burn,
> Yet it is quite beyond the reach of eyes
> Or thoughts, this place and moment oxidize;
> This girl will never turn,
>
> Cry what you dare . . .

If we compare Wilbur's poems with those of the other fourteen poets in John Ciardi's anthology, *Mid-Century American Poets* (1950), his formal strictness and inventiveness stand out even in that company of pattern-makers. And his interest in strict forms is as characteristic of *Advice to a Prophet*, the volume published in 1961, as it is of *The Beautiful Changes* and of the two volumes in between: *Ceremony* (1950) and *Things of This World* (1956).

Wilbur once wrote: "As regards technique, a critic has called me one of the 'New Formalists,' and I will accept the label provided it be understood that to try to revive the force of rhyme and other formal devices, by reconciling them with the experimental gains of the past several decades, is itself sufficiently experimental."[1] This is well said, but it is not followed, as the reader may wish it were, by an essay giving answers to the questions it raises. "To *revive* the force of rhyme and other formal devices"—what theory of the present weakness of rhyme and other formal devices is hinted at here? Unrhymed verse, free verse, loose forms of various kinds have had a certain vogue since Carl Sandburg and Amy Lowell; Ciardi's anthology includes a number of examples. Yet Wilbur's contemporaries had by no means abandoned rhyme; both their poems and their comments in Ciardi's anthology show that. Yeats? Frost? Eliot? Auden? Thomas? Of these only Eliot had given up rhyme entirely in his later work, and all these poets had continued to show in practice their reliance on "other formal devices." The importance of free verse and of loose forms between 1915 and 1945 is often exaggerated. Donald Hall argues truly, I think, that most of the best poetry of the period was Wilbur's kind of poetry—"a poetry of symmetry, intellect, irony, and wit."[2]

What were "the experimental gains of the last several decades" with which the "formal devices" might be reconciled? Wilbur's answer to this question can be inferred, one assumes, from his essay "The Genie in the Bottle," published in *Mid-Century American Poets*.[3] Such gains would include (he would say) the freedom to draw words from all modes and levels of Anglo-American speech, including the "poetic," and on occasion from other languages; an insistence on the value of irony and paradox when properly used; a subject matter ideally limitless; the submergence or transmutation of ideas so that they are not easily extricable in paraphrase; and a refusal to supplement imagery by "equivalent" statement. But, as he warns in that same essay, "works of art can almost never be truthfully described as applications of principles," and the only valid answers to questions about the poet's technique lie in the poems themselves.

II *The War*

Wilbur testifies that although he began to write poems "early," his first serious poems were occasioned by his experience in the war: "One does not use poetry for its major purposes, as a means of organizing oneself and the world, until one's world somehow gets out of hand. A general cataclysm is not required; the disorder must be personal and may be wholly so, but poetry, to be vital, does seem to need a periodic acquaintance with the threat of Chaos."[4] This lucid statement is of interest to the student of Wilbur's work not because of its singularity—most poets writing today probably hold to some version of the doctrine—but because the evidence of disorder is so thoroughly submerged in most of his poems. Some critics would think better of the poems if the struggle were carried on nearer the surface, revealing itself more clearly in whirlpools and bubbles. They find his countermeasures almost too successful, his usual poise an indication that disorder is no match for him. Others see in this poise not only a technical but a spiritual strength. The question is an appropriate one, of course, only if it is asked of poems in which Wilbur is using poetry for "its major purposes." Many of his poems have more modest aims, but no poems in *The Beautiful Changes* could be more properly examined for what they reveal of struggle and imposed order than those based on his experience in the war.

The book includes only seven poems that deal explicitly with the war: "Tywater," "Mined Country," "Potato," "First Snow in Alsace," "On the Eyes of an SS Officer," "Place Pigalle," and "The Peace of Cities." (One other poem, "Violet and Jasper," though it could not otherwise be identified as one of the war poems, is paged with them and may belong in the group.) Each poem seems to be based on some particular experience. Though all are clever in one way or another, some of them show signs of uncertainty or misjudgment; sometimes cleverness is not just what the subject requires. "On the Eyes of an SS Officer," for example, fails to rise to the unavoidable seriousness of its theme. The first and second stanzas present the explorer Amundsen and the Bombay saint as men who worshipped single natural forces of a terrible strength (the northern ice and the southern sun), who found in them a holy purity, and who suffered and died in their service. Stanza three contrasts these two fanatics with a third, the SS officer:

> But this one's iced or ashen eyes devise,
> Foul purities, in flesh their wilderness,
> Their fire; I ask my makeshift God of this
> My opulent bric-a-brac earth to damn his eyes.

The saint's eyes have been burned out, made "ashen," by staring at the sun. The sense in which Amundsen's eyes can be called "iced" is not so clear; he seems never to have gone blind, but possibly we are to recall that he was lost forever, and thus of course frozen, in the Arctic region in 1928. The officer's eyes too are ruined (made "iced or ashen") by what holds them fascinated—and this is flesh, "their wilderness,/Their fire." (I take "Foul purities" to be an epithet not of "eyes" but of "wilderness" and "fire.") Unlike these three fanatics, the poet has a "make-shift God" and lives on an "opulent bric-a-brac earth" where many things are of value. The parallel between the officer's obsession and those of the other two can be worked out, but not without a good deal of straining; and troublesome differences may continue to assert themselves, as they do in my reading of the poem. While at least one of the lines is memorable ("At the cold end of the world's spit") and while stanza two is witty in its diction, the poem reads finally as if it were a device to give the poet a chance to use the cliché "damn his eyes" with a serious meaning. To invest a slang phrase with fresh meaning for a serious purpose is a cherished right of the modern poet, but here I think the moral or human stakes are too high. The loathing required by Wilbur's own conception of the officer is missing, and the hazard fails.

But some of the other war poems are even cleverer without showing any inadequacy of feeling. "Tywater," on the death of an army corporal from Texas, is a good example. It starts with an ironical contrast of the corporal's death with that of a knight in an old romance:

> Death of Sir Nihil, book the *nth,*
> Upon the charred and clotted sward,
> Lacking the lily of our Lord,
> Alases of the hyacinth.

The stanza reminds us of the long history, pagan and Christian, during which men died—or might die—not alone and not with blank finality, but valued and mourned in a sympathetic universe. But stanza four tells us that Tywater's death in "book the *nth*" on a modern battlefield is unceremonious, instantaneous, and final. "When he was hit, his body turned/To clumsy dirt before it fell." The first term of the epithet "Sir Nihil" makes Tywater a member of the ancient profession of knights or fighting men; the second term is appropriate because he no longer exists, but it may hint further that in some sense he has never been a knight.

The second stanza drops the mock-medieval idiom and takes up a racy mock-Texan to describe Tywater's skill at knife-throwing, while the third stanza on his lariat-spinning is a little marvel not only of precise visual imagery but also of word sounds matched to the action and to each other in a tightly woven pattern of internal and end rhyme, assonance, and alliteration. If we consider Tywater's gear and accomplishments, his military role, and more broadly the demands made on any soldier for honorable and courageous service to the point of self-sacrifice, we may be persuaded for a moment by the suggestion of the first stanza that Tywater is a modern knight who has something of the greatness of spirit to which the best medieval or legendary

knights aspired and who is dedicated to some such code of
service as they stood for. But no; the fourth stanza comments on
his limitations: "The violent, neat and practiced skill/Was all he
loved and all he learned." He lacked even the usual range of
interests, sympathies, and aspirations. There is no significant
personal connection between him and anyone else. He is a
specialist, hardly a person at all, only a skilled hand on knife
and rope, a holler and a grin. His death is peculiarly fitting in
its violence, suddenness, and efficiency; it is exactly like that of
the swallow impaled on the blade of his whistling knife.

And there is nothing left over, he was all skill; and that is why
the writer of his epitaph is at a loss: "And what to say of him,
God knows." Though the line has a casual sound, the cliché
"God knows," used carefully, makes its point: the speaker would
not attempt a final judgment, even if he could find the words
for it, because he appreciates the mystery of personality, the
partiality of our grasp of life and fate. The epitaph, when it
comes, is amusingly diffident: "Such violence. And such repose."
And yet how shrewd is that full stop within the line, suggesting,
as it does, not only the speaker's baffled hesitation as he gropes
for the words he needs, and then the spontaneity of the happy
stroke with which the line ends—but suggesting also with a perfect tact the absolute gulf between life and death, our appreciation of which is the more poignant because Tywater is not merely active but violent, not merely violent but skillful, and because
the power of Death is such that his passage from violence to
repose is instantaneous. "Tywater" seems to me a much wittier
poem than "On the Eyes," and yet its wit involves no deficiency
of seriousness or humane feeling.

Often in these early poems, as sometimes later, Wilbur imitates
or echoes the style of other poets. "Place Pigalle" is an exercise,
probably a parody, in several different manners, the easiest of
which to identify is that of Eliot's early poems. In such passages
as these we can enjoy Wilbur's mimicking, but we are out of
touch with his own sensibility. The style of "Potato," on the
other hand, while not without mannerism, retains its individual
character as Wilbur applies to "the mean earth-apples" a freshly
observant eye and nose:

> An underground grower, blind and a common brown;
> Got a misshapen look, it's nudged where it could;
> Simple as soil yet crowded as earth with all.

> Cut open raw, it looses a cool clean stench,
> Mineral acid seeping from pores of prest meal;
> It is like breaching a strangely refreshing tomb:
>
> Therein the taste of first stones, the hands of dead slaves,
> Waters men drank in the earliest frightful woods,
> Flint chips, and peat, and the cinders of buried camps.

Those who survived the war were ready to praise the potato; they had been forced back to the expedients of their remotest ancestors: "It was potatoes saved us, they kept us alive." The potato reminds them that they have lived by "vestigial virtues," upheld by the strength of all who have suffered from hunger and from persecution (or so I interpret the difficult seventh stanza). Men survive not only through meeting the dramatic crises of wartime, but also through patience in dull discomfort. After the potato has been given its full significance as a symbol, the tone relaxes and attention is directed again, as at the beginning, to the object itself, a turn that charms away heaviness:

> Oh, it will not bear polish, the ancient potato,
> Needn't be nourished by Caesars, will blow anywhere,
> Hidden by nature, counted-on, stubborn and blind.
>
> You may have noticed the bush that it pushes to air,
> Comical-delicate, sometimes with second-rate flowers
> Awkward and milky and beautiful only to hunger.

This style, so casual in tone and so indifferent to minor irregularities, is perfectly appropriate to this theme and subject, where elegance would be out of place. It escapes solemnity through its unusually loose rhythm, its avoidance of rhyme, its hints of the speech of ordinary people, its quiet attention to detail. Man brought low and saved by the lowly potato—a low style fits; and how surprising it is, after "Tywater" and "Place Pigalle," to see that Wilbur can command such a style. Though it is not at all his usual style in his later work, he does continue to keep something like it available to use when he needs it.

"First Snow in Alsace" is like "Potato" in being focused on the daily life of villagers in a country at war. The style of the poem is fairly simple, but the figure with which it begins may seem a little precious: "The snow came down last night like moths/ Burned on the moon. . . ." The snow falls as it always does, but this time it "lies rumpled on/What shell-bursts scattered and deranged,/Entangled railings, crevassed lawn," on "the roofs of homes/Fear-gutted, trustless and estranged," on ration stacks and ammunition piles, and, not far from the town, on the eyes "Of soldiers dead a little while." But instead of dwelling, as he might, on human callousness or destructiveness, the poet turns to the pleasure the villagers can still feel "Walking the new air white and fine" or looking at the fresh frost designs on the windows:

> The night guard coming from his post,
> Ten first-snows back in thought, walks slow
> And warms him with a boyish boast:
>
> He was the first to see the snow.

The irony of snow in wartime is sharply presented in the descriptive details, but it is resolved by insisting on the rightness and naturalness, even in the presence of death, of simple pleasures. The poem thus illustrates, like several others among the war poems, Wilbur's refusal to meet "the threat of Chaos" with bitterness. Bitterness and other violent emotions are inescapable in wartime, and for some poets they have been a starting-point, if not a road, to great poetry. But whatever the full range of his feelings, Wilbur shows—not only here but throughout his whole career as a poet—a disposition to avoid the expression of the harsher emotions. One of his later poems, "Another Voice" (*Advice to a Prophet*), makes a pertinent comment on the topic. Meanwhile, these are among the gentlest of war poems.

"Mined Country" is not so good a poem as "First Snow in Alsace," but it is richer in ideas and in this way more interesting. The enemy, withdrawn into the mountains, has left the countryside strewn with mines:

> Danger is sunk in the pastures, the woods are sly,
> Ingenuity's covered with flowers!
> We thought woods were wise but never
> Implicated, never involved.

Seeing the boys search the fields with mine-detectors "hits at childhood more than churches/Full up with sky or buried town fountains. . . ."—that is, childhood is not so deeply disturbed by the rubble and ruin of the villages as by nature made uncertain and dangerous. The nymphs of woods and fields, those presences of wild beauty and innocence ("rightly-called-chaste Bel-phoebe"), have fled; the fine horses too are gone, the kind we admire in calendar pictures.

> Cows in mid-munch go splattered over the sky;
> Roses like brush-whores smile from bowers;
> Shepherds must learn a new language; this
> Isn't going to be quickly solved.

Having vividly and persuasively set the problem, the poem ends with two stanzas of advice to those who must live with it for years to come. They make clear that in speaking earlier of "childhood" the poet meant not only that of the children of this post-war countryside, but that of the adults, educated years earlier in attitudes no longer tenable:

> Sunshiny field grass, the woods floor, are so mixed up
> With earliest trusts, you have to pick back
> Far past all you have learned, to go
> Disinherit the dumb child,
>
> Tell him to trust things alike and never to stop
> Emptying things, but not let them lack
> Love in some manner restored; to be
> Sure the whole world's wild.

Certain ambiguities make the last stanza surprisingly hard to read, and I offer the following paraphrase without perfect confidence: Tell the child in yourself that to come to terms with a mine-implanted countryside, he must eradicate the trust of nature acquired before he could talk (or—preferably—before the age to which present memory reaches back), teach himself anew not to trust some things more than others, and never to stop examining things suspiciously, but once they are seen to be safe, to love them again as before; never to doubt or forget that the whole world, natural and human, is "wild" in several senses of the word: driven to distraction, out of control, untamed, uncivilized—and therefore treacherous. Objectivity and wariness are necessary, but so is love. If this reading is adequate, the poem is true to our post-war experience of war in so many ways that "Mined Country" becomes a symbol, wittily deepened by the pun on "Mined."

III *Nature's True Particulars*

Wilbur included in *The Beautiful Changes* a number of poems that concern themselves in some central way with the strangeness, the uniqueness, the peculiar qualities of natural objects and events. A few, like "The Walgh-Vogel" (dodo) and "The Melongene" (eggplant), are jocular hymns to natural curiosities. The tone of these poems is that of an elaborate spoof in which absurdity is heaped on absurdity while a tenuous gravity is preserved. Of "The Walgh-Vogel" Wilbur says in a note: "Title and first stanza derived from Sir Thomas Herbert's *Travels,* quoted in Phipson's *Animal-Lore of Shakespeare's Time.*" The archaic name for the dodo, the learned source, and the quaint details drawn from Phipson are part of the game. The poem ends:

> Alive the dodo strove for lack of point,
> Extinct won superfluity, and can disjoint
> To joy our fear.
>
> Dive, dodo, on the earth you left forlorn,
> Sit vastly on the branches of our trees,
> And chant us grandly all improbabilities.

The last line parodies the cry of the romantic spirit whose appetite for wonder needs more satisfaction than the world can afford. But it is a sympathetic parody: Wilbur knows, as any romantic does, that the probable is not enough.

Readers familiar with Marianne Moore's poems know that there is a kind of descriptive and reflective poetry made up of odd facts succinctly, formally, elegantly stated; each is true of the subject but comes toward it apparently at random, as if from different angles. We are caught and held by the separate statements, but we do not immediately see how they fit together or whether they add up. The mark of this poetry is not merely an apparent disconnection among the statements of facts, but a certain capriciousness in the choice of the facts themselves, a taste for curious details displayed for their own flavor and interest. An example of this mode, though not a pure one, is in "Cigales," Wilbur's first poem in *The Beautiful Changes.* The poem is a series of statements about what the cicada has meant to man. A small subject, part of the fun is that so much fastidious and amused attention is devoted to it. The subject is elevated by this treatment and memorialized in miniature. The first stanza presents the poet's impression of the cicada's song:

The Beautiful Changes (1947)

> You know those windless summer evenings, swollen to stasis
> By too-substantial melodies, rich as a
> Running-down record, ground round
> To full quiet. Even the leaves
> Have thick tongues.

If the first crickets begin their song then, says the second stanza, they provide a counter-balancing or contrasting note, a welcome "slim false-freshness." The third stanza shifts to the efforts of earlier men to interpret the cicada's peculiar habits. Its quaint phrases ("a simple sign," "his long waiting/and sweet change in daylight") suggest the naïveté of the medieval writers on nature—their appreciation of the marvelous combined with their readiness to see human traits in non-human creatures. Cicadas are noted for their long lives, the larvae of some species spending years underground before being transformed into the pupa, emerging from the ground, and setting free the perfect insect through a slit along the thorax. All this was "a simple sign" that miracles do happen. In spite of these and other attempts at interpretation, the song of the cicada remains puzzling, "uncomprehended." No function has been found for it: it is "gratuitous song." The last three lines enforce this point. If Jean Henri Fabre, the French naturalist and student of insects, drew the right conclusion from his charming and characteristic experiment, cicadas do not even sing for each other, for they cannot hear.

The first two lines of the last stanza are none too clear, and I cannot offer any interpretation of which I feel sure. The difficulty is in the two adjectives "healing" and "binding." An unexplained insect song gives rise to questions among men, some of whom call it a miracle while others draw morals. But why *healing* questions? As he studied insect behavior, Fabre gradually came to believe that the theory of evolution, which claimed to explain so much, was invalid. Can these lines mean that our scientific air is too binding, that it is healthier to have unanswered questions than to imagine we can explain everything? In any case, "a piping tree" remains a kind of mystery, if not a miracle, by which the poet, like the earlier observers of whom he speaks in the fourth stanza, is "puzzled and joyed." He seems to be saying in effect, "Thank God there are things we can't explain," things simply given, things intractable to theorists, wonders on earth.

"In a Bird Sanctuary" takes up again the idea that natural creatures have lives and wills of their own. Men's plans, wishes,

needs, and categories do not constrain them. The prevailing tone
is that of gentle mockery—of the Club, of Commissioners of
Public Parks, and of all men whose clumsy, clouded, well-
intentioned, humane efforts are so inadequate to the swift,
spontaneous, free, and unpredictable ways of birds. Stanza three
is especially witty, stanza four only a little less so. Stanza five is
made up of the random banalities we might expect of bewildered
park men, game but overmatched, forced into the bird-care
business. In stanza six the poet reverts to his own voice for a
comment that seems both fascinating and obscure:

> The liberty of any things becomes
> the liberty of all. It also brings
> their abolition into anythings.
> In order's name let's not turn down our thumbs
> on routine visions; we must figure out
> what all's about.

Perhaps it could be translated thus: If the liberty (independent
existence) of any one class of creatures is recognized, then the
claims of other classes of creatures to liberty come to be recognized also. If, however, all classes of things are granted this
equal liberty, then distinctions among things are obliterated; each
thing (birds, statues, what not) is equally protected by authority
but equally treated as a-thing-to-be-protected, an anything, without special rights or features. The result is such crude gestures or
slogans of protection as those in stanza five, where good will is
evident but the mind breaks down, helpless to grasp the peculiar
nature either of individuals or of each class of things to which
protection is owed. Presumably, the poet regards the abolition of
"any things" into "anythings" as bad, but this is left for the reader
to infer: the last three lines might begin with "nevertheless," but
they do not. The "routine visions" must be those of the park
men, the word "visions" being used of such startling insights as
those itemized in stanza five. Do such "visions" really have some
value? Well, the poet says urbanely, they are better than none;
they show that the park men are aware that birds exist; they are
"a partial wisdom." And since we do not have an adequate
comprehensive view of things, with all things in their places
(statues as well as birds), with relative values attached and
relative freedoms assigned, we should accept such "visions" pro
tem for whatever they may be worth.

For "we" are far more deeply confused than Commissioners of

The Beautiful Changes (1947)

Public Parks. We, or the Club at any rate, are referred to, not the park men, in the lines "Who wills devoutly to absorb, contain,/birds give him pain." The park men are not willing devoutly; they are only doing their duty toward bird-lovers and statue-lovers alike. The more telling satire is directed earlier against the Club, whose cranky and grandiose aim it is to "make men whole." This utter innocence, this failure to take bird-nature after all into account, this absurd inadequacy of means to ends, betray our confusion. Our need is to "figure out what all's about," rather than to tackle the regeneration of man with such pitiful tools and on so restricted a front as the establishment of bird sanctuaries.

Stanza six remains rather obscure. Its ease of style and its apparent assurance are misleading; as in "Mined Country," the concluding utterance is sybilline and thus a weakness, for a strong ending is needed. But one similarity between this poem and "Cigales" ought not to be missed: in each appears the same amusement at the bafflement and absurdity of men confronted with the alien aims and habits of other creatures.

Wilbur's interest in the uniqueness of other creatures extended to the whole relationship of man with the physical world. In "On the Eyes of an SS Officer" he spoke of "my opulent bric-a-brac earth," an earth unsimplified by abstraction or fanaticism, rich in unique objects. There are a number of poems, some in *The Beautiful Changes* and some in later volumes, in which the poet professes his attachment to particular objects rather than to abstractions or to universals. One of these poems is "O," a sonnet on two rhymes only, tortured at some points but provided with some fine lines, particularly the last two:

> The idle dayseye, the laborious wheel,
> The osprey's tours, the pointblank matin sun
> Sanctified first the circle; thence for fun
> Doctors deduced a shape, which some called real
> (So all games spoil), a shape of spare appeal,
> Cryptic and clean, and endlessly spinning unspun.
> Now I go backward, filling by one and one
> Circles with hickory spokes and rich soft shields
> Of petalled dayseyes, with herehastening steel
> Volleys of daylight, writhing white looks of sun;
> And I toss circles skyward to be undone
> By actual wings, for wanting this repeal
> I should go whirling a thin Euclidean reel,
> No hawk or hickory to true my run.

The word "true" is beautifully witty in the context. Geometrical circles, though perfect, and thus "true" in one sense, are not "true" in another sense because they do not describe the curves of particular things. The poem is, of course, a variation on that larger theme, noticed earlier, which might be summarized as the actual versus the ideal. Caught like any man between the two, Wilbur is attracted both ways at once; in any particular poem his logic or sympathetic intuition may take him one way or the other as he feels out some of the consequences of the choice. In this poem as in "Objects," in " 'A World Without Objects Is a Sensible Emptiness' " (*Ceremony*), and in a number of other poems, he inclines toward the pole of actuality. But sometimes his interest in the other pole is evident; and the mere fact that so many poems treat this theme is a sign that, for him, the tension persists.

In studying this theme in Wilbur's early work, I am struck inevitably by the crucial significance of "Objects," one of Wilbur's most brilliant poems, but a difficult one for reasons that recall "Cigales": it leaves gaps in the argument, and sometimes the connections are hard to make. The opening proposition, "Meridians are a net/Which catches nothing," I take to mean "geometrical figures correspond to no reality," as to be "true" a circle must become a wheel. The figure of the net is very fine; the world slips through its meshes and escapes. The gull, out of sight of shore, can "yet/Sense him to land" without any such guidelines; but Hanno, the legendary Carthaginian explorer of the west coast of Africa, could never have heard the song of the Hesperides in the garden of the golden apples without following islands or landmarks along the shore. Hanno's journey is conceived of as the quest of the artist who, if he is to hear "The clear high hidden chant/Blown from the spellbound coast," must keep in touch with objects and not trust to abstractions. The phrases "isles like beasts, and mountain stains along/The water-hem" seem to propose an inherent danger and impurity in particular objects as compared with the pure abstract. Yet the empirical journey along the coast must be risked. And like the Greeks, who imagined that "golden McIntoshes" were a suitable wedding gift for the queen of the gods, one must "Guard and gild what's common, and forget/Uses and prices and names; have objects speak." Uses, prices, names are not inherent qualities but cultural accretions distracting to the explorer on his journey from objects to enchanted garden. (In a review of J. F. Nims' poems published in 1950, Wilbur wrote, "Nims' failures of tone sometimes come, I think, of his having confused the 'object' with the commonplace values, words, and associations which usually surround it—with its *ambiance*.")

"There's classic and there's quaint," begins the fifth stanza casually, "And then there is that devout intransitive eye/Of Pieter de Hooch . . ."—"devout" because so reverent toward true objects like those mentioned in the next four lines; "intransitive" because his eye never ends in an object but travels through—into what?

> Into a day, into magic.
> For is there any end to [any stopping at?] true textures, to true
> Integuments; do they ever desist from tacit, tragic
> Fading away? Oh maculate, cracked, askew,
>
> Gay-pocked and potsherd world
> I voyage, where in every tangible tree
> I see afloat among the leaves, all calm and curled,
> The Cheshire smile which sets me fearfully free.

True textures, *true* integuments—these are the lights and surfaces which we are asked to "see feinting from his plot of paint" in a deception, truer than geometry, that carries us through object to magic. In the "tangible tree," and only there, may be seen "the Cheshire smile," which I take to be the fading away of the tangible into symbolic meaning. The smile invites the poet to find his own analogies for objects, to construct or discover his own enchanted gardens. No enchantment but through things; things are not the end (as in imagism) but the way (symbolism). Hanno made his voyage by objects, and the poet must do the same, past "true textures, . . . true/Integuments. . . ." And when he asks "do they ever desist from tacit, tragic/Fading away?" he means also, perhaps, that though one can—and should—guide oneself by them during all of one's journey, as Hanno kept close to the coast and as Pieter de Hooch made them his whole study, they are endless in extent and fade from the vision as the coastline fades in the distance ahead and behind the moving ship.

Objects fade away not only as we penetrate through them "into a day, into magic," but also more literally as we travel in time and space toward, past, and beyond any particular object or unique configuration of objects. So objects can be "true" though not constant; they are endlessly in view and yet endlessly fading from view, both into the forgotten past (through our own limitations and theirs) and into significances beyond themselves, "Into a day, into magic." Why is this fading "tacit"? I am tempted to relate the word to the clearly very important phrase that ends the first section of this two-part poem at the close of stanza four: "have objects speak." *Can* they speak if they seem never to "desist from tacit, tragic/Fading away?" As they fade out of our sense-range and memory, they cannot speak; but, as they fade into symbols, they can. The question then is *what* symbols; and this, I think, is the question and the mystery that sets the poet "fearfully free." Objects present themselves as a language in which the poet may speak, and he is free to use this language to say what he wants to say, to say what can be said in it, to "have objects speak" as they can and will—but he must give them their voice.

Though "Objects" is an early poem, it is highly characteristic of much of the poet's later work in structure and in style. Because of the steadiness of purpose and direction in Wilbur's work generally through the years since *The Beautiful Changes*, it may not be too fanciful to link this poem with the later poems that celebrate objects and living in time, and even with the recent "Advice to a Prophet," where he speaks of nature as a "live tongue" and a "glass . . ./In which we have said . . . , in which beheld/. . . all we mean or wish to mean." Without that "glass" or mirror, he says, we may be unable to "call/Our natures forth. . . ." In other words, the cost of a failure to "have objects speak" may be the loss of human nature itself. Not that all this is necessarily implied in "Objects," only that a line of thought visible there is developed further in the later poem. In this and in other poems Wilbur affirms his attachment to objects, either directly as a matter of doctrine or indirectly through description, so that we infer the importance this attachment has for him as we follow the gaze of his own "devout intransitive eye." Poets, like the Hesperides, "guard the plant/By praising it." But behind this affirmation we may sense two doubts or fears. One is that his own taste for dreams, visions, or mirages may lead him too far from the world of objects, set him too "fearfully free" of them, so that he is no longer in touch with the stuff of the world. The other is that objects themselves will not be faithful, that "the cow of the world" will not be true, that, in particular, time will come and take his love away. He must remain true to objects; they must remain true to him. But, if he is true to them, he must accept their impermanence, their status in time. As he says in "Sunlight Is Imagination," "All creatures are, and are undone." But this line must be taken in its context to be rightly appreciated.

"Sunlight Is Imagination" is written in six elaborate stanzas, the last five of which pick up in their short first lines the rhyme of the last line of the previous stanza. Run-on lines are the rule; end-stops are scarce. The stanza seems to suit the meditative, somewhat rapt mood of the poem; it starts with a swelling movement and then, as the lines get shorter, slows down so that the short phrases and more frequent rhymes assume more significance, as if the speaker were dwelling on the words. The speaker addresses the woman he loves, who is with him in a sunlit meadow. He begins by noticing that she is always half in sun, half in shadow, as a mermaid is half woman, half fish. Shall he take the view of her that Ponce de Leon first got of Florida, shining in the sun, concealing somewhere

> the fair and noble well
> Of sweetest savor and reflaire
> Whose ghostly taste
> And cleanse repair
> All waste,
> And where was ageless power from the first.

Then he reflects that "thirst/Makes deserts," that yearning for the eternal wastes the temporary; and he resolves to give up the search for "ageless power," to accept his own transitory state, and thus through renouncing inordinate thirst to restore the earth's abundance. Here we begin to catch on to the bearing of the choice the speaker had posed for himself in stanza one: "Shall I say you are fair/In the sun,/Or mermaid you in the grass waving away?" "In the sun" means in nature, implying change and the passage of time; the mermaid is legendary, ideal, immortal. He may love her as a woman; or, if he chooses, he can make her inaccessible, like the fountain of youth in Ponce de Leon's Florida, through the artist's thirst for power over change, for immortality: "My hand/Can touch but mysteries, and each/Of a special shadow." Any object, a girl, Florida—all are mysteries, if imagination can choose to make them what it will— for then what are they in themselves? Each has its shadow, the sign of its mortality, its ghost or shade; and the speaker chooses to accept this mortality rather than to try to transcend it by converting the object into something ideal or symbolic and thus permanent. As noon approaches and shadows diminish, he pleads with the girl to take his view:

> let our love not blight
> The various world, but trust the flight
> Of love that falls again where it begun.
> All creatures are, and are undone.
> Then lose them, lose
> With love each one,
> And choose
> To welcome love in the lively wasting sun.

It is a poem on the *carpe diem* theme, springing out of the poet's anguish as he sees his mistress's beauty and thinks of her mortality. In what sense is sunlight imagination? Perhaps in the most literal sense? If so, it is sunlight that gives things their images; and "imagination" means simply assuming an image in "the lively wasting sun."

IV *Art and Existence*

So, says the poet as lover, we must not diminish the value of what time grants us by thirsting for eternal life. And yet art itself may be an effort to envision and construct a reality superior in some respects to this one. This theme appears in several poems in *The Beautiful Changes* ("My Father Paints the Summer," "A Song," "L'Etoile," "A Dutch Courtyard") and in a number of later poems, notably "La Rose des Vents" (*Ceremony*). In these poems the tension between life (or the world) and art is carefully maintained; the distinction is insisted on while certain claims of each realm upon us are explored and tested. I do not find in these poems any tendency to rest in art as a refuge from the world; each one seems to me to contain within itself an adequate skeptical guard against estheticism. Even "My Father Paints the Summer" has its point, I think, not in the father's turning away from the cold wet reality to "an imagined time," but in the praise of his power to retain the vision of perfect summer through the worst of weathers: "There must be prime/ In the heart to beget that season. . . ." Of the poems in this volume, "Caserta Garden" is one of the most interesting for what it says, hints, and fails to say about the relationship between art and the world.

The Beautiful Changes *(1947)*

A garden is of course itself a work of art, defined or bounded, its contents selected, its design planned and controlled. It is made of the stuff of the earth and resembles the countryside around it; but it differs in being more highly selective, organized, and cultivated. In these respects it is like a painting or even a poem. In the relationship the gardener maintains between the garden and the world outside, we can discern something of his vision of things. So we give "Caserta Garden" our special attention, for it presents the poet with an opportunity to show his feelings about merely "defensive" or "refugee" art.

The poem begins with a stanza on the "silent tall stone-wall," now almost hidden by "drowsing trees and vines." It is called a "barrier," nevertheless, and the next stanza tells

what it's for—
To keep the sun-impasted road apart,
The beggar, soldier, renegade and whore,
The dust, the sweating ox, the screeching cart.

The owners do not understand its function as a barrier, in fact probably don't know the wall is there: "They'd say, 'But this is how a garden's made.'" Wilbur gives two stanzas chiefly to description of the fountain and adds a third which proposes that the circles ever widening on the pool would persuade a child "that the unjustest thing/Had geometric grace past what one sees." Is this a good thing to be persuaded of? How does the question of justice creep into the poem? Is the garden itself, in its exclusiveness, an unjust thing? The poem does not say so, but we may feel a hint of certain scruples between the lines. A beautiful refuge of this kind may be possible only through social privilege, but those who built it would have faith that apparent injustice is ultimate justice or "grace." The next two stanzas remark the richness, the freedom, the delicacy, and the irregularity of the vines, trees, and flowers inside the walls—with "necessity" walled out. Is it being suggested that people who can wall out "necessity" without knowing it develop as these plants do? Or is the description innocent of social innuendo? These questions present themselves because, without a controlling idea, the poem seems aimless and these last two stanzas inconclusive:

And still without, the dusty shouting way,
Hills lazar-skinned, with hungry-rooted trees,
And towns of men, below a staring day,
Go scattered to the turning mountain frieze.

The garden of the world, which no one sees,
Never had walls, is fugitive with lives;
Its shapes escape our simpler symmetries;
There is no resting where it rots and thrives.

The outer reality is recognized and its harshness acknowledged, along with its existence in time, its constant struggle, its complexity. A man-made garden can be understood, its shapes and its peace enjoyed; the world is very different. Is this all? Is there no resolution, no comment on this contrast, no judgment made as to the rival claims of gardens and the world? In his famous poem "The Garden," Marvell describes a paradise to which a man would want to confine himself all his life. Wilbur's Caserta garden is something of a paradise too, but perhaps the snake of conscience—the poet's, not the owner's—has begun to penetrate the "silence dark and cool." But the garden is in any case an inadequate and illusory refuge: it exists after all within the larger "garden of the world," in which rest is impossible. The poem seems a little uncertain of its own drift or import. The uncertainty is not in the detail but only in the expression of the theme. Some readers may feel that the very suggestive delineation of the basic contrast is enough, and perhaps it is.

Two other poems might be mentioned here for their concern with the relationship between art and life, the world, or action: "The Giaour and the Pacha," based on Delacroix's famous painting of that title; and "Up, Jack," based on an equally famous battlefield scene in Shakespeare's Henry IV, Part 1. Both poems are high-spirited and amused. In the scene of the former, the Giaour high on his horse has his "ancient enemy" the Pacha crouching below at his mercy. In a flash of insight the Giaour sees that his victory marks the end of his purpose in life, that the Pacha is "The counterpoise of all my force and pride." This theme, the mortal cost of victory in a quest that organizes and gives purpose to one's whole life, is taken up again, directly or obliquely, in some later poems of more importance, particularly in "Castles and Distances" (Ceremony) and in "Merlin Enthralled" (Things of This World). Another device of "The Giaour and the Pacha" is repeated with more telling effect in "Merlin Enthralled": the Giaour's turning into a figure in a work of art at the very moment when his sense of purpose evaporates:

The Beautiful Changes *(1947)*

> . . . the cloak becomes aware
> Of floating, mane and tail turn tracery;
> Imbedded in the air, the Giaour stares
> And feels the pistol fall beside his knee.

This may be a way of saying that art is a world without practical
ends, radically separate from, though related to and resembling,
the changing, straining world of human effort and desire. The
basic contrast is that of "Caserta Garden."

This distinction runs through Wilbur's work and constitutes
one of his major themes: the rival claims of two modes of reality.
One is the mode of being, of permanence, of vision or dream, of
perfection, the object of desire immune to desire, beyond attain-
ment because beyond life itself. "The end of thirst exceeds experience," says "A Voice from Under the Table" (*Things of This
World*). The other mode is that of becoming, of the "opulent
bric-a-brac earth," of objects and things of this world, of impermanence, imperfection, and partial satisfaction, of the "clambering will" ("The Aspen and the Stream" in *Advice to a
Prophet*). The distinction between the two modes is ultimately
that of the great romantic poets, much like that of Keats in his
odes on the urn and on the nightingale—but the list of poets to
whom it has been an absorbing theme would be a long one. To
which realm do we owe the stronger allegiance or feel the
stronger attraction, and what would be the consequence of at-
taching ourselves deliberately to one realm or the other? These
questions are so important to Wilbur, so fascinating or so nag-
ging, that we may understand his whole poetic career as an
uneasy oscillation between these grand opposites. Time and time
again his poems show this conflict or tension at the center; the
student of Wilbur's work learns to recognize it in many guises.

The idea of the cost of victory implies a faith in the inherent
value of the quest, of unsatisfied desire, a theme to which Wilbur
gives sympathetic attention much later in his published lecture
on Emily Dickinson. The closely related theme that the ideal is
superior to the real, that in fact one reaches the ideal by a nega-
tion of the world and of the worldly self, he considers in a later
essay on Poe. Action may be not merely fruitless; it may be
destructive of the actor, who lives by his quest alone. "Up, Jack"
begins with a leaf from this book:

> Prince Harry turns from Percy's pouring sides,
> Full of the kind of death that honor makes
> By pouring all the man into an act;
> So simplified by battle, he mistakes
>
> A hibernating Jack for dead Sir John.

The Prince makes his affectionate farewell speech and leaves the scene. But if Jack is dead, the Prince and Percy are doomed; for they depend for their lives—that is, their dramatic lives—entirely on the sunny, godlike presence in the play of Falstaff since they are (so the poem implies) merely his foils:

> Up, Jack! For Percy sinks in darker red,
> And those who walk away are dying men.
> Great Falstaff (*rising*) clears his thirsty throat,
> And I'm content, and Hal is hale again.

Prince Hal and Percy are mortal, but Falstaff is immortal and has the power to confer immortality on them. They exist, so to speak, only on his sufferance—in a sense only as his creatures, without any independent reality. Their dependence on him is like that of Gawen and Arthur on Merlin in "Merlin Enthralled": without Merlin they are aimless and ineffectual, mere dim archaic figures in a tapestry. The man of imagination creates worlds and characters that exist only so long as he dreams them. When his dream ends, they die or vanish. Hal is hale not because he kills Percy and walks off the stage; on the contrary, this act of honor produces a "kind of death," a simplification of character that blunts his acumen and reduces our interest in him to the danger point. Only Falstaff can save him from becoming a mere victor and thus a dramatic failure. So into this light-hearted, witty little poem are woven three threads that Wilbur picks up again and again for strands in his later work: the mistrust of action, the cost of victory, and the dependence of existence itself on imaginative power or vision.

V   "... *grace's revenue*"

I have been speaking of poems in which Wilbur is concerned with basic relationships between timeless art and the world. *The Beautiful Changes* includes several poems that take certain qualities of art as their subject; using the term broadly, we might call them poems on "style." They include "A Simplification," "Bell Speech," "Praise in Summer," "Grace," and "Lightness." Of the first two, whose concern is eloquence, "Bell Speech" is much the better and the more characteristic. It begins by complaining that in modern times bells ring the same way for death and marriage:

> The selfsame toothless voice for death or bridal:
> It has been long since men would give the time
> To tell each someone's-change with a special chime,
> And a toll for every year the dead walked through.
> And mostly now, above this urgent idle
> Town, the bells mark time, as they can do.

The language is full of implications, themes hinted at, and we await their development in later stanzas with an interest like that of the audience at the end of the first act of a good play. "The selfsame toothless voice for death or bridal:"— bells lack teeth, though they have tongues, so "toothless" is precise; and perhaps it is hinted that bells are ancient, neglected, of another age, in their last days on earth. "To tell each someone's-change with a special chime"—we remember that the traditional bell-chime patterns are called "changes"; but we are reminded by the wording that people change too at the crucial moments in life when the bells used to be rung for them—that bell changes used to mark human changes. The town, says stanza one, is an "urgent idle/Town," too full of its unimportant business to "give the time" to the celebration of the great human crises. So "mostly now . . . the bells mark time, as they can do." This use of "mark time" refreshes the phrase by giving it a literal meaning; the bells mark the time of day, but they also "mark time" as soldiers do, waiting for orders to do something better. The lively texture of the poem thus stirs up a swarm of minor ideas while the main argument remains perfectly clear.

Stanza two develops the point that in recent times the bells have been confined to work that is beneath their power and dignity. Stanza three offers no solution but foresees that bells will perform a function "Whether or not attended"; that is, whether or not they are heeded or, as of old, waited upon at ceremonial occasions, "bells will chant/With a clear dumb [speechless] sound, and wide of any word/Expound our hours. . . ."

In the fourth stanza the poet addresses Great Paul directly in a difficult but eloquent and fascinating prayer:

> Great Paul, great pail of sound, still dip and draw
> Dark speech from the deep and quiet steeple well,
> Bring dark for doctrine, do but dim and quell
> All voice in yours, while earth will give you breath.
> Still gather to a language without flaw
> Our loves, and all the hours of our death.

These lines convey the impression we commonly get in reading fine poetry: that the language is the willing and utterly flexible tool of the poet, capable of doing things it had never done before and had no notion it could do. Poet and language are like two expert dancers or tennis players discovering, only as they perform, the brilliant steps or strokes of which they are capable. Consider how lucky it is not only that "Paul" sounds like "pail" but that a bell *looks* like a pail, and further that we may speak with the sanction of usage of a "steeple well" from which the bell hung at the top may be considered to draw the air that fills it. The speech of the bell is dark because the steeple well is dark, but also because the message of the bell is obscure: "Bring dark for doctrine." Doctrine is what might come out of a steeple well, but why should any one pray for doctrine that is dark? We should remember that bells "expound our hours" without recourse to words; this exposition consists of "Dark speech from the deep and quiet steeple well," and thus suggests the unverbalized wisdom of an older, more faithful time.

But *what* Great Paul says or should say apparently seems less clear and less important to the poet than that the bell should keep on speaking and drowning out other voices with its "dark speech." This speech is "a language without flaw," characterized, we gather, by a purity unattainable by men who use words. If it is merely bell speech, the tolling of the bell to mark the hours, why is it more flawless than human speech? Perhaps because it is too simple to make mistakes as it celebrates great moments? The last two lines refer to the first line again: "The selfsame toothless voice for death or bridal." But now, as we consider the phrase "and all the hours of our death," we see that the poet has quietly but significantly changed the usual phrase "all the hours of our life." The bell, then, is a reminder of mortality, the proof of which approaches every hour. In marking time for the living, the bell still does something analogous to what it used to do for the dead with its "toll for every year the dead walked through." It is even tempting to see a double meaning in the phrase "while earth will give you breath." That is, the steeple well gives the bell the air that fills it and makes it possible for it to speak, but earth supplies it too with breathing men whose hours can be commemorated.

The last stanza or two remain a little puzzling, to me at least, because of their insistence on the "dumb sound" of the bells, the "dark speech." Perhaps the poet could have suggested a bit more clearly what the bells can say. But he is not inclined to supply easy answers, and we may see some parallel between his refusal to translate into English the "dark" and "flawless" speech of the bells and his pleasure in the incomprehensibility of the cigales' song in "Cigales." One brilliant phase of his performance in this poem is in the whole realm of sound. Some examples of word play and onomatopoeia have been noted earlier, but there are many other passages where assonance and alliteration are a delight and where sounds and rhythms work together in lines not only beautiful to read but remarkably sensitive to meaning. We might consider, among many possible illustrations, the pace of the line "Why should Great Paul shake every window plate" or the dazzling pattern of sounds in the first four lines of stanza four (quoted above), with its repeated *d*'s, *p*'s and *l*'s and the many internal near-rhymes. "A Dubious Night" makes an interesting comparison with "Bell Speech" for its evocation, chiefly through drastically shifting vowel sounds, of the much-flawed speech of distant bells on a windy night.

The sonnet "Praise in Summer" provides further evidence of the young poet's concern with the relationship between things and thoughts, between reality and the imagination that transforms it. The speaker is the poet, who represents himself as on a certain occasion "Obscurely yet most surely called to praise,/ As sometimes summer calls us all. . . ." His praise takes the form of turning things upside down: he sees the hills as heavens "full of branching ways" (mole-tunnels), the trees as "mines in air," the sparrows as burrowers in the sky.

> And then I wondered why this mad *instead*
> Perverts our praise to uncreation, why
> Such savor's in this wrenching things awry.

"This mad instead" is metaphor itself, which for its own purposes (for the "savor") verbally makes of things what they are not. Thus metaphor does not fail to create, but it also "uncreates" by denying the true names and functions of things. Not content with what is, the poet makes it something else. And yet why should a poet intent on praise not be content with what is? "Does sense so stale that it must needs derange/The world to know it?" How much "art" is consistent with respect for the thing praised? Essentially the same question is raised by Shakespeare in the sonnet beginning "My mistress' eyes are nothing like the sun," by Dr. Johnson about "Lycidas," by the romantic poets about wit. Wilbur ends the poem with the question:

> To a praiseful eye
> Should it not be enough of fresh and strange
> That trees grow green, and moles can course in clay,
> And sparrows sweep the ceiling of our day?

Do these lines mean that if one enjoys the natural scene as it is he should not need to write poems at all? Or only that if one does write poems he should not use metaphors that are too extravagant and paradoxical, even though there is "savor" in them? Does all poetry "derange/The world to know it?"—or only highly metaphorical poetry? This question is material because the last line uses a metaphor. It may be that this line is a sly joke, an abandonment of the argument—an admission that, mad or not, poets must use metaphors. If so, the poet answers the question he has asked: Yes, sense so stales that it must needs derange the world to know it. This view is ultimately the Platonic one that the poet, even when he wants to praise, must be a liar. The poem playfully ignores the argument that metaphors may give insights or knowledge by setting forth resemblances that would not otherwise be seen. It is a poem of doubtful seriousness, and yet it may betray a genuine uneasiness about the vitiation of sincerity by virtuosity; for it is clear that Wilbur wanted to reconcile the two in his work.

Two poems in *The Beautiful Changes* are meditations on human qualities that may have an esthetic value. One is aware at once that they are qualities of special importance to Wilbur as a poet. "Grace" uses images and examples from the arts: a quotation from Gerard Manley Hopkins, references to Nijinsky's famous leap, to Hamlet, and to Flaubert. The other poem, "Lightness," is very different; not explicitly concerned with art at all, it is built on two illustrations presented at length rather than, like "Grace," on a series of skipping allusions. "Grace" takes off from Hopkins' comment on Wordsworth's lines "The young lambs bound/As to the tabor's sound." Hopkins quoted these lines in his journal and added: "They toss and toss; it is as if it were the earth that flung them, not themselves. It is the pitch of graceful agility when we think that."

The first stanza of "Grace" is a marvel of speed, a dazzling flight from sheep to "Nijinsky's out-the-window leap" to a cryptic aphorism. Part of the pleasure in these lines comes from the delayed completion of the first clause: "So active they seem passive, little sheep/Please. . . ." Here we think we are through and on to the next illustration, "and Nijinsky's out-the-window leap/And marvelous mid-air pause please too/. . . ." Then, surprisingly, we get an object for each "please": "A taste for blithe brute reflex. . . ." This delay, when it is finally resolved, is itself an example of grace; like Nijinsky's leap, it holds us through a long moment before the sentence lights perfectly on its feet. There is gaiety as well as self-possession in the speed of the stanza, an air of the sleight-of-hand artist's tricks or the acrobat's fall through space while the drum beats—until he catches the bar and swings up to safety.

The packed little epigram that ends the stanza ("Flesh made word/Is grace's revenue") follows, or should follow, from the earlier statement; but it is not apparent instantly that it does, or what it means. "Flesh made word": the reverse of the Word made Flesh in the Incarnation. Flesh, that is, natural grace, "blithe brute reflex," is made word in Hopkins' comment on the lambs and perhaps in poetry generally. The word "revenue" seems to be used here literally for a return, a coming again, as in the term "revenant," which Wilbur uses elsewhere. (Wilbur's French and Latin are always alive.) By this conjecture the line would mean "physical grace gives rise in poems to linguistic grace, a second incarnation of the quality." The dining-car waiter is, of course, another instance of grace, described in stanza two with a dash equal to that of stanza one: ". . . but this is all done for food,/Is habitude, if not pure/Hebetude." The waiter is only doing his job, but Nijinsky was expressing an idea: "It is a graph of a theme that flings/The dancer kneeling on nothing into the wings." Because Nijinsky was unable to explain his acrobacy in words, he could not bring grace's revenue, make flesh word, teach others his art.

We are invited to compare the grace of the lambs, "constrained to bound," and that of the waiter, which is merely habitual, and that of Nijinsky, which is purposive but verbally inarticulate—with "a grace not barbarous," which depends on "a choice/Of courses," that is, on intelligence and will. Even awkward or hesitant speech may then be graceful, and even "fraction-of-a-second action" may require, instead of spontaneity, "a graceful still reserve" from which intelligence may direct the graceful and effective act. So, for the artist, the models are not lambs, Nijinsky, or dining-car waiters, but Hamlet, Flaubert, and others whose "piety makes for awkwardness," whose actions are not spontaneous, thoughtless, or wordless. Thus defined, the quality of grace takes on an importance and a dignity sometimes denied it. We may ask, where is "balance . . . not urgent" in the arts? Or we may object that "what one utters/May be puzzled and perfect" but not also graceful. But the poem attempts to define some different kinds of grace, from brute to intellectual, and to suggest for the latter not only an esthetic but also a moral value. Grace at its most thoughtful is purposeful and conscientious.

In "Lightness," too, though we might expect Wilbur's interest to be primarily esthetic, and though he describes the fall of the nest as a marvel of lightness and grace, the emphasis falls ultimately not on the beauty of lightness but upon its usefulness in conduct, its protective value. This theme may be seen in a passage quoted by Randall Jarrell to illustrate the influence of Marianne Moore:[5]

> Oh risk-hallowed eggs, oh
> Triumph of lightness! Legerity begs no
> Quarter: my Aunt Virginia . . .

Though Miss Moore's influence may indeed be detected in these and in other lines, the structure of the poem is more closely ordered and less apparently capricious than Miss Moore's often is. The stanza is Wilbur's own; an odd but strict experiment (*4a 5a 4b 5b*, etc.), with a good many run-on lines and a good deal of metrical variation, it gives on the whole an impression of vivacity, if not of verbosity. A measured, heavy tread would of course have worked against the subject. These lines are flighty and light-footed, full of little rushes and turns, of short stops and quick starts, the rhythm and syntax cunningly designed to represent the feel and look of the motions described:

The chalice now bobbing above,
Of interlaid daintiest timber, began the chute
Down forty fell feet toward stone and root
With a drift and a sampan spin, and gripped
Loosely its fine-shelled life; now viciously tipped
By a ripple of air, with an acrobat's quick not-quite-
Lost, dipped lower to whirl upright;
Then, with a straight-down settling, it
Descended into sunshine, and, with a hushed touch, lit
On a mesa of strenuous grass.

If the nest had been heavy, it would have smashed in the fall; it is protected by its lightness. Aunt Virginia, too, is protected by her lightness, but as the focus shifts from the nest to her, the word shifts its meaning. Aunt Virginia is uninvolved in life, detached from it since her earlier illness and recovery, as the nest is detached from the tree; in this respect, she is unlike "her great/ Heavy husband" and the friends who visit her. The last seven lines, which seem to me especially fine, are clear enough for separate quotation if it is noted that Aunt Virginia has been described earlier as "all lapped in an indigo-flowered shawl":

And he and the others, the strong, the involved, in-the-swim,
Seeing her there in the garden, in her gay shroud
As vague and as self-possessed as a cloud,
Requiring nothing of them any more,
And one hand lightly laid on a fatal door,
Thought of the health of the sick, and, what mocked their sighing,
Of the strange intactness of the gladly dying.

This quotation, however, does less than justice to the character of Aunt Virginia, who is presented earlier as parrying their pity and gently refusing their offers

To do-something-for-her; she sat in the heart of her days
And watched with a look of peculiar praise;
Her slight voice could catch a pleasure complete
As a gull takes a fish at the flash of his side . . .

If it seems at first a strain to link both the falling nest and Aunt Virginia under the heading "lightness," we may remember the common expression "traveling light," which fits them both and carries the right implications.

VI *Conscience*

Randall Jarrell calls "Water-Walker" "an animal-morality poem about St. Paul . . . , a member of a genre that Miss Moore discovered and perfected. . . ." This comment is less than just in what it says of its subject and derivation, but the poem is indeed strongly moral, more clearly so than are some of the other poems in which an undercurrent of morality may go unperceived beneath a surface elegance. ("Cigales," "Grace," and "Lightness" are examples, but many others have been discussed in this chapter.) In its tone "Water-Walker" is unique in all of Wilbur's work: it is more openly autobiographical, more troubled, less ironical, more clearly the poem of a young man reflecting on alternative ways of life. Jarrell says: "An ambitious and felt and thoughtful poem like . . . 'Water-Walker' . . . is a partial failure, but surely anybody would rather have written it than some of Mr. Wilbur's slight and conventional successes."[6] If the poem is "a partial failure," it is because its three characters, caddis-fly, St. Paul, and the poet himself, while sharing the double vision they owe to their involvement in two worlds and their consequent detachment from each, are not very clearly alike at other points of comparison.

The infidel who appears in the first four lines and then disappears for good is a figure at the heart of the poem; he is an outsider by conviction who suffers but who prefers his suffering to a place in society bought at the price of abandoning his convictions. He is like the caddis-fly that lives on the water-surface, between the two worlds of air and water, knowing both. And speaker and fly are again like "Paulsaul the Jew born in Tarshish," a Jew and a Roman, knowing both worlds. In Virginia, says the speaker, he has also been afraid of being completely absorbed into Virginia life. That would be like the larva's life under water, "armored," "dreaming," almost suffocated at times, possessive, abiding. And in a small Illinois town he has had the same feeling that the life there was narrow, protected, buried, tame, shy, trustful—a larva's life. Saul could have lived this kind of life and been "Loved and revered"; instead, he went on missions to the Greeks and was either adored or cursed. Brought up in one world and venturing into the other, he was a stranger to both, knowing both but inhabiting neither. The speaker also, as an American, is a repository of contrasting cultural experiences and memories. Can he remain a spectator of diverse historical movements and changes and summon the wisdom to praise what deserves praise, that is, the spirit which is permanent, rejecting the local and the ephemeral? A long immersion in one's original element is necessary. He who learns how hard it is to be just cannot escape the dilemma of conflicting points of view, nor does he want to: he will cherish the detachment that makes him suffer.

It is especially the last two stanzas that leave the reader with unanswered questions. But clearly the poet is concerned with a justice that transcends any one set of factional or cultural doctrines, concerned with intelligence or knowing, with venturing rather than abiding—and yet he seems to admit the value of having long experience of one culture before venturing outside. The repeated emphasis on the necessity of suffering is important. The theme is not detachment, but commitment without parochialism to some ideal of justice, however difficult this may be to carry out. A later and much less personal exploration of this theme appears in "Castles and Distances" (*Ceremony*).

It is a fact worth noticing that even though satire or social criticism appear only in muted ways in Wilbur's poems, they are not absent entirely. "In a Bird Sanctuary" and "Cigales" contain an implicit plea for the recognition of the autonomy of non-human life. "Bell Speech" in one of its aspects is an attack on the callousness behind our modern neglect of ceremony. "Folk Tune" presents a "sickly city" tossing in its sleep while John Henry, "our nightmare friend," strains to vindicate our human strength against the machine. "Superiorities" celebrates the courage of two men who face a storm on shipdeck, while lesser men are "Huddled below with wives and buddies,/Comforting, caring, sharing pills,/Prayers and other proper studies." We see in "Water-Walker" an admiration for the fighter-adventurer Paul that is matched by a lower estimate, unexpressed but clearly implied, of those who choose to stay always in one cultural element. "The Peace of Cities" criticizes the inconsequence and the coldness of life in a European city and does so in surprisingly violent terms. Such strains in these poems do not comprise anything like a position on questions of the day, but they are evidence of a capacity for moral feeling and of a willingness on occasion to express it. It is necessary to insist upon the presence of these qualities in Wilbur's poems because his quietness and urbanity have led some readers to overlook his basic moral seriousness and to accuse him of frivolity or blandness.

VII *"The Beautiful Changes"*

One other small class of poems deserves mention: Wilbur's love poems. There are only two in this book: "June Light" and "The Beautiful Changes"; in later books others appear with similar characteristics. In both, the poet indulges in some artful word play without destroying the tenderness and intimacy of tone that he is trying to achieve. The question is whether he overdoes the tenderness and slips over into something too silky and precious. Although it may be too much a matter of taste to pronounce on, I admit to a certain uneasiness about the tone of both these poems. Here I will comment only on "The Beautiful Changes," a poem marked by a subtlety of sound and meaning unusual even for Wilbur. Though the title is grammatically ambiguous, the poem uses "beautiful" as a noun, not as an adjective. The beautiful changes *things,* then, and the first two stanzas give four examples: Queen Anne's lace turns a fall meadow into a lake, the poet's love makes a lake-filled valley of his mind, a chameleon changes a forest by turning green, and a mantis deepens the green of the leaf it sits on:

> The beautiful changes as a forest is changed
> By a chameleon's tuning his skin to it;
> As a mantis, arranged
> On a green leaf, grows
> Into it, makes the leaf leafier, and proves
> Any greenness is deeper than anyone knows.

While the beautiful changes other things around it by intensifying their individual qualities, it too undergoes changes to bring itself into harmony with its surroundings. The chameleon changes its own color to match that of the forest, and the mantis, "arranged/On a green leaf, grows/Into it. . . ." The phrase "the beautiful changes" is thus used here (though not in its second occurrence in stanza three) both transitively and reflexively. We might gather from the examples of stanzas one and two that the poet is saying that the beautiful exerts its influence on surrounding scenes or objects only by increasing their beauty, but stanza three broadens the scope of this influence:

> Your hands hold roses always in a way that says
> They are not only yours; the beautiful changes
> In such kind ways,
> Wishing ever to sunder
> Things and things' selves for a second finding, to lose
> For a moment all that it touches back to wonder.

The Beautiful Changes (1947)

By the argument of the earlier stanzas, girl and roses both take on an augmented beauty as she holds them—but the first line and a half of this final stanza make a different point: that she holds the roses in such a way as to invite others to share their beauty with her. The distinction between "things and things' selves" in line five is one I have not been able to grasp; even so, it seems clearly implied that one of the functions of the beautiful is to restore the freshness of a first encounter with things and to renew our sense of wonder.

In an article on the meters used by the poets of Wilbur's generation, George Hemphill included a metrical analysis of "The Beautiful Changes." He called the meter of this poem "a kind of stress-verse that is . . . hard to distinguish from loose iambic verse. . . ." If the lines are scanned in feet, the stanzas are not identical; but if they are scanned in stresses, the stanzas all fall into the pattern 5a 5x 2a 3b 5x 5b. Stress-reading, he said, makes for naturalness in the sound; and, he added, "a triumph of naturalness which does not destroy but which actually establishes artfulness is not to be despised in any poet and seems to me to be part of the character of Wilbur's achievement, in this as well as in other poems."[7] It is true that the stress pattern of these lines is less regular, more prosy, closer to speech rhythms, and thus more "natural" than is usual in iambic verse. But the sound and the movement of a line of poetry are the product of much more than the stress pattern, and in the whole effect of its complex audible harmonies the style of this poem is highly artificial. Consider the repetitions of sound in lines like "Any greenness is deeper than anyone knows," or "Your hands hold roses always in a way that says. . . ." These artful lines, and most of the others, are much smoother, much easier, more melodious and flowing than speech. As for the rather glamorous diction and the elegant phrasing of this poem, they are inseparable from the effect of the lines, but they are unthinkable in prose. Nobody could ever say "Valleys my mind in fabulous blue Lucernes." Even if the stress patterns are "natural," then, because they are closer than usual to those of prose, the lines of the poem are anything but natural in their whole effect. To speak more generally, Wilbur does not aim, as some poets do, to bring his language close to that of spontaneous speech. He is capable of informality and, as in "The Beautiful Changes," of a silken ease, but as a rule his idiom remains deliberate and literary.

The Beautiful Changes left reviewers with an unusually strong conviction of its merits. Louise Bogan, in the first of several acute and sympathetic reviews of Wilbur's books in *The New Yorker,* wrote that "Wilbur surpasses the majority of his contemporaries in range of imaginative reference and depth of feeling. He has a remarkable variety of interest and mood, and he can contemplate his subjects without nervousness, explore them with care, and let them drop at the exact moment that the organization of a poem is complete. This ease of pace, this seemingly effortless advance to a resolute conclusion, is rare at his age; the young usually yield to tempting inflation and elaboration."[8] One or two reviewers, including Miss Bogan, noticed that Wilbur had not yet thoroughly assimilated his technical lessons from older poets such as Marianne Moore, Wallace Stevens, Rilke, Eliot, and Hopkins. Francis Golffing, though he called the book "a very remarkable . . . job of work," objected that Wilbur "too often spoils his chances by concessions to modishness . . . and by attempts at genres that are outside his range. . . ." Surprisingly, he added that Wilbur "lacks wit."[9] Nevertheless, Wilbur's individual talent displayed itself unmistakably in this early collection. No reviewer I have read failed to recognize that the book was not merely a promise but an achievement with its own permanent value. Oscar Cargill, writing in 1954, quoted T. S. Eliot's remark to an interviewer, "I must admit to a continuing respect for Robert Lowell and Richard Wilbur." And Cargill added, "And well he might, for each of these young men produced in his first volume more memorable poems than were found in the first volumes of Robinson, of Frost, and of—Eliot!"[10] However that may be, it seems, as one looks through the reviewers' comments, that all would have cordially agreed with M. L. Rosenthal that "Wilbur is one of those rare poets who not only can think in verse but who are also a pure joy to read."[11]

CHAPTER **2**

Ceremony (1950)

SINCE I OMIT from my discussion what I consider to be Wilbur's less significant work, I will say here that about half the poems in *Ceremony*, his second collection, seem to me to be first-class. These poems give mature expression to the talent displayed in *The Beautiful Changes* and amply fulfill the promise of the earlier book. Without revealing any important new developments in technique or any new turns of subject or theme, the best poems in *Ceremony* seem to me as rich in implication, as fully worked out, as surprising and delightful, as the best of his later work. Compared with the best poems in *The Beautiful Changes* they show more skill, more self-possession, and often a more subtle and characteristic irony. The lesser half of *Ceremony* includes, apart from translations, a number of exercises and slight poems—some mere music, some merely clever. ("Games One°" and "Games Two:," disguised as trifles, are actually as profound as poems are likely to be.) Most of these are genuinely amusing or otherwise diverting, but it is nonetheless significant that Wilbur omitted quite a number of them from the collection *Poems: 1943-1956* that he prepared for English publication.

The publication of *Ceremony* firmly established Wilbur's reputation as one of the best of the young American poets when he was less than thirty years old. Though reviews of the book were generally favorable, some telling criticisms were made, such as those of Randall Jarrell, who found in the work an excessive caution and composure;[1] of Joseph Bennett, who thought Wilbur was prone to slackness or laziness;[2] and of Peter Viereck, who called for more vulgarity and less blandness.[3] These criticisms, which resemble one another in their demand for more boldness and energy, will be discussed with some of the poems to which they might be applied. Meanwhile, it is worth noting that Viereck found in *Ceremony* "a compelling tension between surface sunniness and subsurface storms" which he considered a new and hopeful sign for Wilbur's development. Without conceding that this tension is absent from his earlier poems, I too find something like it in the most severely disciplined poems of *Ceremony* and also in many later poems.

Tensions are not mere contrasts; they are significant contrasts. Contrasts do not become tensions until practical, esthetic, moral, or other interests are engaged and create in the consciousness a balance of competing motives, moods, or impulses. There is no tension between mountains and sea coast until they are presented as alternatives by the travel agent or the landscape painter. From this point of view a poem, like any other work of art, is a whole system of tensions, some extremely subtle, like the one Viereck names above, and some more obvious. In the last chapter I proposed that one recurrent tension in Wilbur's poems is the tension between the actual and the ideal, between the world that is and some other world that might be or can only be conceived of. This tension is easily visible in some of the poems of *Ceremony* in which observation and description of nature are especially important.

I   *Nature and Spirit*

Among the poems of this general class in *Ceremony*, "Conjuration" is perhaps the most difficult. It begins with lines whose power to evoke a familiar sea-coast scene is remarkable, but equally good are the speed and ease with which we move from the simple scene to the scene as symbol:

> Backtrack of sea, the baywater goes; flats
> Bubble in sunlight, running with herringbone streams;
> Sea-lettuce lies in oily mats
> On sand mislaid; stranded
> Are slug, stone, and shell, as dreams
> Drain into morning shine, and the cheat is ended.

The whole stanza is a brilliant example of the close adaptation of cadence to meaning. The pace of the stanza is perfect; the parallel details are accumulated in sentences cleverly varied in structure until the final clause rounds off the stanza with a sudden authority. The long elegiac sounds of "dreams drain into morning shine" are beautifully set off against the abrupt "and the cheat is ended." What *is* the cheat that is ended by the recession of the sea? The illusion that the blue water was "amenable," tractable, not to be feared or distrusted: "Oh, it was blue, the too amenable sea./We heard of pearls in the dark and

wished to dive." But in the morning sunlight it becomes clear
that under its bland, blue surface the sea has been creating
monsters; like the crab in the snail-shell introduced in stanza two,

> All join, and in the furl
> Of waters, blind in muck and shell,
> Pursue their slow paludal games.

So far "Conjuration" presents no apparent difficulty. Its theme
seems to be the difference between the harmless surface appearance of the sea and the somehow treacherous work of joining
"strangest things" that goes on underneath. This contrast or tension is the familiar one between the beauty and the cruelty of
nature, and we wonder how it is to be resolved. The fourth
stanza begins with an appeal to the pearl to come to the surface:

> O pearl,
> Rise, rise and brighten, wear clear air, and in
> Your natal cloudiness receive the sun;
> Hang among single stars, and twin
> My double deep; O tides,
> Return a truer blue, make one
> The sky's blue speech, and what the sea confides.

Clearly, there is a symbolic meaning for "My double deep,"
and the temptation to try some rather wild hypotheses is strong.
First of all, however odd it may seem, the poet asks the pearl to
take a place among the stars (why "single" stars?), where it
would be visible both in the sky and by reflection in the sea;
thus it would "twin/My double deep"—that is, make twins of
sky and sea. Sky and sea, both "deeps," would then be among
the "strangest things together grown," like snail shell and crab,
"softness" and "bitter claws." The pearl is thus invited to become an agent of reconciliation between the two contrasting
deeps. But how shall the pearl "twin" sea and sky? By showing
that it is possible to leave one and hang in the other, to dwell in
both? In the last lines of the stanza the poet turns from the pearl
to make a parallel appeal to the tides: "Return a truer blue" than
before, he asks. As the tides reflect the blue of the sky, let sky
and sea convey the same meaning, reconcile their speech. This
plea is not quite the same as vainly imploring the sea to change
its character. Perhaps the sky can be regarded as "true blue,"
but what the sea "confides" will presumably remain what it was:
a disturbing, a terrible secret of monsters in the deep. How shall

the tides make their speech one? By suggesting, like the pearl, that the two worlds are one. The sea, more broadly nature, is a source of doubt and fear, for it poses the problem of evil. The sky, more broadly the supernatural realm of the ideal, is a source of faith and consolation. Ultimately, the sky suggests, all will be redeemed into harmony. The poet "conjures" pearl and tides to symbolize this harmony, to signify that in the end the worlds are reconciled.

This poem is one of a common type: a scene is observed in which natural events are not merely noted but tend to assume symbolic significance. The poet learns as he observes; he ponders some truth about the world in which he lives, and he concludes by pleading or praying that the world conform itself somehow to his needs. He encounters the world with delight, wonder, or apprehension; and then he praises or exhorts it. It can tell us something; we can tell it something in return, ask a human question, or make a human request. Man is often uneasy as he confronts nature and desires reconciliation with it. But there is a good range in Wilbur's responses to scenes: he is open to impressions, his feelings about nature remain fresh and flexible, and his inferences or conclusions vary.

"Grasse: The Olive Trees" is another ambitious nature poem in which the objects become symbols. The first two stanzas set forth a wet, hot landscape in southern France, where "luxury's the common lot" and "all is full/Of heat and juice and a heavy jammed excess." "Only the olive contradicts," the trees lying "like clouds of doubt against the earth's array." Faint in color, its leaves "like famished fingers waving," the olive alone is insatiable:

> Even when seen from near, the olive shows
> A hue of far away. Perhaps for this
> The dove brought olive back, a tree which grows
> Unearthly pale, which ever dims and dries,
> And whose great thirst, exceeding all excess,
> Teaches the South it is not paradise.

Thirst, one of Wilbur's recurrent themes, appeared earlier in "Sunlight Is Imagination," in which Ponce de Leon's thirst makes a desert of Florida; it reappears in important roles in "'A World Without Objects Is a Sensible Emptiness,'" in "A Voice from Under the Table" (*Things of This World*), in "Ballade for the Duke of Orléans" (*Advice to a Prophet*), and in his essay on Emily Dickinson (1959). In "Grasse" all things are content except the pale olive with its unquenchable thirst. The olive suffers from romantic incompleteness, from a yearning that makes it unfit for this world.

And unfitness for this world, whether because of excessive thirst or for other reasons, is a plight in which many of Wilbur's poetic creatures find themselves. He may mock these misfits, as he mocks the "Walgh-Vogel" or later the "Black November Turkey" (Things), or as he mocks himself in "In the Elegy Season" or in "Epistemology II"; but his mockery is tempered by a sense of the awkward dignity of maladjustment. Otherworldliness may be, and often is, absurd; but it can be, perhaps must be, the ground of noble action. The olive tree of this poem, however, merely reminds us that the requirements of some creatures go beyond what this world can afford. The suggestion (in the stanza quoted above) that Noah needed this reminder is surprising and puzzling; here the olive seems to have lost its earlier symbolic role to take on the diminished import of a token (with its "hue of far away") merely of the great distance remaining between Noah and the land, or of a token ("unearthly pale") from Paradise itself that conveys hope rather than a warning.

There are some bold descriptive effects in stanza two:

> Whatever moves moves with the slow complete
> Gestures of statuary. Flower smells
> Are *set* in the golden day, and *shelled* in heat,
> Pine and columnar cypress stand. The palm
> *Sinks* its combs in the sky. This whole South *swells*
> To a *soft rigor,* a rich and crowded calm.

I have italicized the more venturesome words, which, though not all the things named here could be seen or felt, help to carry out the implications of the strange and yet persuasive opening statement. While the passage might be cited to meet the objections of readers who do not find enough boldness in Wilbur's language, it may strike others as over-ingenious—as an example of the danger the poet himself hit upon in "Praise in Summer." But this criticism is valid, if at all, only of stanza two; the descriptive details of stanza one and of the later stanzas are vivid and just without strain.

Another poem in which description is especially rich and evocative without being any less the servant of ideas is "In the Elegy Season." For poems like these, we might alter William

Carlos Williams' slogan "No ideas but in things" to "No things but in ideas." "In the Elegy Season" is explicitly about not being in touch with the outer landscape and substituting an inner landscape for it. It is one of those poems in which a playful extravagance of the mind, an intellectual humorousness, amounts to self-parody. As November begins, the poet smells the fallen leaves and remembers summer, which, he says, he could not hold in his head while it was present. His mind therefore makes up a conceptual summer in which it can take satisfaction. But this is an act of pride that his "body" or senses cannot emulate; instead, the body looks forward past winter and longs for the coming of spring. The note is not that of bitter loss and desperate desire; it is lighter than that. No great urgency is here, but rather the poet's mild, rueful exasperation with his inability to live in the present. When people want more from Wilbur than they think he offers, it is likely, I think, to be his playful tone that puts them off. They see that the theme is capable of more serious treatment, and they suspect him of being lazy, or too cautious, or even bland. Without claiming that "In the Elegy Season" is more than a minor masterpiece, two things can be said in response to such criticism. One is that this is not the only poem in which Wilbur takes up the problem of living in the here and now rather than in a visionary world. This problem is touched on, or more fully considered, in a good many poems from the earliest to the latest, and it receives in all these poems taken together a varied and searching exploration. A poet may be permitted an occasional light poem on one of his favorite themes.

Another possible response to the criticism I have mentioned is that this poem shows an energy and a boldness in its language of which a lazy poet would be wholly incapable. Again and again the language surprises and delights, as much in its pace and sound as in its precision. The leaves have fallen, summer is over:

> Haze, char, and the weather of All Souls':
> A giant absence mopes upon the trees:
> Leaves cast in casual potpourris
> Whisper their scents from pits and cellar-holes.
>
> Or brewed in gulleys, steeped in wells, they spend
> In chilly steam their last aromas, yield
> From shallow hells a revenance of field
> And orchard air.

Ceremony (1950)

These "last aromas" could hardly be more brilliantly brought to mind; indeed, the triumphs of phrasing in the poem are too numerous to mention. Any reader should see how much descriptive work is accomplished in these two stanzas, which are undiluted by the pervasive whimsy: the justice of "revenance" (the return of a ghost or spirit after death); the pun on "inspiration" (literally, a breathing in); the bombastic Shakespearean echo in "all the boundless backward of the eyes" ("the boundless backward and abysm of time" from *The Tempest*); the emphatic position of "wings" as the rhyme-word and its onomatopoetic sound, juxtaposed as it is with "soft commotion"; the high-toned reference to Persephone, who climbs the stair from Hades in the spring; and the special richness in the last stanza of such adjectives and verbal forms as "freighted," "cordial," "building," and "hoisting." The language of the last two stanzas is deliberately inflated, self-mocking, amused by the romantic plight of the stranger on earth, the untimely one, the man out of adjustment with things. But if we remember Wilbur's persistent preoccupation in other poems with what he is amused by here, we may suspect that the elegance and the urbanity of this poem, along with its verbal ingenuity, only conceal a serious concern with the subject. Its lightness may be a protective device, one kind of armor against the threat of Chaos; its strict form and intellectual orderliness may also serve this end.

The tone of many of Wilbur's poems, nevertheless, is such that one is not inclined to take them as efforts to reveal an insight or a view of the world held seriously by the poet. Not that they do not deal with the most serious subjects, but they do so as if the poem were a game rather than a mortal struggle with truth. One such poem, still within the class of poems being considered—those that examine or contemplate the state of man in nature—is "A Problem from Milton." The problem is man's consciousness of God's design in the world; once he becomes aware of it, he can never feel free. In the Garden of Eden, trees, vines, streams, and flowers submitted to God's plan without any sense of restriction, freely taking the liberties appropriate to their kind. A wave expresses its sense of freedom every time it hits the rocks, and yet it performs a service, of which it is unaware, when "it leaves the limpet and the whelk ashore." Though it feels free, it is only playing out the role assigned to it in the scheme of things. Swedenborg tried to infer the features of heaven from those of nature, but he left no room in heaven—nor elsewhere in his system, said Emerson—for spontaneity or for the individual. Thus we may bind ourselves in intellectual chains. Only through human knowledge and speculative power do we get a sense of human limitations. It would be better to be ignorant and thoughtless like the sea, "whose horses never know their lunar reins." A familiar argument runs "Knowledge liberates"; Wilbur's wit lies in pointing out that it can also constrain.

"A Problem from Milton" is enjoyable without being at all personal; that is, it is a witty exercise in fitting fresh images to a theme in everybody's possession. The poem differs from "In the Elegy Season" in that, if we look elsewhere in Wilbur's work for its theme, we do not find it. And it is even more frankly playful: for example, the two meanings of the last line of stanza four ("But Emerson was damned if it would do") and the outrageous yet teasing pun on devilled eggs in stanza five. The poem appears to be an example of Wilbur's taste for "games" and paradoxes rather than a statement of anything urgent in his own beliefs. When the mind is flashing and turning among ideas, expressing them in language that amazes and delights, the poet's beliefs are unimportant. What difference does it make what the man believes who contrives and sets off the town fireworks?

But despite Wilbur's enjoyment of the poem as a verbal and intellectual performance, he does return to certain ideas that must be considered his, and one of these is the need to accept the world and to live in it while we may. This theme appears so often, and it is used with so much energy in his work, that it may reflect a strenuous inner struggle. Only a man with a strong ascetic impulse would be moved to so constant a reassertion of his joy in the world. The conflict is explicit in "La Rose des Vents," the first poem in Wilbur's work in which conflicting ideas are presented as drama—that is, in dialogue. The Poet says, "The world disintegrates in time; we must find a permanent home outside it in the imaginary world, in art." The Lady replies, "That world is too far away for me; I would disintegrate there. Let us live in this mortal world while we can." With her own very feminine concern for what is alive and must be cared for, including herself, she says "Forsake those roses/Of the mind/And tend the true,/The mortal flower." She has the last word, a weighty one; but it does not dispose of the poet's perfectly valid fear of mortality. The two urgencies are as evenly balanced in the poem as they are in life. And I propose that what is felt in this poem, as often elsewhere in Wilbur, is not composure but the excitement, the strain, of attraction toward precisely opposed but equally valid ends.

The same conflict between the two impulses seems to be at the heart of "Clearness," in which Wilbur uses the traditional device of the dream to present two realms of being:

> There is a poignancy in all things clear,
> In the stare of the deer, in the ring of a hammer in the morning.
> Seeing a bucket of perfectly lucid water
> We fall to imagining prodigious honesties.

In this passage the range of things conceived of as "clear" extends the meaning of the term beyond narrow limits, and the second stanza expands it to include the crystalline perfection of snowflakes. From these things it is an easy step to "In pine-woods once that huge precision of leaves/Amazed my eyes and closed them down a dream." By now, however, the poet has moved from things simple and clear to things clear-cut in their particulars but infinite in number, and some strain on the term may be felt. At any rate, the pine-woods suggest to him not "the usual southern river,/Mud, mist, the plushy sound of the oar" but a northern city, "a fabulous town/Immaculate, high, and never found before":

> This was the town of my mind's exacted vision
> Where truths fell from the bells like a jackpot of dimes,
> And the people's voices, carrying over the water,
> Sang in the ear as clear and sweet as birds.

A characteristic wit appears in "my mind's exacted vision," in which "exacted" means not only "made more exact" but also "required by the mind" as distinct from "conveyed to the mind in the usual way by the senses." This is a vision of the mind's desire, clearer than sensory vision, perfect in its ministry to the dreaming eye and ear of the mind. Unhappily, the dreamer cannot live in that atmosphere:

> But this was Thulë of the mind's worst vanity;
> Nor could I tell the burden of those clear chimes;
> And the fog fell, and the stainless voices faded;
> I had not understood their lovely words.

It is as if he had had a glimpse of heaven but found that the angels spoke a language unintelligible to man. "Stainless" is fine here; but "lovely," weakened as it is by thoughtless use in everyday speech, entails a great risk. It must establish itself as the best choice against two other possibilities: either no adjective at all, which would be passable at this point, or an adjective that would attribute another quality to these "words" as sharply defined, as fertile in suggestion, and as pertinent to the whole meaning as "stainless." "Lovely" must in this particular use of the word be meant literally, as "lovable" or "inexpressibly beautiful"; but on the whole it seems to fall short of Wilbur's usual standard of precision. The vision fades and the mystic returns to this world as always, without the saving word. But while Wilbur might have expressed the desire for another such vision, he pointedly does not. Instead, in condemning the vision as "Thulë of the mind's worst vanity," he implies that it is an error to dream of the perfect city; the dreamer should recognize that he is radically disqualified for citizenship there and should refrain from making his application. And since it is a city of *clearness*, not of some other quality, he must be resigned to living a life in which vision is inescapably muddied, in which "prodigious honesties" are always a little out of reach.

"Clearness" is only one of a number of poems in which Wilbur warns himself against embarking for the Happy Isles. The central document of this doctrine is probably " 'A World Without Objects Is a Sensible Emptiness.' " In earlier poems the ideal season appears as spring ("In the Elegy Season") or as summer ("My Father Paints the Summer" or "Grasse: the Olive Trees"). His dream of the north in "Clearness" is unusual, as he acknowledges in the lines "I lost to mind the usual southern river,/Mud, mist, the plushy sound of the oar . . . ," a landscape of peace, ease, plenty, beauty. In " 'A World Without Objects . . .' " he is drawn toward a desert landscape, characterized so that certain dangers in it are clearly perceived. The question is that of the value of dreams of the perfect in a world like ours. Are they mere illusions, idle self-indulgences? Do they find themselves so consistently mocked by the world's realities that they mislead and destroy the dreamer? Do they unfit him, through averting his eyes, for life in his own world and time?

Wilbur often seems fearful that his dreams are a sort of Belle Dame sans Merci; as in "Clearness," he calls himself back from them—but to what compensatory view of this world? " 'A World Without Objects . . .' " takes its title, a little altered, from the following passage in Thomas Traherne's *Second Century*, Meditation 65: "You are as prone to love as the sun is to shine;

it being the most delightful and natural employment of the soul of man, without which you are dark and miserable. Consider therefore the extent of love, its vigor and excellency. For certainly he that delights not in love makes vain the universe and is of necessity to himself the great burden. The whole world ministers to you as the theatre of your love. It sustains you and all objects that you may continue to love them. Without which it were better for you to have no being. Life without objects is sensible emptiness, and that is a greater misery than death or nothing." As Wilbur's poem opens,

> The tall camels of the spirit
> Steer for their deserts . . .
>
> .   .   .   .
>
> And move with a stilted stride
> To the land of sheer horizon, hunting Traherne's
> Sensible emptiness . . .

"Sensible" seems to mean "knowable"—apprehensible to the consciousness. The spirit moves out of this world toward the horizon "where the brain's lantern-slide/Revels in vast returns."

> O connoisseurs of thirst,
> Beasts of my soul who long to learn to drink
> Of pure mirage, those prosperous islands are accurst
> That shimmer on the brink
>
> Of absence; auras, lustres,
> And all shinings need to be shaped and borne.

Why are these islands "accurst"? Because they are "out of this world," yes, but not merely because they are remote; they are also "pure mirage." They are "prosperous islands," rich perfections of some kind; they are congenial, even fascinating to the spirit, but ultimately fatal to it. The poet calls his spirit back from them with the warning that "auras, lustres,/And all shinings need to be shaped and borne"—meaning, I gather, not thin or insubstantial, but constructed of the solid materials of experience, as were the haloes of saints painted by the "early masters." He is still addressing the camels of his spirit as he pleads in the long fourth sentence that ends the poem:

> Turn, O turn
> From the fine sleights of the sand, from the long empty oven
> Where flames in flamings burn

Back to the trees arrayed
In bursts of glare, to the halo-dialing run
Of the country creeks, and the hills' bracken tiaras made
Gold in the sunken sun,

Wisely watch for the sight
Of the supernova burgeoning over the barn,
Lampshine blurred in the steam of beasts, the spirit's right
Oasis, light incarnate.

Objects themselves are "light incarnate"; unlike mirages, they are substantial; further, they have their own glory and mystery, their own holiness—the imagery insists on that. These objects are blessed, not accurst; and only in returning to and celebrating them can the spirit find its "right oasis." This poem thus affirms a sort of responsibility toward the physical world, one based on a belief in its blessedness and in its power to refresh us. The imagery of trees, creeks, and hills may suggest at first that the poet's love for objects has a narrow range, excluding love of persons as Traherne's does not. But the last stanza, with its delicate evocation of the nativity scene at Bethlehem, brings out the full responsibility of love implied in the Incarnation: of God for man, of man for God, and of man for man.

The poem is clearly a rejection of the quest for visions, however beguiling, that are not firmly based in this life. But on the positive side, in what the poem approves as the spirit's right oasis, is it in touch, after all, with urgent modern fears and needs? Some readers with a strong sense of the elements of crisis in contemporary life may feel that what Wilbur calls his spirit back to in this poem has its own remoteness and irrelevance. It seems to me, however, that in its rejection of the dreams that remove us from life and reduce its importance, as in its insistence on the blessedness of whatever exists, the poem implies attitudes that could hardly be more responsible. Despite their traditional role in Christian history, these attitudes have not always served as an effective guard against destructive impulses, and yet it is possible that no better guard exists.

Technically, " 'A World Without Objects . . .' " is one of Wilbur's most successful and assured poems. Again and again the phrases are right beyond expectation, right with an ease that is astonishing because it mocks the difficulties of the form. A few phrases, perhaps are not quite expressive enough, in particular "auras, lustres,/And all shinings need to be shaped and borne," a key statement but not an easy one. And the adjective "halo-dialing" may seem both clumsy and puzzling, as it does to me. But the climactic images of "the super-nova burgeoning over the barn,/ Lampshine blurred in the steam of beasts" are richly suggestive and delightful, as are the details of the desert earlier. The "camels of the spirit" are "tall," "slow, proud,/And move with a stilted stride," as if there were something remote and self-absorbed about them. And as "connoisseurs of thirst," they are like Ponce de Leon, whose thirst, in "Sunlight Is Imagination," turned all Florida into a desert.

The poem relates itself in various ways with "Objects," with "Clearness," with "La Rose des Vents," and with some later poems, particularly "Love Calls Us to the Things of this World" (*Things*). "'A World Without Objects . . .'" lacks the sense of the hurrying-on of life that informed "Sunlight Is Imagination" and also the stress on the particularity and uniqueness of objects and textures, the "gay-pocked and potsherd world" of "Objects" or the "opulent bric-a-brac earth" of "On the Eyes." The speaker in "'A World Without Objects . . .'" can see things as eternally blessed; but the unresolved "La Rose des Vents" presents them as eternally vanishing. Some may think the speaker in "'A World Without Objects . . .'" trades one "accurst" mirage for another: instead of textures and integuments that fade into mystery, he has haloes that transfigure forever, a much harder proposition to accept. But he doesn't represent his spirit as finally persuaded or as saved. Rather, "'A World Without Objects . . .'" is a prayer for success in overcoming the temptation of a divided spirit.

Wilbur's consciousness of the hurrying-on of things, of the impermanence of spirits and of objects, reappears in "Lament," another difficult but important poem. He starts from the line "Queens have died young and fair" in the famous poem of Thomas Nashe, "Adieu! Farewell Earth's Bliss!" The queens have "bartered" their light tiaras for ponderous headstones, but the poet wishes to think of them as if they were alive, to recall their fine bodies and their beauty. Then, with a brilliant pun, he introduces a surprising argument: "It is, I say, a most material loss." This assertion means both that the loss of the queens is a loss of their material bodies and also that the loss of their bodies is very much to the point. The next assertion, "Kept spirit is corporate," is a paradox—for how can spirit be corporate? There are two ways: first, our memory of some one else's spirit is based on, inseparable from, our knowledge of his body, his appearance and gestures; second, it is a joint enterprise, for his thought of his lover, says the speaker, grew "out of my wishes and your being," or substantial existence as a body. Both are needed in the delicate mixture of elements that makes up his thought. "Kept spirit" is not abstract but is an image, and an image is a perception, a recollection, or a representation of an object. The implication seems to be that the spirit cannot outlive the body, at any rate not for long enough to be "kept spirit." Clearly, this idea is one we have encountered in "La Rose des Vents" and "'A World Without Objects . . .'"; we may even notice the opportunity of a gloss on the lines (from "'A World Without Objects . . .'") "auras, lustres,/And all shinings need to be shaped and borne"; that is, incarnate or corporate. But, the poem continues, the metaphor of water and air is not satisfactory; though these are durable substances, air is not visible, water not firm enough to serve as symbols for "rarest things." "But rarest things are visible and firm"—a return to the idea that "kept spirit is corporate," that the rarest things (most precious and uncommon, with a beautiful paradox on its other meaning of least dense, even less dense than air) are the bodies themselves that we remember and love.

The poem is a mosaic of such paradoxes. "Grace falls the fastest from our failing past" echoes Nashe's line "Brightness falls from the air" and also glances back at the earlier lines in this poem: "doubly the thought of you,/As air fills air, or waves together toss,/Out of my wishes and your being grew." Grace in both senses of the term evaporates from things we have loved as we forget the images of these things in "our failing past." The poet laments the necessary shortness of the life of grace in his love's bodily gestures "whose spirit only sense can understand." He laments, he says, that he can understand only through his senses, which have their own short life in years as in the failing record of impressions kept by the memory. And he laments the sure passing of the times when his lady's spirit, mortal and unique, "doomed and single, flows/Into the speeches of your eye and hand." These "speeches" are recorded and kept in his memory only through the senses, and her spirit will live only as long as he can recall his sensuous impressions.

This poem is the richest and least sentimental of Wilbur's love poems. The surprising thing is that the intellection remains happy in its effects and that we feel the force of the lament when the poet turns to his own mortal love in the final stanza. Wilbur tellingly joins the ancient theme, the mortality of love and beauty, to a theme of his own: the primacy of the particular body without which spirit is nothing. In this poem, as in some of the earlier ones, he swears by particulars (as the artist must, if he swears at all) without blinking the truth that particulars fade beyond the power of thought to retain their images and thus their spirit.

Before leaving the topic of the poet's concern with his relationship to illusions, to abstractions, to images, and to particulars —in short, his metaphysical interests—we might consider the two couplets Wilbur entitled "Epistemology." Both are expressions of his skeptical and speculative temperament. They are Berkeleyan, of course, and ultimately Platonic, and well within the public domain; no new philosophic insights are presented in them; they are witty statements of old ones. "Kick at the rock, Sam Johnson, break your bones:/But cloudy, cloudy is the stuff of stones." The story is in Boswell's life of Johnson; when Johnson was told that Berkeley doubted the reality of matter, he kicked at a rock in his path and cried, "Thus I refute Berkeley!" In the couplet, "cloudy" may be read in two senses: first, as composed of tiny particles or electrical charges in whirling motion, with vast spaces between particles; and second, as not well perceived or understood even now, mysterious not only to physicists but to all those who are teased by the ancient puzzle of appearance and reality.

The second of these couplets, "Epistemology II," is built on one of the funniest images in modern poetry: "We milk the cow of the world, and as we do/We whisper in her ear, 'You are not true.'" In these lines the word "true" can mean both "real" in the metaphysician's sense, and faithful, reliable, constant, or honest as it does in some of Wilbur's other poems ("O," "Objects," "Conjuration," "La Rose des Vents"). There is a certain self-mockery in this poem, for the poet himself is one of the skeptics. But the wit in both couplets is inseparable from the way they move; they are tiny marvels of ease and grace. In the first one, there are the four separate alliterative pairs, two in each line; there is also the sudden violent beginning and first line, the line of impatient mockery and action, then the slowing down enforced by the sounds of the second line, the line of ominous reiteration of a stubborn truth. In the second couplet, there is the slower middle part after the initial assertion and before the punch at the quotation, a pause craftily located to give the understanding time to take in the first part and prepare for the last. Each couplet is thus perfectly easy in its sounds and witty in its timing; they are a pleasure to say aloud and to think about.

II *Heroic Figures*

Some of the poems already discussed, though primarily epistemological or metaphysical, have also a moral significance. "'A World Without Objects . . .'" is the poet's plea to his spirit to turn away from "pure mirage" to the glory of natural objects and, by implication, to live in this world rather than to withdraw from it. But living in this world is not merely a matter of adjusting one's attitude to objects; it includes establishing a responsible relationship with other people. "La Rose des Vents" also has a moral purport, indeed the same one exactly. The moral element is at least as strong in "Lament," although in this poem, instead of saying "Let us love particular objects, including people," he is saying "I do love a woman in just this way." But these poems are moral chiefly by implication; other poems take up and explore moral topics more openly and directly. Among these, one of the most intricate and elaborate is "Castles and Distances." The interest with which we follow the argument of this poem is a witness to the boldness and discrimination of Wilbur's mind; the confidence we feel in the ultimate coherence of the pattern is a proof of the skill with which he keeps his intellectual and linguistic balance as he develops the argument through its several phases and applications.

The first two stanzas of the poem call up brilliantly the distance, which is not merely geographical, between the austere northern sea where the walrus lives and the frivolous city, whether the modern city of "film palaces" or that of James First with its royal palace. In either city the walrus is laughed at, but Wilbur has located its origins in such a cold sea, one so indifferent to us, that we can sense the vanity in our amusement. There is a hint, too, of a theme touched on in several of the poems discussed earlier: the sin of appropriating wild creatures heartlessly for our own needs and diversion: "The serious face made for surprises/Looks with a thick dismay/At the camera lens which takes/Him in. . . ." But the focus in this poem, as stanza three shows, is on what such hunting does to men who laugh or say "most strange" and let the captured walrus die. So the strangeness of creatures hunted at such a distance steels us to their slaughter and kills our curiosity. Only the hunters, Wilbur says in stanza four, feel regret and love the beasts they kill. In this beautiful and witty stanza the poet sees the hunter and the prey not with the modern pragmatic eye but with the eye of the mythmaker, from whose viewpoint the hunter is forever destined to hunt and the prey, forcing its own doom from the hunter, to be killed. Each has his mystic vocation.

And in the next three stanzas, in a scene depicting the conversion of St. Hubert in the forest, we have an emblem of the hunt, a sign that beasts are God's creatures; but also, in the trophies of real antlers hung high on the chapel wall, a reminder that the truce is miraculous and momentary, that hunters must continue to hunt and stags to die from their arrows. The sweetness in these lines is like that of some medieval sculpture and painting, yet the passage is full of bold figures and phrases. The comparison of the ring of antlers with the tatters left in the target by the "sped thrust" of the "updrawn/Vanishing godbound stone," in which the steeple itself is likened to an arrow shot upward, not only leaves a powerful visual impression; it is symbolically true to the mystical idea that the hunter's role, though destructive, is holy, its spirit a kind of worship. Man must hunt, but creatures must be given their due. When hunting had to be done for human survival, it was only this spirit that could absolve the hunter from the butcher's guilt: "Oh, it is hunters alone/ Regret the beastly pain. . . ."

Though castles and distances appear briefly in the first section of the poem, they do not yet have the central position promised by the title. Part II presents them as symbols whose meanings are posed in contrast. Castles, built by hunting lords, provide views of the distance; they stand in the nearby clearness, set off by contrast from the far haze. Castles, set in their formal grounds, are seats of order; but distance means wilderness, difference, or disorder. Castles mean (imperfect) justice; distance, mercy or escape from justice. Castles are the "world," distance is unworldly; the king in his castle must rule, but to rule is to risk wrong and perhaps inevitably to do harm to others. Distance means an avenue of escape from this responsibility,

> Through Ardens out to Eden isles apart,
> Seeking a shore, or shelter of some spell
> Where harmlessly the hidden heart
> Might hold creation whole.

The hunter's need to kill and the king's need to order, to judge and to punish, to live by strife—these two motifs are linked as twin instances of the tragic inseparability of power and guilt. If we would live harmlessly, we must give up the world. Prospero, who tried both lives, reached in his exile such an isolation in distance that "the world became as island mists"; yet he returned to his dukedom,

> And Duke again, did rights and mercies, risking wrong,
> Found advocates and enemies, and found
> His bounded empire good, where he could hear
> Below his walls the baying hound
> And the loud hunting-song.

So Duke Prospero resumes his life in the world of mortal error, and the hunt goes out from below his walls into the distances in a rite parallel to that of government (the use of force for survival) and perhaps reminds him, and other governors, "to love the foe that quarries out their force." The essential sin is not to risk wrong while seeking right, nor even to do necessary harm, but to remain indifferent to those we harm—as we laugh at the walrus in our "film palaces."

In "Castles and Distances," a kind of rumination, the poet's mind links a number of things rather freely in symbolic patterns; it is, therefore, a highly intellectual poem both in its method and in its preoccupations. "Beowulf" reaches into a remoter time than "Castles and Distances," and its spirit is very different. It seems to use a shifting point of view, so that some things are seen as Beowulf himself would have seen them and others as some modern but highly sympathetic interpreter of his ancient spirit might. "The land was overmuch like scenery"—whose feeling or judgment is this? Beowulf's? Or the poet's? Or that of some persona who can tell us what Beowulf probably thought? On the whole, I think it is that of the poet, but of the poet caught up in a rapt and highly subjective mood, free to give his impressions of Beowulf's story and to interpret Beowulf's mind as if he were receiving messages from the past. Details emerge that no one would think of who was not possessed, and the tone seems strangely sympathetic. A melancholy, weary but heroic mood, like that of Beowulf himself, suffuses the poem. The remoteness of this mood sets Beowulf off from common men, and a strange simplicity in the lines takes us close to the hero's mind and feelings.

When Beowulf arrived in Hrothgar's land to drive out Grendel, the "child,/Grown monstrous," he found himself in "a childish country"; the landscape was too bright for his taste, the people "strangely warm," but

> in all was a vagueness and a strain,
> Because they lived in a land of daily harm.
> And they said the same things again and again.

After he meets Grendel and overcomes him, the country is subtly changed, "And the people were strange, the people strangely cold." The country seems to have lost its childishness and developed another kind of strangeness; but whether this is Beowulf's own moody impression only, some effect of his trial and the deep rest that followed, or a change that occurred in the people themselves, it is hard to say. He had conquered a monstrous child. Was Grendel in some sense the spirit of that "childish country"—childishness itself, perhaps, by which the people had been enchanted and enslaved? When they gave Beowulf gifts and he departed, he "wept that he could share them with no son."

> He died in his own country a kinless king,
> A name heavy with deeds, and mourned as one
> Will mourn for the frozen year when it is done.
> They buried him next the sea on a thrust of land:
> Twelve men rode round his barrow all in a ring,
> Singing of him what they could understand.

Beowulf remains a mystery to his own people, monolithic in courage, magnanimity, grandeur, and inarticulacy. Something of the spirit of the hero's isolation, as well as some of the dark stoic mood of the age, may be felt in this fantasy. One feels that the poet has made an extraordinary effort of the sympathetic imagination. If we compare this entranced elegy with any of Wilbur's brighter and wittier poems, we are struck by the range of which the poet is capable.

Very different from "Beowulf" in every way but one—its interest in the isolated, responsible hero—is "Still, Citizen Sparrow." In "Beowulf," the tone is remote, elegiac, primitive in some sense of the word. We are not sure whose tone it is, but it is triumphantly evocative of an age and a personage. The tone of "Still, Citizen Sparrow" is modern, urbane, casual, reasonable in argument, but ironical in such a way that some lines carry a perplexing ambiguity. The poem begins as if it were breaking into an argument just as the poet is about to have his say. Citizen Sparrow has been claiming that a certain political leader, now out of office, is not only a vulture but unnatural, a monster. The poet defends this vulture, arguing that if he can be given a chance to climb again to the altitude where he is at home, he will be both beautiful and powerful. If he is to re-assume power, he must be elected to office, but to "a rotten office." If, as I assume, this "rotten office" is also the "carrion ballast" that the re-empowered vulture would carry aloft, then its rottenness may imply that it is outmoded and functionless; though it might serve to launch the vulture on a new political career, it could not constrain him by any firm limitation of his powers. As "carrion," however, the office would provide the vulture with a living; and, as "ballast," it might, through some residual authority, exert a steadying influence upon him.

Once far up above such small, low-flying birds as the sparrow ("you/Who dart in the orchard aisles") he "shoulders nature there," assuming great responsibilities and meeting them with heroic courage: "it is he/Devours death, mocks mutability,/ Has heart to make an end, keeps nature new." The appropriate meaning of the word "mock" seems to be "mimic" or "imitate." With his capacity for facing necessity, the vulture will clear away those remnants of the past which obstruct healthy change. The poet asks the sparrow, therefore, to pardon this hero. He is like Noah, whose clamorous preparations for the voyage were an annoyance to all small-minded men; if they are tempted to accuse him of callousness, they should not forget his strength:

> Forget that he could bear
> To see the towns like coral under the keel,
> And the fields so dismal deep. Try rather to feel
> How high and weary it was, on the waters where
>
> He rocked his only world, and everyone's.
> Forgive the hero, you who would have died
> Gladly with all you knew; he rode that tide
> To Ararat; all men are Noah's sons.

Weaker men should try to understand and appreciate the burdens of strong ones, to whom they owe so much. "Forgive the hero" is an ironic request: it is only because the sparrows *are* small birds that they condemn big ones. But in a democracy even the smallest citizens have the power to choose whether or not big men shall lead them. The last statement in the poem ("all men are Noah's sons") has a special richness beyond its dialectical point; it means not merely "you owe your life to such men" but also, of course, "we too inherit and harbor within ourselves the capacity to do great things." The poem is thus a plea for keeping the faults of great men in perspective. The vulture is not, after all, "unnatural": greatness is a human quality, as natural as the fears of the sparrows.

"Driftwood" celebrates different but equally heroic qualities: those which enable a man to retain his individuality through all vicissitudes. It is a great theme, and a fine poem comes of it—a poem, moreover, of a distinctly individual character. It is written in a four-line stanza whose lines have a 5342 stress pattern. The meter is basically iambic, but the stress is kept irregular so as to produce a rough, free rhythm with heavy pauses. These features, together with the constant alliteration, result in a distant, melancholy, pounding movement that recalls Anglo-Saxon poetry. The verse seems gnarled, bumpy, tough, with something of the "dense,/Ingenerate grain" of the driftwood; and its sound and movement may remind us of the restless suck and surge of the sea in which these worn timbers have spent their years:

> Brought in the end where breakers dump and slew
> On the glass verge of the land,
> Silver they rang to the stones when the sea
> Flung them and turned.

The rhyming pattern, though Wilbur does use it elsewhere, is not a common one: xaxb, xaxb, xcxd, etc. The Anglo-Saxon flavor is strengthened by touches of archaic diction and syntax. These properties of the style have a genuine role to play in a poem about old things that have served and survived their purpose without losing their character.

The poem is a flight of fancy that recreates the history of "these relics" as it might have been, controlled by a sense of the loose analogy between their story and human experience. When we understand that "the old engine of grief" is not only the sea but life itself—the restless medium of harsh experience, the agent of fate—we see that the first two stanzas evoke not only the life of young trees, though they do that with sympathy, but also some features of human childhood and of the possible origins of durable character, of a "dense,/Ingenerate grain." When they were old enough, "Their solitude was taken" for work in the world; they were given a useful shape and function and, to take the human side of the analogy, set to arduous and (it is hinted) fabulous tasks. They performed them greatly and survived voyages and battles into a time beyond their usefulness. The poem is thick with abstractions on which the poet sometimes puns. Stanza four provides an example, with its pun on "lost ends" (geographical limits but also purposes or causes), but stanzas five and six are better worth quoting, not only to demonstrate the richness of the diction but to display their brilliant evocation of the sound and movement of the sea:

> Then on the great generality of waters
> Floated their singleness,
> And in all that deep subsumption they were
> Never dissolved;
>
> But shaped and flowingly fretted by the waves'
> Ever surpassing stress,
> With the gnarled swerve and tangle of tides
> Finely involved.

Calling the sea "the great generality of waters" is a fine stroke, evoking with admirable economy its vastness, its inclusiveness, and its undifferentiated character in order to dramatize the situation of single pieces of wood on its surface. Literally, "to subsume" means "to take under or into"; figuratively, to take one item under a heading, as the single wood into that "great generality." Thus the word "subsumption" is used with a delicate justice not only to the argument but also to the patterns of imagery and sound required in this passage. There are puns also, of course, in "fretted" (to be vexed, to be eroded, to be shaped into frets) and in "involved" (to be rolled in or on, to be wrapped up in).

Now, as the pieces of driftwood lie silver on the "gold sand," they look to the poet like "Curious crowns and scepters,"

> Warped, wry, but having the beauty of
> Excellence earned.
>
> In a time of continual dry abdications
> And of damp complicities,
> They are fit to be taken for signs, these emblems
> Royally sane,
> Which have ridden to homeless wreck, and long revolved
> In the lathe of all the seas,
> But have saved in spite of it all their dense
> Ingenerate grain.

By introducing what seems an unnecessary new metaphor for the driftwood, this crown and scepter imagery may seem to obscure the idea of the preserved identity of human character. But the metaphor is to some extent prepared for: the sea was a melting pot for metal in the first stanza; the driftwood rang "silver" to the stones in stanza seven; and "the lathe of all the seas" in the last stanza might be a metal or a wood lathe. But, because the metal of crowns and scepters has no grain to preserve, one feels a strain in accepting them, in this poem where grain is so important, as metaphors for either wood or human character. Even so, "Driftwood" seems to me one of Wilbur's finest poems, as it is one of his most individual. The human qualities celebrated in it are indeed akin to those celebrated in the other poems discussed in this section, but nowhere else does he present so powerful a symbol of the stubborn assertion of moral identity against erosion, engulfment, and dissolution by vast impersonal forces. Anyone still inclined to think of Wilbur as a poetic dandy, as a mere stylist or virtuoso, is shutting his eyes to the moral preoccupations revealed in the poems of the group just discussed—and in many others.

III ". . . the man/We are"

While Wilbur's usual tone is that of amusement, praise, or delight, and while he seems in general among the least angry, frightened, or despairing of contemporary poets, there is in his work, nevertheless, a persistent concern about human shortcomings. No major progress toward discontent characterizes his development; even in his earliest work there is some protest, and in his latest he retains his old pleasure in man and nature. The number of poems that are critical of certain faults in mankind nonetheless gradually grows as the intensity of the criticism strengthens. Turning to "Marché aux Oiseaux," we see Wilbur protesting against cruelty in one of its commonest forms. The puns on musical terms in the first stanza (on "minor" and "burden") are not so telling as the comparison of the birds' song with a fountain "lightly loud." How sad it is that caged birds will sing! And what does the song mean? The *travailleur* is enraged, but his hearers think his chirr is joyful. The eighth line should be heard: "He batters softly at his wooden cage." We should hear too the names of the birds imprisoned in the cages: they suggest not only brilliant color and daintiness, remote exotic origins, but uniqueness. Each bird is a singularity, a treasure of its kind. Then we notice the implications of the word "stacked": to the sellers all are alike in that all are merchandise, like eggs or potatoes. "Termless" is a good and characteristic pun, meaning both endless and unconditional. The buyers' need for love is "outrageous," a tyranny and a perversion.

Who the buyers are is apparent in stanza four. Their need is explained by their shortcomings. But the "we" of stanza five identifies the buyers with the rest of us to suggest that destructive love is a human trait, one more clearly seen in the less perfect specimens of the race, perhaps, but not confined to them. There should flash through our minds the untold damage we may do, not only to birds but to each other, by the kind of love that keeps control at any cost, even that of retarding the full development of powers in the person loved. The destructive power of love is a major theme. But in the unusually angry lines that make up stanza five, I feel a certain failure of tone as the poet speaks through the character of these desperate, pathetic bird-lovers. To test this opinion, the reader might try leaving off the last stanza entirely. The poem would still make its point. It would make it more delicately, to be sure, but I think the last line of stanza four would linger in the mind with all the disturbing power of the poem behind it.

"The Puritans" resembles "Marché aux Oiseaux" in describing a scene while preparing for an angry or at least a highly critical comment on it. The poem implies an idea: Puritans are those who denounce in daylight the very crimes they commit at night. The title seems too inclusive—that is, there are honest and dishonest puritans—but the shot nevertheless hits a target. Atonement for these people consists simply in denouncing "the sunk murder" while the corpse itself poisons the river. The second stanza contains some of Wilbur's best descriptive writing:

> Blam. In the noon's perfected brilliance burn
> Brief blooms of flame, which soil away in smoke;
> And down below, where slowed concussion broke
> The umber stroll of waters, water-dust
> Dreamily powders up, and serves to turn
> The river surface to a cloudy rust.

In this stanza sound and sense are brilliantly matched and fused; alliteration and assonance are rarely so happily employed; and the lines move as deliberately and inevitably as the events themselves.

Just as interesting in its language, and even more penetrating in its suggestions about human nature and the human condition, is "Year's-End." Stanza one describes a village in the snow on New Year's Eve:

> From the soft street the rooms of houses show
> A gathered light, a shapen atmosphere,
> Like frozen-over lakes whose ice is thin
> And still allows some stirring down within.

The next three stanzas are devoted to reflections on the postures in death of frozen leaves, fossilized ferns, mammoths frozen in ice and preserved for ages, the sleeping dog at Pompeii. These things die perfect and complete. But human beings at the moment of death are always incomplete: "We fray into the future, rarely wrought/Save in the tapestries of afterthought." And with the next words, "More time, more time," the poem returns to the scene and to the moment of its opening: it is because they always need more time that human beings cheer on the eve of the new year: "Barrages of applause/Come muffled from a buried radio./The New-year bells are wrangling with the snow." The snow is a symbol of death or the end of time; the bells are the voice of new life, another chance for another year. The poem is introduced by lines that contain a flurry of puns: "Now winter downs the dying of the year,/And night is all a settlement of snow." If puns on "downs" are intended (puts down, covers with white down, makes downs of), they do not seem entirely satisfactory; but those on "settlement" are in Wilbur's wittiest vein (a coming down of snow through the air, a community or village, a final arrangement).

While the poem presents mankind as always unready for death, there is in this plight potentially as much to be praised as deplored. All depends on whether a man has done much or little—or done what he should have done. But when Wilbur speaks of "the random hands, the loose unready eyes/Of men expecting yet another sun/To do the shapely thing they had not done," the words suggest slackness and a foolish hope. Even so, the power of the poem is not so much in the criticism of unready man as in the collocation of things with their associations of meaning—the New Year as an end and a beginning, its similarity to other ends of time, the relative grace and perfection of the deaths of leaf, mammoth, fern, dog—and in the language that orders these details and makes them vivid.

In "Giacometti," on the other hand, the poet is concerned with the whole style and circumstance of modern man. In the late 1940's the Italian painter and sculptor Alberto Giacometti was producing the extremely thin and elongated human figures in roughly textured plaster and bronze for which he is now famous. Wilbur seems to have visited Giacometti's atelier, "a room/Dim as a cave of the sea," and he may have seen there a plaster figure of walking man, "Towering like a thin/Coral, out of a reef of plaster chalk. . . ."[4]

In any case Wilbur finds in Giacometti's sculptures a relentless attempt to see modern man as he is. The poem, which consists of ten six-line stanzas, begins by arguing that "Rock insults us" by its hardness, its unfocused scorn, its power to strike without stirring. We respond by carving it laboriously into the human image. "So we can baffle rock, and in our will/Can clothe and keep it." But as time passes and we change, then we are mocked and oppressed by these very emblems of our older selves. Typically, these figures of the past are individuals, represented as religious, or thoughtful, or firm of purpose,

> While we on every side,
> Random as shells the sea drops down ashore,
> Are walking, walking, many and alone.

Indeed, the poet suggests, stone is not a suitable material for representing modern man: he is too changeable, various, numerous, mobile. Not stone, but Giacometti's walking plaster figures represent him truly: "This is the single form we can assume." In four brilliant and haunting stanzas, Wilbur seeks and finds our modern nature in Giacometti's emaciated walkers:

> We are this man unspeakably alone
> Yet stripped of the singular utterly, shaved and scraped
> Of all but being there,
> Whose fullness is escaped
> Like a burst balloon's: no nakedness so bare
> As flesh gone in inquiring of the bone.
>
> He is pruned of every gesture, saving only
> The habit of coming and going. . . .
> .   .   .   .
>   . . . we are
> This starless walker, one who cannot guess
> His will, his keel his nose's bony blade.

And volumes hover round like future shades
This least of man, in whom we join and take
A pilgrim's step behind,
And in whose guise we make
Our grim departures now, walking to find
What railleries of rock, what palisades?

I have not been able to read the first line of the final stanza in any way that seems adequate. For the rest, we recognize in "this least of man" our own epitome, take on his semblance, and walk in his steps. In the final line the poet recalls his earlier thought that, even in its natural state, rock insults and resists us. As we pass into the future, its antagonism—and by synecdoche, perhaps, that of the whole natural order—will express itself in ways that we cannot foresee. The word "palisades," which refers us back to the mocking "cliffs" of the third stanza, seems to carry the connotation, "barriers set in man's path by an antagonistic nature." The poem is so responsive to Giacometti's reduction of man to a solitary, anonymous, purposeless walker that we can use it as an illustration of Wilbur's capacity to take an un-flattering—though not an unsympathetic—view of humanity to-day. And yet the strongest impulse in the poem is Wilbur's ad-miration for Giacometti's art—for his willful, assertive control over rock in the service of self-criticism. We are not simply aim-less and helpless if we can see ourselves so clearly in Giacometti's work and admire the justice of the portrait. This gusto is a counterweight to the impulses toward despair and self-contempt that may be felt in the poem, and another is the assurance im-plied in the central image that, moving, we will surely change.

IV Three Metamorphoses

Of "The Death of a Toad" Wilbur has said that the poem is "the only instance in which I went straight from something that happened to me to writing a poem about it, with very little violation of the actual circumstances, though I put more into it before I was through than I'd felt at the time."[5] This poem pro-vided the critic Randall Jarrell with an instance of what he took to be over-fine writing. This is his comment:

When you read "The Death of a Toad," a poem that begins "A toad the power mower caught,/Chewed and clipped of a leg, with a hobbling hop has got/To the garden verge," you stop to shudder at the raw being of the world, at all that "a hobbling hop" has brought to life—that toad is real, all right. But when you read on, when Mr. Wilbur says that the toad "dies/Toward some deep monotone,/Toward misted and ebullient seas/And cooling shores, toward lost Amphibia's emperies," you think with a surge of irritation and dismay, "So it was all only an excuse for some Poetry."[6]

But Wilbur's lines might be taken—more plausibly, I think—as "Poetry" of a deliberate extravagance, used half-mockingly of a subject that is inadequate to it. There was a time, of course, when toads and their kind ruled the earth. In proposing that the toad at the point of death can recall and review the day of "Amphibia's" glory and dominion, Wilbur is already within a fantastic realm which may justify inflated language. In short, the poem may be read as another of those gentle but high-spirited mockeries so common in Wilbur's work, and the language enjoyed for its strange power and beauty:

> The rare original heartsblood goes,
> Spends on the earthen hide, in the folds and wizenings, flows
> In the gutters of the banked and staring eyes. He lies
> As still as if he would return to stone . . .

Even the ambitious adjectives in the last two lines ("To watch, across the castrate lawn,/The haggard daylight steer") justify themselves if we imagine that the dying toad looks on the modern world as a world in the last stage of decline. When an interviewer asked Wilbur whether he had encountered the word "emperies" in the poetry of Donne, he replied: "I may have found it in John Donne in the first place, but I think I wanted to use it here as a kind of confession that I'm doing rather a lot with that toad. I'm turning him into the primal energies of the world in the course of this poem. And so I get a little bombastic as a way of acknowledging that I'm going rather far."[7]

"A Simile for her Smile" has its humor too, as we see what an impressive ceremony the lady's smile must be. It comes like the packet with its bells and paddle wheel, and all the suggestions of elaborate gallantry are implicit in the way the halted traffic waits for it to pass. And yet the speaker's tribute is not merely a joke: the lover means to honor the lady and does so. If he exaggerates, the teasing remains admiring and affectionate. "He Was" is based on the poet's memory of a gardener "all but dumb" who was outlived by an orchard he had planted in the fall

> . . . with so great care
> In that last year that none was lost, and May
> Aroused them all, the leaves saying the land's
> Praise for the livening clay,
> And the found voice of his buried hands
> Rose in the sparrowy air.

Just the right degrees of sadness, affection, and playfulness are mixed into this poem which honors an inarticulate man for good work done without despair at the end of his life.

"Five Women Bathing in Moonlight" seems to me one of Wilbur's subtlest poems. Ostensibly a descriptive poem, as the title suggests, it is full of passages that go beyond description. The very first sentence presents a statement, not an image:

> When night believes itself alone
> It is most natural, conceals
> No artifice. The open moon
> With webs in sky and water wields
>
> The slightest wave. . . .

This first sentence needs "specification": it does not, as it stands, awaken in us any recognition of a mood of the night. What artifice does the night conceal when it knows it is not alone? Even if we could imagine how to illustrate or give body to this statement, we could not be sure that our imaginings would be similar to Wilbur's. There are ambiguities enough in such terms as "natural," "conceals," and "artifice" to make us dizzy. But, if we take "artifice" to mean an apt contrivance, perhaps it refers to the "webs in sky and water" by which the moon "wields/The slightest wave." The poet's fancy would be that, when night believes itself alone, those "webs" (lines of force or attraction?) can be seen, or sensed, as in a "vision." "Wields" emphasizes the firm, purposeful, and practiced control of the moon over even "the slightest wave," all the more remarkable in that it can be done with webs, though we accept this feat as a miracle. But now the poet's attention is drawn to another aspect of the scene:

> . . . This vision yields
> To a cool accord of semblance, land
> Leasing each wave the palest peals
> Of bright apparent notes of sand.

The sand throws on the waves a pale reflection of its own bright color. Here we may feel some strain: the surprising analogy be-

tween the gleams on the waves and a peal of bells, apparently
suggested by the possibility of the pun on "notes," can be followed with pleasure, but "leasing" seems far-fetched and "apparent" is hardly needed. It should be noted that the quatrains
themselves are linked by rhyme: *abab, bcbc, cdcd,* etc.—an unusually difficult scheme to carry out.

The rest of the poem traces the implications of the phrase "a
cool accord of semblance" by showing the outlines of the women's bodies and their voices blurred and blended into the seascape until the women, "unaware/How lost they are . . . begin"

> To mix with water, making then
> Gestures of blithe obedience,
> As five Danilovas within
> The soft compulsions of their dance.

These last three stanzas seem to me very fine, not only pictorially
and audibly, but also in their evocation from mythology and
folklore of a whole complex of notions about the close dependence of women on the moon and its cycle. Though "unaware
how lost they are," they are in the moon's power—lost to the eye
and ear of the observer, first of all; and second, lost as individuals with their separate wills. They are diffused, mixed
with water, their hair like seaweed, their voices "plucked with
words." They have become mermaids or sea-nymphs, compelled
or charmed out of their humanity and enlisted in a dance of the
moon-worshippers. (One is reminded of "Merlin Enthralled," in
which something like this happens to Merlin, whose fatal creature, the sorceress Niniane, "receives him as the sea receives a
stream.")

As we look for clues to an attitude toward this enchantment,
we must examine the surprising words: "The moon's misprision
salves them in-/To silver. . . ." It is a wrongful act, a crime, for
the moon to have effected this transformation; and the women,
though they dance most beautifully, are "lost." "Salves" can
mean two things: (1) soothes or mollifies, and (2) saves or
rescues, or salvages from loss or destruction. If they are already
lost, the second meaning seems impossible; but perhaps the
first may be taken to suggest the gentleness or insidiousness of
the moon's influence, which so acts upon them that "they are
unaware/How lost they are. . . ." The poet stands helpless and
abandoned on the shore.

V *The Ceremony of Art*

As in his earlier collection, Wilbur included in *Ceremony* a number of poems directly or indirectly concerned with the artist's problems. Some of these have been briefly discussed. "La Rose des Vents" gives us a glimpse of the poetic character and the poet's dreams. The title is explained by Wilbur's note on the poem in *Mid-Century American Poets* (p. 12): "The French call the compass-rose the Rose of the Winds." (The compass-rose is the often ornate figure on the face of old compasses.) Appalled by mortality and mutability, the poet is intent on the rescue mission of which poetry is capable. He and his lady, he says, will dwell forever "On the rose of the winds,/Which is the isle/Of every sea. . . ." But the lady rejects his plea that they "rise and go" and holds out for life, though only for the hour, in this world. Her objection to going with him is stated as follows:

> That roving wave
> Where Venus rose
> Glints in the floods
> Of farthest thought;
> What beauty there
> In image goes
> Dissolves in other
> And is not.

The Greek myth tells us that Venus was born in the sea and floated ashore at Kythera. But the sea of this poem is that of mind or imagination, "the floods/Of farthest thought," the mother of myths and of all the arts. By "farthest thought," perhaps the lady means remote, in the sense of not immediate, not concerned with the here and now; or perhaps she means extended to the limits of the conceivable, almost beyond imagining. In any case, as the second half of the quoted stanza shows, she does not envy Venus nor aspire to the immortality by which the poet has hoped to tempt her. Indeed, if my reading is adequate, she sees very shrewdly that the poet is in a sense predatory, that his aims run counter to hers, that he will use her mortal "beauty" to create an immortal "image," but that *she* will be destroyed in the process. She has, in fact, identified her poet as one whose views and desires are not unlike those of Poe, who, says Wilbur, argued that "the poet begins with earthly things (Rowena, Mary Chaworth, the City, the Sea), subverts

their identities and accomplishes their imaginative destruction."[8]
Fully understanding what the poet's invitation implies, the lady
of "La Rose des Vents" refuses to sacrifice her identity and insists on the value of her doomed and single life:

> There are some shores
> Still left to find
> Whose broken rocks
> Will last the hour;
> Forsake those roses
> Of the mind
> And tend the true,
> The mortal flower.

The happy phrase of these concluding lines, "the true,/The
mortal flower," is a terse reminder of Wilbur's trust in particular
things, expressed earlier in such poems as "O" and "Objects." A
difficult but delightful comparison may be made between the
lady of "La Rose des Vents" and the apparition of the much
later poem "She" (*Advice*), which is written entirely from the
poet's point of view.

Some of the formal qualities Wilbur seems to value most in
poetry are illustrated and celebrated in "Juggler," which gives
us also a theory of their function. In its way, the poem is another
attempt to deal with the problem of Poe's "mechanism of destructive transcendence" (Wilbur's phrase), the problem of "La Rose
des Vents," the problem on which "Praise in Summer" was an
early, tentative comment. The question is: What does art do to
the world? Poe says it must destroy and transcend it. The lady
of "La Rose des Vents" agrees—and refuses to be destroyed and
transcended for art's sake. "Praise in Summer" says that art—or,
at any rate, metaphor—"perverts our praise to uncreation" and
asks "Does sense so stale that it must needs derange/The world
to know it?" "Juggler" answers "yes," and gaily re-creates a performance in which the poet saw the world deranged and known
anew:

> A ball will bounce, but less and less. It's not
> A light-hearted thing, resents its own resilience.
> Falling is what it loves, and the earth falls
> So in our hearts from brilliance,
> Settles and is forgot.
> It takes a sky-blue juggler with five red balls

> To shake our gravity up. Whee, in the air
> The balls roll round, wheel on his wheeling hands,
> Learning the ways of lightness, alter to spheres
> Grazing his finger ends,
> Cling to their courses there,
> Swinging a small heaven about his ears.

The writing is brilliant in its swiftness and ease, in the sensitivity with which the verse follows the action in sound, pace, and phrasing, and in the justice and interest of the central metaphor. The world fades from our consciousness; we don't see it as we once did, for we are too grave. Happily, it can be shaken up ("deranged") and lightened; its tendency to dull and deaden can be defied by a master who can create of its elements an ideal world ("a small heaven") and control it as he will for the term of the illusion.

Then comes a wise and witty comment from the author of " 'A World Without Objects . . . ,'" in which he implored "The tall camels of the spirit" to turn from mirages to reality:

> But a heaven is easier made of nothing at all
> Than the earth regained, and still and sole within
> The spin of worlds, with a gesture sure and noble
> He reels that heaven in,
> Landing it ball by ball,
> And trades it all for a broom, a plate, a table.

Not to be the victim of one's imaginative powers, not to be destroyed by one's own creatures, not to lose touch with the world while maintaining the artistic illusion—these are the scruples of a canny spirit who believes, unlike Poe, that the earth is worth regaining. Donald Hall has suggested that there may be a significant difference between the balls and the broom, plate, and table. Trading one for the other may amount to the artist's renouncing more easily manageable materials or forms in favor of the awkward objects and experience of everyday life— the things of this world.

The next stanza is a masterpiece of tone and pace, to say nothing of the skill it shows, worthy of a juggler, in handling its clever rhymes without the slightest awkwardness. The suddenness with which the scene ends in the last line is, I think, one of the most pleasing effects in all of Wilbur's work:

> Oh, on his toe the table is turning, the broom's
> Balancing up on his nose, and the plate whirls
> On the tip of the broom! Damn, what a show, we cry:
> The boys stamp, and the girls
> Shriek, and the drum booms
> And all comes down, and he bows and says good-bye.

Wilbur concludes by returning to the theme: the revivifying of
the world through art (or certain kinds of art), the artist's
victory over its normal recalcitrance:

> If the juggler is tired now, if the broom stands
> In the dust again, if the table starts to drop
> Through the daily dark again, and though the plate
> Lies flat on the table top,
> For him we batter our hands
> Who has won for once over the world's weight.

The juggler's is a temporary victory. We cannot live forever in
that "small heaven," but it is a great deal that, through the
artist's mediation, we can reach it at all. Those who love good
poems can reach it through "Juggler," for "the world's weight"
includes not only that of objects but that of language—the lightness, resilience, precision, and grace of which Wilbur revives
here from its mundane heaviness and flatness.

It is worthwhile to compare the function of art implied in
"Juggler" with the rather different one acknowledged in "Giacometti." In "Giacometti" the artist is less a master of illusion
than a moral and intellectual force who tells us who we are,
suggests our powers and failings, stubbornly seeks the human
truth. Something is proposed in "Giacometti" about the artist's
struggle to subdue his materials and their power to mock him
later, in the forms he shapes, as the times and his own will
undergo changes. But mainly we see in the poem a study of the
artist's power to devise a convincing image of contemporary
man. We become this man more surely under Giacometti's influence; for better or for worse, his insight guides us and thus
contributes something to our fate itself. The poem concerns the
broadly educational effects of art and acknowledges their importance.

But, in the arts, everything must be done through form.
"Ceremony," Wilbur's title poem, takes its start from a painting
by the French nineteenth-century painter Jean Frédéric Bazille:

> A striped blouse in a clearing by Bazille
> Is, you may say, a patroness of boughs
> Too queenly kind toward nature to be kin.
> But ceremony never did conceal,
> Save to the silly eye, which all allows,
> How much we are the woods we wander in.

The lady in the striped blouse seems too superior, too gracious toward the surrounding trees, to be a part of nature herself. She looks too dainty, too artfully got up, too fashionable. But ceremony—formal dress and address, manner and gesture—never did conceal, except to the naïve observer who is taken in by any disguise, how much a part of nature we are underneath. If the lady were not dressed for "society" but appeared instead as a water-nymph, naked on a bed of ferns, proclaiming her kinship with streams and flowers, then the scene would lose its lively incongruity, that of nature versus art, and become wholly natural, idyllic, harmonious—and dull. In the "feigning lady" the poet finds an art which conceals nature without denying it, an art to which he gives the name "wit." When he says "What's lightly hid is deepest understood," he compliments the lady on her wisdom. The difficult closing lines of the poem push the argument a little farther:

> And when with social smile and formal dress
> She teaches leaves to curtsey and quadrille,
> I think there are most tigers in the wood.

Teaching the leaves to assume manners and graces, the lady is doing for them only what she has done for herself. The desire to submit nature—whether outer or inner nature makes no difference—to ceremony implies a deep respect for the power of natural forces. The lady shares more than her stripes with the tiger, and she is therefore more interesting to the poet than the languorous and insipid Sabrina.

In choosing "Ceremony" as a title for the book, Wilbur seems to have intended the term to include poetry, or at least his own kind of poetry. A poem may be considered a ceremony which teaches or forces our wildness to order, control, and gentle itself. A high degree of formality may be the expression of an unusually acute sense of the unruly, whether in human or in non-human nature. Readers of the poem "Ceremony" may usefully recall Wilbur's description of poetry as a way of ordering the chaos of one's world and also his aphorism "the strength of the genie comes of his being confined in a bottle." The bottle is a shape, a form, a ritual pattern, a ceremony. In this volume of poems, and "most typically" in the closing lines of "Ceremony," Peter Viereck found evidence of a "subsurface Dionysian storm."[9]

VI The Poet as Critic

Before *Ceremony* appeared Wilbur had published at least two reviews of the work of other poets and some notes outlining his own poetic credo. The reviews are not only excellent as reviews; they also inevitably reveal something of his poetic outlook, tastes, and convictions. In the first, writing on Cecil Day Lewis' *Poems 1943-1947*, Wilbur offers some conjectures about the reasons for the decline in the technical skill and power of Lewis' work since the 1930's. To the student of Wilbur's poems, the most significant passage is perhaps his warning against the dangers of trying to reach a wide audience by "approaching poetry to the public speech . . . : loss of subtlety and spontaneity; neglect of contradictions; the orator's fake clarity; discomfort about 'obscurity'; assumption of a too dissociated persona; ingratiation" (*Poetry* [May, 1949], p. 17).

Wilbur's other review is of John Frederick Nims's *A Fountain in Kentucky and other Poems*. Like Lewis, Nims had resolved in his poems "to court the commonplace" (Lewis' phrase); but unlike Lewis he was making no special effort to communicate with large numbers of readers. Though much of what Wilbur says about Nims's poems is merely—though shrewdly—descriptive, his own standards appear when he identifies two sources of strain in some of Nims's poems: one, an excessive attention to the surface of the verse, a self-conscious wordiness and contrivance; the other, "a fatal excess of deference to his 'object,' or to a mistaken notion of objectivity" (*Poetry* [November, 1950], p. 107).

Wilbur was one of a number of poets who were represented in John Ciardi's anthology *Mid-Century American Poets* (1950). The poets had been asked to give their answers to a series of questions on poetry and on their own working principles, and these were printed with several of their poems. Wilbur's statement, entitled "The Genie in the Bottle," begins with a warning against taking any artist's comments on his own work too seriously. The penetrating little essay that follows is an affirmation of *poetry* (not something else), an acceptance of its limits and its special resources, an attempt to define it and to express confidence in it. Throughout, Wilbur shows an unusually sharp awareness of the dilemmas that poets were confronting at the time; and what he says about contemporary poetry has the balance and breadth that comes from a good understanding of older poetry. Curious readers are urged to consult the essay itself, for only the scraps that follow can be given here. The questions are Ciardi's; the answers are Wilbur's but much of value has been omitted.

1. *Is the poem meant to be read aloud?*
   Any poem written by a man or woman with an ear profits by being read aloud. . . .

2. *To whom is the poem addressed? How difficult may a poem be?*
   A poem is addressed to the Muse. It is one function of the Muse to cover up the fact that poems are not addressed to anybody in particular. During the act of writing, the poem is an effort to express a knowledge imperfectly felt, to articulate relationships not quite seen, to make or discover some pattern in the world. It is a conflict with disorder, not a message from one person to another. Once the poem is written and published, however, it belongs to anyone who will take it, and the more the better. . . .

3. *What is your attitude toward the language of the poem?*
   . . . one does not, merely by referring to the dying god or what not, evoke a legitimate emotional response. The value of the reference must in every case be proven.

5. *What is your attitude toward irony and paradox?*
   There should be no flight from irony and paradox in writing poetry, rather an insistence on them. They are often the source, I think, of what richness and honesty we may sense in a poem. But "the corruption of the best is the worst," and it is unfortunately the case that these devices . . . can also be the slickest tools for saying nothing at all.

6. *What is your attitude toward subject-matter?*
   Ideally, the "subject-matter" of poetry should be limitless. For the individual poet, however, limitation in subject-matter seems often to be a condition of power. . . .

7. *Do you have anything to say about imagery?*
   I think it a great vice to convey everything by imagery, particularly if the imagery is not interrelated. There ought to be areas of statement. But the statement should not equal and abolish the "objects" in the poem, as Arnold's does in *Rugby*

Chapel. All those rocks and cataracts gone in a puff of piety! The statement should have obliquity, and congruence to the imagery, as Marianne Moore's does—not vitiating the objects, but rather finding in them another and ideal dimension.

8. *What about rhyme?*
Aside from its obvious value in the finished poem as a part of poetic form and as a heightener of language, rhyme seems to me an invaluable aid in composition. It creates difficulties which the utterance must surmount by increased resourcefulness. It also helps by liberally suggesting arbitrary connections of which the mind may take advantage if it likes. . . .

9. *What is your attitude toward the structure of the total poem?*
. . . The use of strict poetic forms, traditional or invented, is like the use of framing and composition in painting: both serve to limit the work of art, and to declare its artificiality: they say, "This is not the world, but a pattern imposed upon the world or found in it; this is a partial and provisional attempt to establish relations between things."

There are other less metaphysical reasons for preferring strictness of form: the fact, for example, that subtle variation is unrecognizable without the pre-existence of a norm; or the fact that form, in slowing and complicating the writing-process, calls out the poet's full talents, and thereby insures a greater care and cleverness in the choice and disposition of words. In general, I would say that limitation makes for power: the strength of the genie comes of his being confined in a bottle.

These opinions are not particularly surprising or original: they are based on an intelligent appreciation of, and a general sympathy with, the best criticism of the 1930's and 1940's. But they are expressed with a rare firmness, lucidity, and point, and they give us a closer acquaintance than we could otherwise have with Wilbur's taste, if not necessarily with his working principles.

Not much need be said here about Wilbur's one short story, "A Game of Catch" (*New Yorker* [July 18, 1953]). Less than four columns long, it tells how a seventh-grader named Scho, excluded from a game of catch by two other boys, climbs a tree to watch them play and then retaliates by insisting that all their actions are the result of his wishes. This ploy baffles and annoys the others, and one of them finally sets out to force Scho into silence. They are frightened, however, when Scho is scared into falling from his tree; for they do not really want to see him hurt.

Scho persists to the point of hysteria, undeterred even when badly shaken by his fall and unmollified by apology. His triumph is somehow real, but so is his misery; and one sympathizes with him as the least complacent and assured of the boys, one who is desperately using his wits to assert a psychological domination over the others. In his final short-winded croak from under the tree one might perhaps hear the voice of whatever in a fiction-writer's complex make-up may be power-seeking and compensatory: "I want you to do whatever you're going to do for the whole rest of your life."

VII   *Critics' Opinions*

At this point in his career, with two books of poems published, Wilbur had earned the admiration of many critics concerned with contemporary poetry. Despite the dissatisfaction that Randall Jarrell expressed in 1951 in *Poetry and the Age,* he granted that Wilbur "seems the best of the quite young poets writing in this country, poets considerably younger than Lowell and Bishop and Shapiro and Roethke and Schwartz. . . ." (230). About the same time, in an article on "American Poets Since the War," Donald Hall came to much the same conclusion. "Wilbur is less exciting than Roethke," he said, "and less moving than Robert Lowell, but produces with his particular genius poems which are among the best written in America in many years."[10] Still later, Hall wrote an article based on interviews and entitled "Method in Poetic Composition (with special attention to the techniques of Richard Eberhart and Richard Wilbur)." Eberhart appears in the article as "the contemporary vates. To him it seems that poetry is spontaneous, and the expression of a divine madness." Wilbur, on the other hand, appears as a slow, deliberate craftsman who "often carries the idea of the poem in his head for some time," perhaps making notes for it before writing. The writing itself "is a condition of intense self-absorption, rather than a 'manic state.' It is an effort, of the intensest variety, to force the poem into a whole." Hall concludes that while "method has no consistent relation to quality," it does have a relation, in these two poets, to style: "Wilbur's poems move carefully and elegantly, step by calculated step, to a sure conclusion; Eberhart's are like fireworks left in the rain; many of them have their powder wet, and only fizzle, but when one goes off there is a real explosion."[11]

A balanced estimate appears in Oscar Cargill's survey of "Poetry since the Deluge," in which he links Wilbur with Yvor Winters for his adoption of conventional meters and forms and with Stevens for his whimsicality. But Cargill suggests that "his real forte is to imbue the apposite descriptive phrase or image with expansible meaning." Only Lowell among Wilbur's contemporaries, he thinks, can match his mastery of technique. Viereck had said that Wilbur "has all the qualities of a great artist except vulgarity." Cargill's word for what Wilbur lacks is "virility," but he thinks this will come: "there seems to be a consistent philosophy behind his writing which will force its way through and impart virility to his verse."[12]

Finally, in an article called "The New Poetry: Notes on the Past Fifteen Years in America," Donald Hall remarks that Richard Wilbur "is the youngest of the leading poets of the day; his reputation is exceeded only by Robert Lowell's." He cites, as among Wilbur's best, two poems which later appeared in *Things of This World*, "Beasts" and "A Voice from Under the Table"; and he comments "in the last especially there is a successful attempt to move away from the elegant pose. Much as we enjoy the elegant Wilbur, perhaps it is healthy for a poet to try new ways of speaking. Wherever he moves from here, Wilbur's survival as a poet of infinite delight is secure."[13] Thus Hall, like Viereck and Cargill, greets with favor what he takes to be the signs in Wilbur's work of a slackening interest in what is merely elegant and an attempt to move toward something more virile, more vulgar, more ferocious. Wilbur himself would have been well aware of the danger and the waste of confining himself to too narrow a range, however successful he might be within that range. He was indeed beginning to try new ways of speaking, but the results appear more clearly in *Advice to a Prophet* (1961) than in *Things of This World* (1956).

CHAPTER 3

Things of This World (1956)

FOR SOME YEARS BEFORE *Things of This World* appeared in 1956, Wilbur had been perfecting his skill as a translator of poems from French. *Ceremony* had included a translation from La Fontaine and two from Villiers de L'Isle-Adam; *Things of This World* included one from Baudelaire, one from Francis Jammes, and one from Paul Valéry. Many reviewers have praised these translations, and even the reader who does not know enough French to judge them can see that in English each poem has its own character and the distinction of style: the lines move and show point whether the original is La Fontaine or Valéry. Sometimes, if not always, the poems chosen for translation illustrate some aspect of technique or mood in which Wilbur is especially interested in his own writing. As we might expect, he enjoyed finding English equivalents for the word play in Valéry's sonnet "Helen"; and the very different spirit of Francis Jammes's "A Prayer to Go to Paradise with the Donkeys" has its analogue in some of the original poems of *Things of This World*.

Wilbur's main work as a translator was his poetic version of *The Misanthrope* of Molière. First produced at The Poets' Theatre in Cambridge, October 25, 1955, and later at Theater East in New York in 1956-57, it appeared in book form in 1955.[1] Wilbur's brief but thoughtful introduction to the book includes a noteworthy defense of his choice of verse rather than prose for his translation. Verse was necessary, he says, to reproduce the effect of Molière's parodies of "Cornelian *tirade*" and for other reasons also—and his own words reveal his interests as poet and translator: "The constant rhythm and rhyme was needed, in the translation as in the original, for bridging great gaps between high comedy and farce, lofty diction and ordinary talk, deep character and shallow. Again, while prose might preserve the thematic structure of the play, other 'musical' elements would be lost, in particular the frequently intricate arrangements of balancing half-lines, lines, couplets, quatrains, and sestets. There is no question that words, when dancing within such patterns, are not their prosaic selves, but have a wholly different mood and meaning" (x-xi). Finally, he says, verse was the best medium for preserving two peculiarities of Molière's dialogue, which he designates as "redundancy" and "logic." Translated into prose, a series of couplets that say the same thing in several ways loses the power "of stabilizing the idea against the movement of the verse, and of giving a specifically rhetorical pleasure"; in prose, moreover, "Molière's logic loses all its baroque exuberance," as well as its clarity. Clearly, Wilbur finds in Molière a poet whose technical interests were in many respects like his own.

But even those who admire this translation of *The Misanthrope*, or who have enjoyed hearing Wilbur read excerpts from it, have sometimes doubted that it could be used successfully in a stage production. The problem is that the constant rhymes, despite Wilbur's care to subdue them by running lines on, tend to stand out more emphatically in English than they do in French. For example, we may consider a short speech of Philinte to Eliante:

> What most intrigues one in our friend Alceste
> Is the grand passion that rages in his breast.
> The sullen humors he's compounded of
> Should not, I think, dispose his heart to love;
> But since they do, it puzzles me still more
> That he should choose your cousin to adore.
>
> (Act IV, Scene I)

The danger is that the rhymes will become monotonous and distracting. But William Becker, who attended the production at The Poets' Theatre in Cambridge, reported that "Wilbur's version is stageworthy—and even durable . . . the verse itself came through extraordinarily well. . . ." The actors did not slur over the rhymes but concentrated instead "on the strong internal wit and logic of the speeches as a whole." Becker called the play not only "the best translation of Molière ever done into English," but "a workable theatre piece."[2]

For the comic operetta based on Voltaire's *Candide*, produced in New York in December, 1956, Lillian Hellman adapted the book, Leonard Bernstein wrote the music, Tyrone Guthrie directed, and Wilbur wrote the lyrics—with some assistance from

Dorothy Parker and John La Touche. *Candide* was not a great success on the stage, either in New York or in a later English production. Though the critic Wolcott Gibbs considered the whole show only intermittently satisfactory, he called the lyrics "unusually funny and appropriate."[3] Brooks Atkinson was more enthusiastic: the operetta was "the first musical of the season that has distinction," and he added that the lyrics, droll, "pithy and idiomatic," deserved much of the credit.[4] Of the lyrics he wrote for *Candide*, Wilbur has reprinted only one, "Pangloss's Song," in *Advice to a Prophet*.

Things of This World was not entirely new to readers when it appeared. Of the thirty-two poems in *Things*, three had appeared in *A Bestiary*, seven in *The New Yorker*, and at least eighteen in other magazines. Still, book publication is always an opportunity to make judgments that cannot be made easily while the poems are scattered; and Wilbur's readers looked hard at *Things* to discover new ventures in technique, subject, spirit, or theme. They were not easy to find. Superficially, the book looks much like *Ceremony*, which was not very different from *The Beautiful Changes;* but the differences in the first two books are more clearly marked. In four poems with Italian settings, *Things* shows the influence of Wilbur's year in Italy (1954-55), but not very obviously otherwise. Wilbur continues to be concerned with the power of imagination to shape the world and history; with the rival claims of the ideal and the actual; with certain threats to the welfare and freedom of the spirit; with the celebration of certain virtues, often humble or gentle, in men and even in animals; and with autobiographical episodes of several kinds. Precedents are easy to find in his earlier work for all these interests, if we state them thus in general terms; yet each new poem is such a delicately individualized complex of meanings that even if the themes are not precisely new, the poems are. Many of the poems need the most sensitive analysis for proper appreciation, and the reader is often aware of something crude and incomplete in comparing poems as to subject and attitude. The difficulty of some of the poems is produced or compounded by Wilbur's tone, in which a subtle irony makes for uncertainty about what he is saying. He is, of course, saying several things at once in the various ways of poetry. I think it is true to say that, although *Things* includes only thirty-two poems compared to *Ceremony's* forty-two and about the same number of translations, the proportion of Wilbur's best work in *Things* is higher.

I *Italian Virtue*

The poems that show the mark of Wilbur's year in Italy are
"Altitudes," "Piazza di Spagna, Early Morning," "A Baroque
Wall-Fountain in the Villa Sciarra," and "For the New Railway
Station in Rome." In the opening lines of "Altitudes," the poet
speaks as a sightseer in an Italian church:

> Look up into the dome:
> It is a great salon, a brilliant place,
> Yet not too splendid for the race
> Whom we imagine there, wholly at home
>
> With the gold-rosetted white
> Wainscot, the oval windows, and the fault-
> Less figures of the painted vault.

In style and execution the poem starts out as one of Wilbur's
most brilliant and characteristic performances, and it broaches a
theme adequate to major poetry; but its conclusion—as it seemed
to me at first—may seem blurred or unachieved. And yet, through
rereading, I have come to see more clearly the parallels between
Part I and Part II, and the poem has taken on an integrity for
me that I could not feel in it before. The last sentence of the
poem now seems justified, its casual near-pointlessness just what
is needed there at the ending. The high intensity of the climax
in the next-to-last stanza carries the reader along into the last
stanza, which brings him gently down from "a wild shining of
the pure unknown" to garden-level, the language relaxing and
declining into everyday, though some hint of Emily's ecstatic
mood is still abroad and felt in Amherst. As for the parallels, the
"great" and "brilliant" and "splendid" dome of the Italian church
corresponds with Emily Dickinson's sunlit "little cupola" up the
"spiral stair"; the windows, paintings, and other appointments
of the dome correspond with the cupola's "clear/Small panes, its
room for one"; the "dark" in which the observer stands to look
into the dome corresponds with that of "the dark house below";
the gazing crowds and "massed voices" of the church are set off
against the "eyes/In mirrors" and the buzzing "shut-in flies" of
Emily's house. More generally, in its splendor, its spaciousness,
its beauty, its social atmosphere, its publicity and visibility, the
upper dome is all that Emily's house is not. "How far it is from
here" says the opening of Part II, suggesting both the geographical and the cultural distance of Puritan New England from
Catholic Italy.

But the house is not merely "Emily Dickinson's father's house in America"; it is Emily Dickinson herself, and she is her own church:

> Like the dark house below, so full of eyes
>   In mirrors and of shut-in flies,
> This chamber furnished only with the sun
>
>   Is she and she alone,
>   A mood to which she rises . . .

Not only the bright sunlit chamber but also the darkness, the eyes in mirrors, and the shut-in flies are features of Emily Dickinson's internal architecture. She herself is such a dark lonely house; in it she observes herself; in it she and the flies live similarly confined and baffled lives. But the cupola is "a mood to which she rises" as into a church dome, a mood "in which she sees/Bird-choristers in all the trees/And a wild shining of the pure unknown/On Amherst." Unlike the populace who gather beneath the Holy Family, the angels and the saints in the Italian church, Emily Dickinson can rise from below to a vision of holy things, not of art but of nature. Her vision is composed not of the familiar elevated, but of the unfamiliar, the unknown, the utterly mysterious and otherwise from ourselves. What she attained to as a transcendentalist was "All that the world cannot in fact afford." In the beautiful ambiguity of this line, which uses both "world" and "afford" in two senses to supply two different but equally telling meanings, we may enjoy Wilbur's characteristic wit in one of its most brilliant flashes. Even the common phrase "in fact" has an uncommon justice here.

The last stanza seems to suggest that Emily's mood is capable of bringing to her neighbors' windows, which I take to imply their attention or consciousness, something of that "wild shining of the pure unknown" in the light of which she sees Amherst. A neighbor becomes aware of it; he comes out of his house "To pace about his garden, lost in thought." Her mood has its public effect, not because she is visible like the Italian dome dwellers, not even through her writing, about which her neighbors knew so little, but through more subtle influences. An extraordinary amount is conveyed through the imagery of this poem. Yet there is no strain; all is ease and good humor. The poem has a new subject in the contrast of Catholic and Protestant modes of keeping the most elevated visions and sentiments alive in the community. Wilbur glimpses something of the Italian social genius and contrasts it with the solitary way of the transcendentalists. He never commits himself to a preference—if we disregard the tone of the poem. But if we are alert to the tone of the first part, we feel that the poet keeps the Italian experience at a distance with the subtlest of mockery. In Part II Emily is not mocked; she is his saint, and Amherst has his heart. Here the tone does what in another poet might require an overt statement of allegiance: it indicates his sympathies. Of this technique of statement through tonal commitment and disclaimer only, the poem is a perfect example. There are others in Wilbur's work. Readers who miss the delicate tonal indicators may feel that his poems tend to be unresolved; yet some resolve themselves as "Altitudes" does.

The English poet and critic G. S. Fraser cited "Piazza di Spagna, Early Morning" as evidence of the existence of a distinct attitude of young American poets toward poetry, and he argued that English poets share a different attitude. The young American poet, he said, is concerned above all not with "the right basic attitude to life," not with the rival claims to our attention of the ideal or the actual (these, he implied, are the subjects of serious poetry), but with "what a poem is, with the shaping of a poem as an object." American poems are "luxury products"; the American poet is "expensively and deliciously adding something to life, rather than expressing, perhaps awkwardly, something urgently arising out of life." American poems show the flaws of insubstantiality, derivativeness, preciousness, "faults especially of the poet who feels he has not much of an audience except other poets, or, say, the very specialized audience, largely perhaps consisting of university teachers of literature, that reads and writes for the more abstruse American quarterlies." Taking "Piazza di Spagna" as an instance, he pointed out that the diction is "poetical," the properties "glamorous," the aim a "beautiful" poem. The poem is important not for what it says, but for what it does. "It dances like the girl," he truly observed, and added: "The life of Mr. Wilbur's poem is in its form; the form specifies, realizes the 'meaning.'" But he found in it no "particularly original or striking insights into life" and suggested that its achievement is one of manner only and thus insubstantial.[5]

Fraser's criticisms of "Piazza di Spagna" seem to me to be sound enough. Though it accomplishes perfectly what it attempts, I doubt that Wilbur's readers can easily share the mood it evokes;

the poem remains, I think, a brilliant exercise in the adjustment
of line movement and image to the actions described. What is
missing may be a protective irony of some kind—humor, or a
delicate mockery like that of the first part of "Altitudes," or a
shrewd shift in the point of view, so that the girl's and the
speaker's mood might be caught and criticized in a crossfire of
the poet's perceptions. Wilbur leaves her glamor undisturbed,
and we feel the need of a touch of real life for perspective.
Nevertheless, Fraser made too much of this single example. No
one who reads with care Wilbur's first three books, or even
Things of This World, can doubt that "the right basic attitude to
life," or the rival claims to our attention of the ideal and the
actual, are among his constant themes. These are the themes of
most of the poems I have discussed thus far, from "Tywater" to
"Altitudes."

Another poem from Wilbur's Italian journey, "A Baroque Wall-
Fountain in the Villa Sciarra," shows him again, as in "Altitudes,"
considering rival attitudes to life and weighing their merits. The
poem consists of fifteen stanzas of the same construction as those
in "Altitudes" (*3a 5b 4b 5a*); the long sentences run through the
line-ends and stanza divisions in the same way; all but one of the
sentence endings fall within the stanza. In his film interview
Wilbur spoke of some of the special virtues of this form: "I think
one reason why one finds in a lot of poetry nowadays very long
sentences trickling down through the stanza is that in the long
sentence you can have a more complex grammar and hence more
freedom in placing the important words where you want them,
at the beginnings and ends of lines. Of course, a lot of the length
in this poem—a lot of the length of sentence—has to do with an
effort to imitate the trickling down of the water."[6]

The first six stanzas describe the Roman fountain referred to
in the title. Nowhere else in his poems is Wilbur's descriptive
talent more evident; the sounds of the language suggest at every
point the flashing, splashing pattern of light, shade and sound
that he wants to convey:

> Happy in all that ragged, loose
> Collapse of water, its effortless descent
>
> And flatteries of spray,
> The stocky god upholds the shell with ease . . .

Beginning with stanza seven Wilbur moves easily into the question at the heart of the poem: what human ideal this fountain ex-

presses and how it compares with a different, more strenuous
ideal implicit in another set of fountains described with equal
brilliance in these lines:

> Yet since this all
> Is pleasure, flash, and waterfall,
> Must it not be too simple? Are we not
>
> More intricately expressed
> In the plain fountains that Maderna set
> Before St. Peter's—the main jet
> Struggling aloft until it seems at rest
>
> In the act of rising, until
> The very wish of water is reversed,
> That heaviness borne up to burst
> In a clear, high, cavorting head, to fill
>
> With blaze, and then in gauze
> Delays, in a gnatlike shimmering, in a fine
> Illumined version of itself, decline,
> And patter on the stones its own applause?

We see in the following stanzas what Wilbur has in mind: that
the fountains of Maderna, unlike the wall fountain, express human aspiration upward, away from the actual toward the ideal,
away from earth toward heaven: "If that is what men are/Or
should be, if those water-saints display/The pattern of our areté
[virtue] . . ." But he immediately supplies an apology for the
fauns as an emblem of a different set of virtues equally Christian
—not the yearning for what is not, but gratitude for what is:

> What of these showered fauns in their bizarre,
>
> Spangled, and plunging house?
> They are at rest in fulness of desire
> For what is given, they do not tire
> Of the smart of the sun, the pleasant water-douse
>
> And riddled pool below,
> Reproving our disgust and our ennui
> With humble insatiety.

The Maderna fountain is shown "struggling aloft until it seems
at rest/In the act of rising, until/The very wish of water is reversed . . . ," but the fauns "are at rest in fulness of desire/For
what is given. . . ." The repeated phrase "at rest" serves to make

the contrast sharper, and the ease with which this true and significant contrast is expressed is elegance.

Now, at the end of the poem, where another poet might say "As for me, I choose . . . ," Wilbur characteristically stays out of sight; but his voice continues, rapt, contemplative, and visionary as he refers us back to Saint Francis of Assisi for the tradition in which the wall fountain belongs:

> Francis, perhaps, who lay in sister snow
>
> > Before the wealthy gate
> > Freezing and praising, might have seen in this
> >   No trifle, but a shade of bliss—
> > That land of tolerable flowers, that state
>
> > As near and far as grass
> > Where eyes become the sunlight, and the hand
> >   Is worthy of water; the dreamt land
> > Toward which all hungers leap, all pleasures pass.

This final allegation is tentative ("Francis, perhaps . . . might have seen in this"), but the vision of a blessed world in which we are perfectly assimilated and at home, "a shade of bliss" ("shade" meaning dream, ghost, shadow, copy, adumbration)— the vision inspired by the wall fountain is authentic and compelling. Despite the tentativeness, this is not a weak conclusion, but a strong one, in which the wall fountain in all its distracting glitter and homeliness is suddenly seen in perspective, its charm explained and justified. There are two opposite modes of sainthood—one lying in a perfect rejection of the world, the other in a perfect acceptance. The way of St. Francis may be no less difficult and blessed than the other. The last two stanzas show a heightened rhetoric, a subtle extravagance in the terms, that suggest both the dream and the consciousness that it *is* a dream, both its powerful charm and the ironic regret that it can never be realized; but the dream itself is real.

Do the descriptive passages in this poem show too much ingenuity? Do they distract us from the theme, which, as I have said, seems to me serious and important? I do not think so. I think the poem needs the fully detailed presentation of both fountains so that the contrast is well established. This is a highly elaborate poem; but if it were somehow cast in a more severe form, renouncing the pleasures of sound and sight, giving up rhyme perhaps, and refusing to play its high-spirited game with its formal hurdles, I cannot think it would be a better poem. The very central point of the poem is a rejection of a spare and severe ideal.[7]

Not from Italy but from a Mexican or possibly a Spanish setting comes "A Plain Song for Comadre," another poem in which humble virtues are celebrated ("comadre" means a woman who does manual work). "Plain Song" can mean a theme chosen for contrapuntal development or merely a simple melody or air, but neither is clearly appropriate here. Bruna Sandoval had swept and scrubbed a church for seventeen years "for love and in all weathers." Although she sees no more visions than those without faith, she believes in the constancy of holy things in daily life. Good work and things well made during the day are blessed by the coming of dark and by the turning evening sky. Though she does her work well without a sign from the unseen,

> Sometimes the early sun
> Shines as she flings the scrubwater out, with a crash
> Of grimy rainbows, and the stained suds flash
> Like angel-feathers.

Perhaps, then, there are visions to be seen in the very scrubwater. The ending is characteristically unforced, for we are given earlier a vivid sense of Bruna Sandoval's devotion to her daily chore and of the satisfactions she feels in it. The confident questions of the first three stanzas, though expressed in the poet's witty language, are hers:

> Though the unseen may vanish, though insight fails
> And doubter and downcast saint
> Join in the same complaint,
> What holy things were ever frightened off
> By a fly's buzz, or itches, or a cough?
> Harder than nails
>
> They are, more warmly constant than the sun . . .

Those who care for "holy things," the candlesticks, the plaster statues of the saints, the clay porch and the white altar, need have no fear of the vanishing unseen or of failing insight. The humble Catholic's attachment to and trust in "holy things," evoked here so sympathetically, is seen to produce not only good works but a steady spiritual health. Though Wilbur makes little of the point, it is obvious that Bruna Sandoval drinks at "the spirit's right oasis, light incarnate" ("'A World Without Objects . . .'"). "Doubter and downcast saint," in their search for the vanishing unseen, are like "those connoisseurs of thirst," the "tall camels" of the poet's spirit. How to live in this world is still the poet's study. "Holy things" are all things seen in the right light:

> Harder than nails
>
> They are, more warmly constant than the sun,
> At whose continual sign
> The dimly prompted vine
> Upbraids itself to a green excellence.

Bruna's "grimy rainbows" and "stained suds" flashing like "angel-feathers" are her reward for tending "the true, the mortal flower" ("La Rose des Vents"). We may think of other lines from earlier poems: "Kept spirit is corporate . . . rarest things are visible and firm" ("Lament"), or "auras, lustres,/And all shinings need to be shaped and borne" (" 'A World Without Objects . . .' "). We see that "A Plain Song" supplies new terms for an old theme. And who can fail to see also that in doing so it involves precisely the rival claims of the ideal and the actual and poses the question of a right basic attitude toward life?

The last of the Italian poems is "For the New Railway Station in Rome," with which the book ends (it begins with "Altitudes"). Like the other Italian poems, this one treats of a human beauty, excellence, or aspiration—virtue—of which Wilbur seems to have had a glimpse in Italy. A poem of exultation, it is an unusually strong statement. Nowhere else does the poet appear more clearly confident of man's creative powers, nowhere else so scornful of those who predict and hope for human defeat. Let me ask Hyam Plutzik's question here: whether Wilbur shows enough consciousness of the odds against man, both within and outside himself. "How can he be so good-natured in an abominable world?"[8] The answer must be by his absorption in the modes and the products of human excellence, which is no less real, and no more real, than human depravity. The poet's subject must be whatever captures his imagination and spurs it along into creative territory. In any case, in the opening stanzas of this poem, Wilbur speaks of bygone pessimists and misanthropes with an asperity unusual in his work:

> Those who said God is praised
> By hurt pillars, who loved to see our brazen lust
> Lie down in rubble, and our vaunting arches
> Conduce to dust;

Those who with short shadows
Poked through the stubbled forum pondering on decline,
And would not take the sun standing at noon
For a good sign;

Those pilgrims of defeat
Who brought their injured wills as to a soldiers' home;
Dig them all up now, tell them there's something new
To see in Rome.

The new railway station is constructed so as to build onto and echo the "broken profile" of the ruined Servian Wall,

. . . defeating

That defeat
And straying the strummed mind,
By such a sudden chord as raised the town of Troy,
To where the least shard of the world sings out
In stubborn joy,

"What city is eternal
But that which prints itself within the groping head
Out of the blue unbroken reveries
Of the building dead?

"What is our praise or pride
But to imagine excellence, and try to make it?
What does it say over the door of Heaven
But *homo fecit?*"

The exuberance of these last three stanzas is a little bewildering: we may assent and cheer without quite hearing. The juxtaposition of the modern booking-hall roof, with its "light/And cantilevered swoop of reinforced concrete," and the ancient stones of the wall is so happy as to stimulate the poet's mind to a vision of ruins singing out a definition of the Eternal City, a city in which the dreams of "the building dead" are understood and in some sense given expression by living builders. Like Troy, like Heaven itself, Rome deserves the epithet, "The Eternal City," because it stands for a persistent desire of the spirit for a kind of excellence, and calls on the imagination to express this desire in tangible forms.

II *Hazards of the Spirit*

In another group of poems Wilbur is more concerned with threats to the spirit than with its triumphs. In these, instead of dwelling on what human beings are capable of at their best, what ideals or models they have to look to if they wish, where their sources of strength and joy are to be found, his imagination senses and defines certain spiritual hazards. What he finds menacing in the course of his explorations in five or six widely different poems is not easy to summarize: the adversary takes various shapes and occasions, and perhaps each poem should be allowed to speak for itself, to make its own distinctions. But in these poems, if anywhere in *Things,* we encounter what Plutzik missed in Wilbur: "our old friends the devils and trolls." Such poems as "Speech for the Repeal of the McCarran Act," "Marginalia," "Beasts," "After the Last Bulletins," and "All These Birds" either confront some evil openly and confidently or reveal obliquely a strain of apprehension so strong as to dominate the poem.

In its tone, "Speech for the Repeal of the McCarran Act"* is like nothing else in Wilbur's work. Its confident public manner may remind us of some poems of Archibald MacLeish or of William Carlos Williams' "Tract." The stanza is unusual in Wilbur in its lack of rhyme and in its line-lengths (4635); its rhythms are prosy and rather irregular, yet strongly stressed. The poem uses the figure of a spider web to stand for spiritual strength, but it does not disclose the full import of this symbol until its final lines:

> As Wulfstan† said on another occasion,
> The strong net bellies in the wind and the spider rides it out;
> But history, that sure blunderer,
> Ruins the unkempt web, however silver.

The next two stanzas insist that the destruction caused by our bombing of churches and railways in Europe is not so important as what Wulfstan called "oathbreach, faithbreach, lovebreach." Europe will recover; and we will be forgiven if we remember our common humanity and honor it. The last stanza pleads for freedom of thought and for the testing of ideas in a healthy spiritual atmosphere:

* The McCarran Act of 1952 limited the opportunity for immigration into the United States at a time when distressed European refugees needed it most.

† Wulfstan, archbishop of York until his death in 1023, wrote a famous prose address to the English in which he described the devastation of the country by Danish raiders and also attacked English vice and demoralization.

Let thought be free. I speak
Of the spirit's weaving, the neural
Web, the self-true mind, the trusty reflex.

The poem defines a real danger to the spirit, a danger given the authority of law, and it takes a firm stand against the law and the fear behind it. Oscar Cargill found in "Speech . . ." the signs of a strength and consistency of philosophy that, he predicted, would serve Wilbur well as he continued to develop as a poet. But the poem was of a poetic mode that Wilbur returned to only once, in "Advice to a Prophet," which appeared in 1959.

Unless I am mistaken, "Marginalia" is not a developed poem but three separate stanzas on a single theme, composed perhaps at different times and brought under the present title merely for convenience. But this hypothesis has its difficulties; while it is easy to see that the first and second stanzas treat of margins, the third does not obviously do so. Perhaps the title is meant to suggest instead that the stanzas were written separately, as it were in the margins of his books, in response to something in Wilbur's reading.

The first stanza presents, as one kind of margin, a pond-surface in sharp, close focus: "Things concentrate at the edges; the pond-surface/Is bourne to fish and man. . . ." This image had been used earlier in "Water-Walker," but in "Marginalia" the significance of the opening assertion is limited, not enlarged, by the description that makes up the stanza. Stanza two speaks of the margin between waking and sleep:

Descending into sleep (as when the night-lift
Falls past a brilliant floor), we glimpse a sublime
Decor and hear, perhaps, a complete music,
But this evades us, as in the night meadows
The crickets' million roundsong dies away
From all advances, rising every distance.

Certainly this stanza is very beautiful, particularly, it seems to me, in the rhythm (given the subject) of "as when the night-lift/Falls past a brilliant floor," in the internal rhymes of "floor" and "decor" and of "dies" and "rising," in the delicate falling-away of the lines with unstressed endings, and in the justice of "roundsong" (a round or part-song, the lines of which are sung consecutively and repeatedly by singers who take different starting points). It is a happy analogy for the sound of a field full of crickets. The "sublime decor," the "complete music," the "roundsong" are perfections glimpsed at the margins—things valued for beauty, sublimity, brilliance, completeness; but things out of reach, evasive, haunting the mind as visions or dreams. The theme is that of the thirst for the ideal so common and persistent in Wilbur's work.

Whether or not one takes the notion of "Marginalia" as a clue, stanza three is difficult to interpret, and I have not been able to arrive at a reading that I find entirely satisfactory. But if we take "riches" as equivalent to "dreams," and "dreams" as the burden of the speech or song of the "remote consummate chorus," we begin to get a consistent framework of meaning. Each of us sails his ship in the whirlpool of life. The chorus of our "final dreams" rides on the outer rim of the pool, and we ply our trades in the circling current between that margin and the central vortex into which finally we are all sucked down. By this reading the "which" in the clause "past which we flog our sails," refers not to "rim," as one would at first assume, but to "whirlpools," the destructive center. As we live our lives, then, we compose our dreams; and they sing or speak to us from their distance on the rim of the pool. These dreams are "riches" in a sense that is unstated in the poem but easy to imagine: perhaps they guide and encourage us; perhaps they amount to our store of insights into the meaning of life. The senses in which they are "final" and in which their chorus is "remote" and "consummate" are more difficult to determine. A "good drowning" might be a life that had not lost touch with the chorus of its dreams, but one feels that this conjecture is not based firmly in the text. Another possibility is that the chorus heard by the individual is that of all mankind, rather like the chorus in some Greek plays; and a "good drowning" would be one the chorus could approve. Despite these uncertainties, the stanza presents a striking image of doomed human life engaged in its characteristic struggle.

The reference in "Beasts" to "suitors of excellence" is echoed in the later poem "For the New Railway Station in Rome," with its praise of those who "imagine excellence and try to make it." But in "Beasts" the attitude of the poet toward the "suitors of excellence" is very different. The poem is a strange one, reminiscent of Auden in its terse and modish phrases, the briskness of its rhythms, and the surprise and violence of the details that imply a menacing atmosphere. The six stanzas present three scenes in contrast under the moon: beastly, mixed, and human; the natural realm of beasts, the bedroom of a werewolf at the moment of changing from man to beast, and the "high windows" of the human "suitors of excellence." "Beasts in their major freedom/Slumber in peace tonight" in perfect harmony with their surroundings—not only those beasts who sleep, but even "the ripped mouse, safe in the owl's talon." "Safe," here a bold and witty word (the line sounds like Auden), suggests that the violent death of beasts is only an aspect of the peace of the natural order; indeed, the owl's peace depends on the mouse's death; and the whole scheme is harmonious and acceptable even to the mice. Why "major" freedom? The word means "larger" or "greater" if we take it in its strictly comparative sense, and perhaps it implies that the werewolf and the men have less freedom than beasts. At any rate,

> . . . . Here there is no such harm
> And no such darkness
>
> As the selfsame moon observes
> Where, warped in window-glass, it sponsors now
> The werewolf's painful change. . . .

This unnatural or monstrous change is more harmful and darker than anything in normal nature. In stanza one, the moon on "the moon-plucked waves" (a musical image) below the sleeping gull seems beneficent. In stanza three, however, "warped in window-glass," it has a malign influence that overpowers the werewolf and turns him into a beast who lacks the characteristic peace of the true beasts. He hears "the wind's exciting minors,/ The leaves' panic, and the degradation/Of the heavy streams." These are the sounds of a perverse and corrupted nature, internal and external, to which the werewolf comes indeed reluctantly. In a striking and poignant phrase, "he tries to remember/The mood of manhood"—but fails, a beast in spite of himself, without the self-control needed to prevent the violation of his own nature and without the integrity of the true beasts.

The "suitors of excellence" may perhaps be men unbalanced in the other direction, without enough of the beast about them, "far from thicket and pad-fall." They work late, sigh, and "construe again the painful/Beauty of heaven. . . ." At odds with nature, they live not at peace but under a strain, though a self-imposed one. And the dreams they make will break men's hearts, ruin cities, bring death through warfare, and resign all to the beasts. Who are these "suitors of excellence" whose dreams are ultimately so destructive? Do they represent intellect without instinct, mind without guts, body without sweat, Lawrence's drained and sterile upper-class "thinkers"? Are they modern scientists, Faustian and condemned? Are they to be blamed when their dreams go wrong, or is it the fault of "history, that sure blunderer" ("Speech for the Repeal of the McCarran Act")? Or is it the fault of ordinary man who cannot remember "the mood of manhood," so that in despair he always turns visions of excellence to corrupt uses? Is there any such thing in the world of the poem as a balanced man, a man we could set beside these unbalanced ones as a norm from which they have strayed? Man seems to be presented in "Beasts" as a total loss in practice, though he has good intentions. Divided into body and mind, he is dominated by one or the other, and either kind of imbalance brings ruin. Without any hint of the human capacity for making constructive use of dreams, the poem is unusually pessimistic for Wilbur—pessimistic enough, I should think, to satisfy Plutzik's call for devils and trolls.

"After the Last Bulletins" is also about things going wrong at night, but I am not sure how serious it is. While the city sleeps, the wind rises; and the newspapers and news-magazines revolt anarchically against statues, buildings, police, and the very words printed on their pages. But in the morning, as news bulletins come on the radio, peace is restored, people return from home to the city again, the trash is cleared up. This is the outline of the tale, but much more is intended, as the imagery lets us know. The rebellion comes at night:

> After the last bulletins the windows darken
> And the whole city founders readily and deep,
> Sliding on all its pillows
> To the thronged Atlantis of personal sleep . . .

The city gives up its public life and retires in "personal sleep"— not retires, but "founders," sinks, joins others on the lost sunken continent Atlantis. The imagery suggests a loss of control. In the morning we return from the personal to the public:

> Oh none too soon through the air white and dry
> Will the clear announcer's voice
> Beat like a dove, and you and I
>
> From the heart's anarch and responsible town
> Return by subway-mouth to life again,
> Bearing the morning papers. . . .

The announcer is a peace bringer, a comforter, as are the morning papers. And in the park "saintlike men,/White and absorbed" like hospital attendants, "remove/The litter of the night, and footsteps rouse/With confident morning sound/The songbirds in the public boughs." Things are reassuringly public now, back to routine, order, normality. During the daytime we feel in control, but we spend the night in "the heart's anarch and responsible town." This puzzling phrase is an important one. The heart is in revolt, but against what? Against the imposed order of the day with its consolations in the news? But isn't the news disturbing rather than consoling? Apparently not, for, while we have radio and newspaper bulletins, we feel safe; perhaps the very familiarity of these bulletins is calming. Only in "personal sleep" are we uneasy; only as our public life is interrupted do our responsible hearts take over and worry us. This much seems fairly clear, but the poem leaves one with the sense of unexpressed meanings.

III   *Forming and Transforming*

In "All These Birds" Wilbur takes up arms against a threat of a different kind: the scientific fact. It is one of his most brilliant poems, composed in one of his own intricate and lovely stanzas (*3a 6b 5c 5c 3a 2b 3d 3d,* and the next stanza begins with the *b* rhyme). The stanza is even beautiful to look at. And the tone is not in the least anxious, but confident and gay. For this reason, the poem may serve as a bridge between the uneasy warning poems just discussed and another group of poems: those that explore and celebrate the power of imagination to transform the world. "All These Birds" is an exhortation to the imagination to assert itself "lest it be undone" by the scientific habit of apprehension and observation. It is a hymn or invocation, as the last lines show: "Come, stranger, sister, dove:/Put on the reins of love."

A preoccupation with the power of the imagination informs many of Wilbur's poems, early and late. What the imagination brings to reality is as important as reality itself. The things of this world must be bathed in this active, transforming, and enriching light; otherwise, as in the theory of Wallace Stevens, by whom Wilbur seems influenced, they are of no use to the spirit. As early as "Poplar, Sycamore" in *The Beautiful Changes*, Wilbur prayed/that "My eye will never know the dry disease/Of thinking things no more than what he sees." In *Things*, the more conspicuous examples of poems that show this interest are "All

Things of This World *(1956)*

These Birds," which serves as a kind of invocation to the muse,
"Merlin Enthralled," "An Event," "A Chronic Condition," "The
Beacon," "Mind," "Looking into History," "Digging for China,"
and perhaps "John Chrysostom." There are strains of this theme
in some poems already discussed, such as "A Baroque Wall-
Fountain" and "For the New Railway Station in Rome." But
the fifth stanza of "All These Birds" might serve as a motto for
the whole group:

> Let us, with glass or gun,
> Watch (from our clever blinds) the monsters of the sky
> Dwindle to habit, habitat, and song,
> And tell the imagination it is wrong
> Till, lest it be undone,
>   it spin a lie
> So fresh, so pure, so rare
> As to possess the air.

The lie gives us possession of things, or dominion, as nothing
else can. We create our world in this sense. But, as Stevens insisted and as Wilbur insists, the lie also is, or becomes, a part
of reality:

> Oh, let it climb wherever it can cling
> Like some great trumpet-vine, a natural thing
> To which all birds that fly
>   come natural.

Some other less striking or weighty poems might be cited here
because they touch on the theme of the world as dream or fic-
tion: "Digging for China" is one. In it the poet recalls how,
when a boy in New Jersey, he had been spurred by some adults'
casual remarks to dig a hole through the earth to China. What
he wanted was to find a country where, as they told him, "Nothing looks the same." After digging all morning with his head
down the hole, "I stood up in a place I had forgotten. . . . Until
I got my balance back again/All that I saw was China, China,
China." The poem has some Frostian touches and is generally in
Wilbur's "low" style—relaxed, conversational, unrhymed pentam-
eter without stanzas. On a small scale it is a parable of the
quest for the other world and of the strangeness of this world
seen through the eyes of the dreamer returned from his quest.
Absorption in the "other" makes the familiar seem strange.

"Mind" begins by establishing a witty correspondence between the mind's activity "in its purest play" and the flight of a bat through the black air of a cave. The purest play of the mind suggests mathematics and other highly logical enterprises; but, as the third stanza makes clear, it includes poetry, too—or at least the construction of similes. The bat flies its "perfect courses" not by observing the irregular interior of its cave, but by "a kind of senseless wit" that keeps it clear of obstacles. The cave, then, is the known limit of the mind's domain, and obstacles within the cave would presumably be logical contradictions or other impasses:

> And has this simile a like perfection?
> The mind is like a bat. Precisely. Save
> That in the very happiest intellection
> A graceful error may correct the cave.

The simile "The mind is like a bat" is itself an example of such perfect flight or mental play, and yet mind and bat are unlike in one significant respect: the mind may through "a graceful error" (a lucky or inspired straying) either make its own domain larger or discover that it *is* larger or differently shaped than had been thought before. To "correct the cave" is to correct one's conception of it by extending the limits of intellection. A new thought is a new shape for the cave, but the changes come through "hunches" that take the mind out of familiar patterns of flight. This idea of mental activity seems to be that of some scientists and poets who like to stress the role of intuition or lucky hits, rather than sustained reasoning or method, in the effort to make "breakthroughs." But Wilbur's point is that mind can make or shape its world. In its assured movement, its logic and economy, its directness, and its witty wordplay, the poem is in Wilbur's most elegant style.

"An Event" describes brilliantly the impetuous flight of a flock of small black birds who suddenly leave their trees and fields and "convene" in the air, the many behaving as one. "What is an individual thing?" the poet asks, marveling and delighted; and their figure in the air stirs him to a striking simile: "They roll/ Like a drunken fingerprint across the sky!" When they scatter, "as if refusing to be caught/In any singular vision of my eye/Or in the nets and cages of my thought," he stays in his place, "Shaping these images to make them stay." The philosophizing, both in its use of the occasion and in its expression, is lightly and happily done. The thoughts arise exactly and spontaneously out of the observation, and stanza and rhyme are handled without the slightest clumsiness. The movement of the birds is captured and conveyed in all its protean mobility. The poet tries to contrive some image of their flight "to make them stay"—in his mind or in his poem. "Stay" must mean both remain and stand still. "Meanwhile, in some formation of their own,/They fly me still, and steal my thoughts away." Here are the "crosspurposes" mentioned in the next stanza.

The last stanza lightly touches on the major theme we have been tracing in the poems of this whole group:

> Delighted with myself and with the birds,
> I set them down and give them leave to be.
> It is by words and the defeat of words,
> Down sudden vistas of the vain attempt,
> That for a flying moment one may see
> By what cross-purposes the world is dreamt.

In what sense does he "set them down and give them leave to be?" He sets them down in words; so his "leave to be" is leave to exist in the images of the poem. Or does he mean he gives them leave to go free of "the nets and cages" of his thought? To be themselves, untransformed or un-"deranged" in his images? For his words are defeated: it has been a "vain attempt." The "crosspurposes" are of course his and the birds'. Now perhaps it appears that he is saying that only as he and the birds encounter each other in this "event" do they exist. "The world is dreamt" as the birds go their way and he his. His permission for them to exist, then, implies the artist's claim that what exists does so only in his imagination. The world is in this sense his dream, and he gives the birds a place in it.

The happiness of expression in "An Event" is extraordinary—in the whole poem but particularly, against great odds, in the final stanza. How cleverly Wilbur builds on the earlier experience—"a flying moment," "by what cross-purposes"—and also on his own presentation of it, on the connotations of his own language. The poem is concerned also with the nature of reality: "the world is dreamt." Such propositions are offered not as theses to defend but as glances at the truth, as products of the mind at play. We try to capture elusive, recalcitrant reality and hold it in images. Another "event" would have served as well as a basis for these reflections (though Wilbur loves birds and their ways). The poem illustrates Anthony Hecht's remark that Wilbur is concerned with "the search for reality," which "though it is discovered in the most casual epiphanies [like the flight of birds] is characteristically fugitive and uncertain."[9]

The search for reality and the modes by which we apprehend it are themes also of "The Beacon." The sweeping beacon, as it appears in the first three stanzas, is an eye that can blink and gaze; but it is also a cutlass that can sever the Gordian knot and therefore also a mind that can solve puzzling problems by drastic means. Its "brilliance," at which it "blinks," seems then to be an intellectual as well as a physical brilliance. After stanza three the intelligent point of view is not the mind of the beacon but that of the speaker in the poem, for whom the beacon "gives clearance to/Our human visions . . ." (stanza seven). The seascape in the beacon's light is intelligible to human eyes because it presents itself in the familiar terms of analogy, metaphor, and myth (stanzas two and three). But all that seems familiar disappears as the light blinks "and the dark of the eye/Dives for the black pearl/Of the sea-in-itself." The "sea-in-itself" is that venerable will-o'-the-wisp, the reality independent of our senses and in this case free also of the linguistic tricks and fictions by which we normally accommodate ourselves to the sea. Could we come to grips with it, "the sea-in-itself" would be a metaphysical prize of incalculable value, a "black pearl." But the mind is unequal to the task; though we can hear the sea in the dark, it is unintelligible to us: its noises

> Warn of the pitchy whirl
>
> At the mind's end. All of the sense of the sea
> Is veiled as voices nearly heard
> In morning sleep; nor shall we wake
> At the sea's heart.

Not only the mind but the soul is baffled and defeated. But as the beacon light returns, "Our human visions . . . assume the waves again. . . ." How many of the several distinguishable senses of "assume" Wilbur intends is a question. The primary meaning seems to be "appropriate," but "take on" and "take for granted or without proof" also hover in the offing, the last casting light back on the language of stanzas four and five. The mind at the mind's end must assume what it cannot know. Then comes the cryptic summary statement: "Let us suppose that we/ See most of darkness by our plainest light." I take these lines to mean that we understand mysteries best by not confronting them directly. When without light we dive for "the black pearl/ Of the sea-in-itself," we quickly reach our limits and encounter a baffling, even a frightening, mystery. "Our plainest light" must then be our analogies, metaphors, myths, fictions for ordering and explaining what would otherwise remain inhuman and alien. Human history and purpose tame the sea, as the two final examples suggest. There is a distinction worth noticing between "endears" (engages our affections) and "assembles" (orders and makes intelligible). This sea that we can know, which is not the sea-in-itself, is humanized.

For "The Beacon" is really about a moment's vision of that Chaos which, as Wilbur has said, it is the business of poetry to confront. The sweeping beacon shows us the sea in the light of human imagination and purpose; the beacon is faith in the power of our minds and of our creative talents. Without this faith, in the moment of darkness, without our heritage of myth and science, what do we have left? Then

> Watching the blinded waves
> Compounding their eclipse, we hear their
> Booms, rumors and guttural sucks
> Warn of the pitchy whirl
>
> At the mind's end. . . .

In this moment of terror the spectator catches a glimpse of mindlessness. But the moment passes, and light is restored: "Let us suppose that we/See most of darkness by our plainest light." The paradox perhaps amounts to this: that once our most brilliant intellectual and imaginative achievements are known and appreciated, we can see the more clearly what we do not know and have no access to. Only through acquaintance with order can Chaos be known; only through love can terror be known. If we can so interpret the lines, the poem reaches a metaphysical conclusion, and the ordering mind is given the power to sharpen our sense of mysteries outside its purview.

In *The Modern Poets* M. L. Rosenthal praises Howard Nemerov for certain characteristics which he does not find in Wilbur. Both poets are in the liberal predicament: "There they stand, the thoughtful people of good will, dreaming of peace and kindness and education and progress, while their hair stands on end at the horror, moral and metaphysical as well as political, that is everywhere. Nemerov wishes to report the horror frankly.

He also wishes, at least by implication, to put the case for melioristic faith" (258). Rosenthal shrewdly illustrates this point from Nemerov's poems and commends him for reducing "the necessary liberal dependence on near-sentimental wish to an almost invisible point" (259). Nemerov is left with a "minimal idealism," just enough to protect himself "against the more extreme effects of insight into the world's emptiness" (260). Rosenthal uses a phrase of Wilbur's in describing Nemerov's position as a "hypothetical, liberal-tinged commitment to whatever positive can be wrung out of the 'things of this world.'" The commitment is like that of Wilbur and Elizabeth Bishop, but Nemerov more closely approximates the nervously uncertain moment-by-moment immediacies of the sensibility they all share" (261). And he then discusses W. S. Merwin as a poet who has surrendered this commitment altogether, who "has in his best work tried to envision what the resulting sense of empty fatality, of a continuous, all-eroding wash of impersonal reality, would mean" (261).

"The Beacon" is of course a poem about getting a glimpse of this "impersonal reality." But Wilbur does not leave it at that; he returns, as the light returns, to a human reality, a more amenable sea. Does he, as Rosenthal suggests, permit himself too much consolation? Is he obliged in the name of seriousness and contemporaneity to try to throw off the Western heritage (if that is what nereids, meridians, and ships do represent) and to match his soul, unequipped and untempered by history and tradition, against an indifferent and unfathomable nature-in-itself? Is it merely sentimental to conclude that "the Nereid's kick endears/ The tossing spray; a sighted ship/Assembles all the sea"? Perhaps "our plainest light" is really the ignorant or innocent eye— light or vision unequipped by our learned capacity to interpret and to mythologize the landscape. And to what modern observer is it "the Nereid's kick" that "endears the tossing spray"? Even Wordsworth complained that he could not apprehend the sea in such terms as these. Wilbur seems to be suggesting that we can— or does he mean only that if we are to come to terms with the sea we must devise some modern equivalent of "the Nereid's kick"? These are not easy questions to answer, but we must remember that in other poems ("The Waters," "Conjuration," "La Rose des Vents") Wilbur sees some aspects of the sea as strange and terrifying, and also that in "The Beacon" his vision of chaos is as vivid as his vision of order.

Things of This World *(1956)*

In another difficult but rewarding poem, "Looking into History," the poet tries to believe in the reality of five Civil War soldiers in a Matthew Brady photograph, but he fails until he sees that the trees beyond their tents are sycamores. The men and their gear look strange and outdated, but the familiar trees bring the scene to life because they look the same in every age. The opening lines of Part II suggest that the same trick may help us to enter sympathetically into the world of *Macbeth* or *The Iliad*. There follows a difficult—if not obscure—comparison of "history's changes" with the sea's, the point of which seems to be that—although both, in constant motion, disguise and transform what they have consumed—the relics persist in a natural setting that remains familiar to us, as even in the sea we find the familiar shapes of trees. The contrast is that between superseded individuals and a constantly renewed vegetation.

In Section III Wilbur draws—magnificently—certain conclusions. The "old man of the sea" is Proteus, a seer who would advise and prophesy only after attempting to escape from his captors through changing into various forms. "The will will find no stillness/Back in a stilled land"—the will, that is, of the seeker for historical truth or reality, specifically the poet who speaks here. Though the past is "stilled" to the eye and ear, it is not changeless but is constantly changed in the sea-wash of history. We must make a great effort if we wish to salvage it; and what we find will have been transformed by time. The poet-historian cannot bring the dead to wake, to speak, to "command" or direct him until he himself musters them by making "some present fatal choice."

But what sort of "fatal choice" is meant? It is an unspecified commitment which the poet must make, by which he may "in the end stand fast/And by some fervent fraud/Father the waiting past." "Father" is a breath-taking pun meaning not merely "beget" but also "furnish with fathers." (The five soldiers of Part I are his "spellbound fathers," "breathless in their amber atmosphere," with "the hermit faces of a finished year.") The past waits in its "stilled land" for the poet to bring it to life again, whereupon the dead will find their voices and become his effective fathers—that is, nourish, protect, and teach him. But the poet can father the past only by assuming, like Proteus, shapes other than his own. It seems he must enter the past in disguise, perhaps through identifying himself with such figures as those of the trees in the photograph. But, he adds, let me

Yet in the end stand fast . . .

Resembling at the last
The self-established tree
That draws all waters toward
Its live formality.

The "self-established tree," then, is the poet who draws on history ("all waters") for nourishment and vitality. The poem is concerned with ways of making history available to the imagination. My interpretation is not adequate at every point, and I suspect that the poem, though much more exciting in its texture than I have suggested, is too complex in its imagery for perfect coherence. Still, the major theme seems clear enough: the past lives through our deliberate effort to bring it to life, as the world lives or exists through the creative consciousness we bring to it; and once alive it can feed our roots.

"Merlin Enthralled," which gathers up and employs several of the recurrent themes in Wilbur's work, is beyond a doubt one of his finest poems. Merlin, after arranging for Arthur to prove his right to the kingship by pulling the great sword Excalibur out of the stone in which it had been embedded by his magic, acted for some time as Arthur's counselor, magician, and seer and then disappeared mysteriously from the scene. According to some accounts, Merlin had fallen in love with Niniane, a water-nymph, who had teased from him enough secrets of magic to bewitch him and to seal him up alive in a rocky tomb or tower. The poem begins at the moment when Merlin is first missed by Arthur and Gawen, whose bewilderment is suggested in an irregular movement of the opening lines, as aimless as their ride:

In a while they rose and went out aimlessly riding,
Leaving their drained cups on the table round.
Merlin, Merlin, their hearts cried, where are you hiding?

The drained cups are a perfect symbol for finished careers, connoting as they do not only an end, but an end of lives lived completely and heroically. The poignant cry of the third line suggests that the era is over and that despair has set in. The fourth line in contrast moves ominously, surely, and finally: "In all the world was no unnatural sound." The knights long for a sign of the "unnatural," of which Merlin was the priest and the demi-god. The whole poem is adumbrated in the first stanza with the most astonishing ease and grace.

"Mystery" in stanza two is the incomprehensible in a nature to which, without faith and without vision, man is alien. (Versions of this theme have often appeared in earlier poems, including "Objects," "All These Birds," and "The Beacon," as well as in Wilbur's prayer in "Poplar, Sycamore" that his eye "will never know the dry disease/Of thinking things no more than what he sees.") To the searching knights, only the surface of things is visible, but behind the surface, they know, is a mystery. In Arthurian story the "water-top" was not always shut; every reader remembers the arm clothed in white samite that reached above the lake surface and caught the sword Excalibur as Arthur was preparing to leave the world.

After the "unnatural" hint about Merlin's fate comes from the whitethorn, Wilbur recounts the story of Niniane's conquest of Merlin:

> That Siren's daughter
> Rose in a fort of dreams and spoke the word
> *Sleep,* her voice like dark diving water;
>
> And Merlin slept, who had imagined her
> Of water-sounds and the deep unsoundable swell
> A creature to bewitch a sorcerer,
> And lay there now within her towering spell.
>
> Slowly the shapes of searching men and horses
> Escaped him as he dreamt on that high bed:
> History died; he gathered in its forces;
> The mists of time condensed in the still head
>
> Until his mind, as clear as mountain water,
> Went traveling toward the deep transparent dream
> Who bade him sleep. And then the Siren's daughter
> Received him as the sea receives a stream.

This passage is one of the happiest examples in Wilbur's work of his perfect control of pace and his power to convey meaning through sounds. The cunning variations in the length of the sentences and lesser rhetorical units; the fitness of the length and movement of these units to the successive events of the story and to the play of the reader's feelings as he reads; the quiet achievement of Merlin's liquidation in lines full of long deliquescent vowel and consonant sounds—these are only a few of the felicities of this handsome passage. Niniane's part in the story is left to some degree mysterious. She "Rose in a fort of dreams . . ."—impregnable as she charms him into a dreamless sleep. The amazing though ambiguous hint of stanza five ("And Merlin slept . . .") that she is the "creature" of Merlin's imagination is given its development in the next stanza. The whole Arthurian era is Merlin's dream; he has brought it into existence and held it together around the concept of the quest. When he dreams of Niniane ("a creature to bewitch a sorcerer") and succumbs to her spell, not only he is lost but the age also is lost, because it depends on him for its faith, its sense of purpose, its very reality. While he dreamed, the Arthurian world was; when his mind becomes transparent, that world dissolves. The water images through which his dissolution is expressed are beautifully in keeping with the idea of Merlin's enchantment and absorption by Niniane. If her "fort of dreams" is really impregnable, she alone will escape the fate of Merlin's other creatures and persist outside history, ageless and inimical to order. But Merlin's era passes; "Fate would be fated," as Wilbur says with a subtle and delightful play on the word; "dreams desire to sleep." The forsaken knights lose their vision and their special powers, grow merely quaint, and take their place as decorative figures in legend and tapestry: "Their mail grew quainter as they clopped along./The sky became a still and woven blue." Another age with other dreams will succeed them. So skillfully constructed and phrased, this poem carries its heavy ideological freight very lightly. It takes the time to say with authority what needs saying, and other things are not said. There is a spaciousness about the poem, a fullness of expression and a harmony among the parts, that are the marks of a masterpiece.

IV Things of This World

High spirits, sheer exuberance, pervade all of Wilbur's best poems; and no doubt he would be willing to say with Stevens that "poetry is the gaiety of language." A number of poems in *Things,* as in the earlier books, cannot or ought not to be read solemnly. Some of them Wilbur has called "Games," for they play with ideas rather than testify to their truth or tenability. Of this general class "Lamarck Elaborated" is a particularly witty example; its five stanzas on the theme "The environment creates the organ" are a dazzling exercise in word-play and paradox. In "A Chronic Condition" the poet represents himself as enveloped in so thick a fog that he is not certain of the world's continued existence. To be is to be perceived, said Berkeley; but what if one can perceive nothing at all? Perceptible objects having disappeared, the poet struggles to retain his faith in reality, but he has lost his bearings: "I sway and lean above the vanished ground."

This sort of witty exercise merges into seriousness in some of the best poems in *Things*, including "Love Calls Us to the Things of this World" and "A Black November Turkey." Both of these, if we disregard their playfulness, might be classed with those earlier poems in which Wilbur persuades himself to give up asceticism and to live in the world; but the reader is made wary both by their exuberance and by a hint of self-parody in them. Another poem, "A Voice from Under the Table," a more unmistakably serious poem than either, has much of the same characteristic extravagance about it. All three, whatever the precise degree of levity the reader may see in them, are explorations of the theme "things of this world." Their ultimate focus is on fact, not dream; on adjustment to, not escape from fact; on acceptance of the human condition (though perhaps under protest), not on an equally human detachment from or aversion to it.

The title "Love Calls Us to the Things of This World" is taken from St. Augustine. "Plato, St. Teresa, and the rest of us in our degree," says Wilbur, "have known that it is painful to return to the cave, to the earth, to the quotidian; Augustine says it is love that brings us back."[10] The poem begins as the soul awakes in the morning:

> The eyes open to a cry of pulleys,
> And spirited from sleep, the astounded soul
> Hangs for a moment bodiless and simple
> As false dawn.
>   Outside the open window
> The morning air is all awash with angels.

The immediate impression is that of the tone, the mock-seriousness or mock-astonishment conveyed by the high impersonality of the language, the fastidious eloquence accorded a low subject, the Quixotic caprice that takes laundry for angels. This is one of Wilbur's few unrhymed poems, but one in which the line movement is most sympathetically varied in accordance with the spontaneous yet orderly progress of the observations and reflections. Humor is everywhere in the diction: "spirited" means "carried away mysteriously or secretly"; but this time the agents are actually spirits, the angels in the laundry; "awash," itself a pun, is followed by the "calm swells" of line 9 and by the "white water" of line 14. And the proposal that angels are in the laundry is followed by a witty description, the tone of which is appropriately amazed:

> Now they are flying in place, conveying
> The terrible speed of their omnipresence, moving
> And staying like white water; and now of a sudden
> They swoon down into so rapt a quiet
> That nobody seems to be there.

The soul as it wakes is "bodiless" and wishes to remain so, like the laundry. The poem tells of its painful acceptance of the body, its descent to daily life:

> Yet, as the sun acknowledges
> With a warm look the world's hunks and colors,
> The soul descends once more in bitter love
> To accept the waking body . . .

Here "as" means not only "while" but "in the same way as." Both sun and soul have been absent from the world in the night. The soul has a "false dawn" as the sun might, but both then come to acknowledge in a real dawn "the world's hunks and colors," "the waking body" in all its substantial variety. "In bitter love," but nonetheless persuaded, the soul approves the use of the clean clothes not by angels but by men:

> "Bring them down from their ruddy gallows;
> Let there be clean linen for the backs of thieves;
> Let lovers go fresh and sweet to be undone,
> And the heaviest nuns walk in a pure floating
> Of dark habits,
>   keeping their difficult balance."

The spirit's progress in this poem is like that in " 'A World Without Objects . . .' "; it moves away from pure vision and back to the impure, "absurd," or paradoxical world in which "clean linen" is not for angels but for "the backs of thieves" and for lovers about to be "undone"; in which nuns, who may incongruously be heavy, must keep not only their feet but also the "difficult balance" at the heart of this poem, the balance of the spirit between the two worlds of angels and men.

It is good to follow this free and playful excursion of the mind, so unbound by anxiety, so unhurried, serene, and good-humored. Good humor—once again let it be said—is one of the primary aspects of Wilbur's charm. Yet all moods have their place in poetry. A bitter or an anguished poet, if he is equally skillful and equally just in his response to his experience, may strike even more deeply into our feelings.

"A Black November Turkey" consists of eight identical stanzas, two stanzas for each of four sentences, in the form *3x 3a 5x 2a*. As so often in Wilbur's poems, there is a constant dialectic or tension between the strict rhyme and stress pattern and the long, supple sentences that run through the stanzas; often the natural pauses do not coincide with rhymes and line endings, and enjambment is the rule. Meter and word-sounds working together produce some delightful effects, as in stanza one:

> Nine white chickens come
> With haunchy walk and heads
> Jabbing among the chips, the chaff, the stones
> And the cornhusk-shreds . . .

The normal iamb at the beginning of line three is replaced by the trochaic "Jabbing," which surprises us because the stress comes earlier than we expect it to; but this premature stress, along with the sudden sound of the stressed syllable itself, is exactly what is needed to suggest the sudden violent jabbing motion of the chickens' heads. The third line is varied significantly from the first two in its stress-and-sound pattern, not only at "jabbing" but elsewhere. It really has only four strong stresses, "among" having a much weaker stress than the other stressed syllables. Thus "chips," "chaff," and "stones"—following as they do a series of four relatively weak syllables and having themselves each a sudden, sharp, appropriate sound—take on a more than usual vigor and decisiveness. The next line is delicately appropriate for similar reasons, and "cornhusk-shreds" is an expression happily matching sound to sense. Later we encounter another perfect example:

> Shuddering its fan and feathers
> In fine soft clashes
> With the cold sound that the wind makes, fondling
> Paper-ashes.

Again and again the lines appeal irresistibly to the ear, even when there is no onomatopoeia; it is a pleasure merely to speak

the first two lines of the second stanza: "And bit by bit infringe/
A pond of dusty light. . . ."

In its images "A Black November Turkey" is equally successful, and everywhere it is humorous. We smile at various ex-
travagances of diction and imagery, such as the use of the word
"infringe," with its solemn legal connotations, in the lines just
quoted, and at the comparison of the turkey-cock to objects of
epic grandeur, as "a cloud over thrashed branches, a calm ship/
Over choppy seas." Above all, we smile at the absurdity of the
turkey-cock's role in the situation and his contrast with the vulgar
chickens: his magnificent aloofness; his spectacular size, bearing,
and coloring; and his apparent consciousness of his distinction
as a doomed figure, an isolated visionary in a petty world, out
of place in daily life and thoroughly out of touch with it. In this
portrait, there is no malice, no annoyance, no moral heaviness—
only the most urbane amusement.

"A Voice from Under the Table" is so full and complex that
one tries at once to relate it to Wilbur's other poems. Does it
really, as Donald Hall thought in 1956, point to a new direction
in Wilbur's development? Not at any rate in its initial question:
"How shall the wine be drunk, or the woman known?" Not by
what devices, as the poem makes clear, but in what spirit: As we
quickly see, it is Wilbur's old question of the rival claims of the
actual and the ideal. The poet does not spurn this world and the
pleasures it affords; hence, his present "low distress." Even so,
his "distress" is the result of a thirst not merely for the wine of
this world: it is a thirst that "conceives a fierier universe," a more
intense order of experience, symbolized by the Yeatsian "birds
in the burning trees/That chant their holy lucid drunkenness."
I am puzzled by the line "I swallowed all the phosphorus of the
seas"; possibly it is a way of saying that he himself had been on
fire in his attempt to make his way to that conceivable other
universe.

Stanza two continues: You up there who are not drunk have
felt desire and heard the wind in the woods whisper of a love
beyond any the world has to offer (a parallel with what the rose
carafes suggest of a "fierier universe"). Love of women is only
a way of breaking the grip of this desire for a perfect love. (The
pun on "spell" must not be missed: it means both "to act out
with gestures," as in charades, and also "to exorcise, to drive
out.") But love has been no more successful than wine in sub-

duing the speaker's excessive desire. The next three stanzas present examples of perfectly beautiful but unattainable women. The speaker concludes that whether one yearns as a religious man for the other world or makes this world his prize, he will never have all he desires: "The end of thirst exceeds experience." But, he adds, may God not permit me to quit desiring, trying, and failing. Helpless at the moment, he can only wait patiently until his strength returns. But the frustrations of love and drink are sweet, and he will not give up his efforts to satisfy his inordinate desires.

The speaker follows the gleam, reaching with human faculties toward inhuman perfections, conceiving transcendental pleasures and achieving only the partial pleasures of this world. But this is the poet's chosen state, the drunkard's, the lover's, the anchorite's—that of anyone who can conceive of some perfection. The theme of inordinate thirst for an ideal state is a strong and recurrent one in Wilbur. In "Sunlight Is Imagination" and in "'A World Without Objects . . .'" such desire turned the world into a desert, but in "A Voice from Under the Table" the poet accepts his yearnings and lives with them, oscillating from effort to frustration and back to effort. In this poem, the poet avoids the excelsior note through humorous extravagance, ribaldry, and self-deprecation: "God keep me a damned fool, nor charitably/ Receive me into his shapely resignations." This pledge of spiritual restlessness is a good omen for his art, and the poem is a fine one, but it does not seem to me to consist of any important new elements or to mark any new turn in Wilbur's development.

All the poems in *Things* I have not discussed so far seem to me minor, though some are perfect; perhaps some readers would wish to challenge my judgment in the case at least of "Statues." The first stanza is a study in internal rhyme; there are beautiful sound effects of other kinds, and the diction is rich with puns. Children in a public garden are playing "statues," a game in which the players, swung by the arm and then released, must hold for a moment any position the body may take in motion:

Above their heads the maples with a stiff

Compliance entertain the air
In abrupt gusts, losing the look of trees
In rushed and cloudy metamorphoses,
Their shadows all a brilliant disrepair,

A wash of dodging stars, through which
The children weave and then again undo
Their fickle zodiacs. It is a view
Lively as Ovid's Chaos . . .

John Ciardi pointed with admiration to the play and paradox in the phrase "stiff compliance" and praised the way Wilbur "works his diction in depth."[11] "To comply" now means "to yield to," but its Latin root meant either "to fold up" or "to be filled up with." "Stiff" comes from Latin *stipes*, a tree trunk or vegetable stalk. "To entertain" means at root "to hold between" (*inter* and *tenir*). These learned but rewarding effects are amazingly frequent in Wilbur. It pays to examine also the origins of "relents" in the next to last stanza, or "compels" in stanza five.

Wilbur's virtuosity in representing the moving, light-and-shadowy, melting and freezing scene of "statues" is nothing less than marvelous. (Those who agree should study also "Part of a Letter" in *Ceremony*.) But the poem doesn't, after all, add up to much more than the scene itself. The nuns ("Moving along a path as mountains move/Or seem to move when traversed by a cloud"), the soldier, the lovers all stop to watch the game; all break their typical poses for a moment (even the trees lose "the look of trees"), as the children break theirs. Something of a theme is suggested: the onlookers are struck by the implications of the game—that "all definition" is "outrageous." So for a moment "every role/Relents" sympathetically in response to parody—except the bum, who has no stiffness of his own, no shape but "an adamantine shapelessness," no pose or role to break. So he sees his own shapelessness carried to extravagant lengths in the game; his refusal to define himself permanently is like that of the children; and the absurd and fickle gestures of the game are thus "the image of his kingdom come."

The sonnet that begins "The winter deepening" is pleasant but needs no long analysis. There is comfortable humor in the octave and a lively or scary quality in the image of the sestet. The night, the snow, and the gestures of the farmer's scarecrow in the wind suggest vividly the elements in the winter that the farmer has worked to shore himself against. "Apology," in another mood and style entirely, is one of Wilbur's exquisitely phrased and cadenced love poems. Finding terms of endearment in country scenes and things, it breathes softly but urgently of love, not of possessiveness or sex. On the other hand, it is not clear why the rapt lover feels the need to apologize for calling his love by the private names he has devised for her. " 'Exeunt,' " said Wilbur in his filmed interview, deals with "rather small things on which I try to make a great deal turn." Wilbur is a lover of fields, and he can take a close view of what goes on in them. The most remarkable sample of this vein in Wilbur is "A Grasshopper" (*Advice to a Prophet*), but "Exeunt," while smaller and less ambitious, brings to mind beautifully the feel of early fall in the fields of New England:

> Piecemeal the summer dies;
> At the field's edge a daisy lives alone;
> A last shawl of burning lies
> On a gray field-stone.

The descriptive details carry their associations and stir the feelings. The daisy has the pathos of all creatures who live in crowds but survive their fellows. The phrase "lives alone" has not only the right elegiac sound but more: "to live alone" is a cliché, used by the poet here with a subtle shift of emphasis that restores its freshness; the word "lives" in this line has its full value since other things, including daisies, are mostly dead. In the cliché "live" has no such force. The phrase "shawl of burning" suggests a red moss glowing in the sun, or perhaps only the sun's red glow. The second stanza too is very fine:

> All cries are thin and terse;
> The field has droned the summer's final mass;
> A cricket like a dwindled hearse
> Crawls from the dry grass.

The "thin and terse" cries are almost disembodied, utterances of the outworn. The field is a choir, "the summer's final mass," the mass for the dead. And then comes a slightly comic or macabre note, as if the tone of the second line had been a bit too full: "a cricket like a dwindled hearse/Crawls from the dry grass." Wilbur's ear is at its best here. The whole poem is kept slow, but we should notice especially the melancholy effect of the last line of each stanza. Neither is regularly stressed; each lacks a syllable of being a full iambic trimeter line; each uses consecutive long stressed syllables in slow drawn-out phrases with quick ones between; and each gets its effect in different ways. The stanza itself (3a 5b 4b 3a) is unusual but demanding, and it shows Wilbur's interest in experiment.

Does Wilbur have a new subject-matter in *Things of This World?* New subjects must be distinguished from new ideas or themes. New subjects he certainly has, but I think his ideas in *Things* are extensions or new explorations of ideas he was working with earlier. The extensions are real but minor; there is no major turn of attitude or thought. Nor do I see in *Things* any genuine new commitment to subject-matter in general—to "things of this world" or to any other. But I do find in the book the vigor, the mastery of expression, and the seriousness one expects of major poetry.

CHAPTER 4

Advice to a Prophet (1961)

*T*HINGS OF THIS WORLD is so good a book because it brings to a culmination the style in which Wilbur had begun to write. In the best poems of *Things* ("Altitudes," "Love Calls Us to the Things of This World," "A Black November Turkey," "Merlin Enthralled," "A Voice from Under the Table," "A Baroque Wall-Fountain") there is an amplitude, a self-possession, and a vitality that is not found in his next collection, *Advice to a Prophet* (1961). Where the same qualities are present in the new book—as they are in the title poem, in "She," in "To Ishtar," or in "The Undead"—they do not have quite the former happy balance: these poems may strike us as essays in the old style without the old joy and conviction. The less ambitious poems of *Advice*—"October Maples, Portland" or "A Summer Morning"— are as clever as ever; but they introduce nothing new in the way of style, and some of these may be a little too comfortable to take for a good sign. The contents of *Advice* seem, on the whole, slimmer or smaller. But, side by side with poems that hint of exhaustion, we find poems of several kinds that Wilbur had never or seldom tried before: experiments with short lines, new personae, dialogue, and satire that give the collection an air of interim work. From this point of view the ten or a dozen poems least like his earlier ones are the most interesting (though not always among the best) poems in the book. And they are interesting not only for stylistic experiment, and not only for considering, as they sometimes do, a subject or theme or occasion that the earlier Wilbur would probably have passed over, but chiefly for a new outspokenness, an open commitment to personal views and feelings—a commitment requiring the sacrifice of the amused and playful elegance of his earlier style.

Some reviewers, among them Babette Deutsch and Dudley

Fitts, found *Advice* a better book than any of the earlier ones. Mr. Fitts praised it chiefly for qualities already familiar in Wilbur's work: an "unobtrusive virtuosity," "a true elegance," "a memorable energy," amusement and wit.[1] Miss Deutsch, however, fixed on the newer note of involvement or commitment which I have mentioned above. Quoting from "Another Voice," she said: "It is his emphasized refusal to unlearn 'Anxiety and hate,/Sorrow and dear concern' that gives this collection a greater strength than its predecessors. . . ."[2] M. L. Rosenthal particularly admired the title poem, but he had more than that in view when he wrote that Wilbur's most incisive work was the result of his preoccupation with the subject of the death of civilization and the need for the heart to see what this death means.[3] As I have argued in earlier chapters, a concern for our human plight and destiny is a recurrent theme in each of Wilbur's collections of poems; and Rosenthal himself had remarked on it briefly but shrewdly in *The Modern Poets* (1960). It is not a concern for the human plight itself but the more personal, more troubled, less ironical acknowledgment of his own involvement in it that gives to certain poems in *Advice* a tone new in Wilbur's work. Of these the clearest examples are "Someone Talking to Himself" and "Another Voice."

But *Advice* stirred up more disagreement among reviewers than any of his earlier books had aroused. Theodore Holmes charged that the poems typically show "things seen from the Parnassian heights of wealth, privilege, ease, refinement, and education, looking down on the permanent sufferings of humankind without being part of them"; and he found in *Advice* a "waning of interest," a loss of force, triviality, mannerism: "the ritual that once shone with the light of belief now fallen to the motions of a code no longer adhered to." But in the title poem and a few others he heard what Miss Deutsch and others had heard: "an openness, a straightforwardness, a giving voice to his own heart, a compassion out of involvement that almost makes recourse to device superfluous. . . ."[4] One other criticism worth mentioning was made at length by Reed Whittemore: that Wilbur's poems were full of echoes from other poets. These echoes—of image or phrase, of rhythm or tone or verbal play—conceal Wilbur's own voice, said Whittemore: "I do not emerge from his poems, as I do from Lowell's, with a sense of what is peculiarly, distinctively the poet's own manner, method, outlook."[5] Most, if not all, of Whittemore's illustrations are con-

vincing (Ransom in "Loves of the Puppets," Auden in "The Undead," Yeats in "Another Voice"); but it is clear that many
readers do not find these echoes damaging to their enjoyment
of Wilbur's poems, as Whittemore did. In any case, I imagine
that the trying out of other voices is part of Wilbur's deliberate
strategy for going beyond *Things of This World,* an effort to
break away from a manner, method, or outlook that (he may
have felt) was becoming too confining.

I *Nature's Tongue*

Let us start, as before, with a group of poems that take nature
in some sense as their subject. "October Maples, Portland" is not
an attempt to represent the appearance of things; the poem is a
set of reflections aroused and set in motion by the appearance
of things. The first three stanzas are built on the pun on "un-
fallen" in the second line:

> The leaves, though little time they have to live,
> Were never so unfallen as today,
> And seem to yield us through a rustled sieve
> The very light from which time fell away.
>
> A showered fire we thought forever lost
> Redeems the air.

This saving rinse in the blessed light transfigures the street and
forever alters "eye and brain." The last five lines of the poem
happily do not belabor the message or dwell on the nature of
the "lasting stain." The "pretty" tale of Mary's mantle lightens the
whole effect, though it concedes nothing to the skeptical reader.
The lightness and wit of the poem procure a hearing for the
grand idea, long out of fashion, that nature is a language
through which God may speak to man. Elsewhere Wilbur sometimes, though not usually, puts the doctrine of "things of this
world" in religious terms ("'A World Without Objects . . . ,'"
"A Plainsong for Comadre," and others). But even when his
imagery remains secular, these things in their symbolic or emble-
matic import are often things of both worlds, holy objects, with
a redemptive power for those who can understand what they
have to say. A secular poem in which nature is explicitly called
a "tongue" is "Advice to a Prophet."

"A Grasshopper" is a minor masterpiece in a form (*2a 3b 3a
2b*) that seems perfect for the tiny scene of a moment presented

in it. The first two stanzas exhibit the verbal economy, the bug's-eye view, and the exactly observed detail characteristic of the whole poem:

> But for a brief
> Moment, a poised minute,
> He paused on the chicory-leaf;
> Yet within it
>
> The sprung perch
> Had time to absorb the shock,
> Narrow its pitch and lurch,
> Cease to rock.

The next three stanzas describe a sinister quiet, "peace like a plague," that settles on the field as the grasshopper sits on his perch. Then the grasshopper leaps again, and everything goes back to its former activity:

> In gay release
> The whole field did what it did,
> Peaceful now that its peace
> Lay busily hid.

The peace of a field, then, is not in an unnatural quiet but in the normal business of its life. The reader may ask himself whether this is not true also of human life, individual or social; but the poem itself does not generalize. One source of its charm lies in its efficiency as it makes its distinction and discovers its idea in the slightest of natural occasions.

"Fall in Corrales" is, in contrast, a full-scale attempt to define the human role as it changes from season to season in a dry Southwest landscape. The language of the poem has a strange remoteness, a distinct formality of tone, and the reader must wonder who is speaking. The rhythms vary from the usual iambic to something much less regular, with a good many pairs of adjacent stressed syllables. In the seven stanzas on the pattern $5x\ 5a\ 5x\ 4a$, the x endings are usually feminine off-rhymes, while the true rhymes are masculine. A difficult poem and an ambitious one, it is to be commended to the attention of those who, like Jarrell, urge Wilbur to "take a chance."

The poem begins by making some surprising distinctions. Winter and summer are alike in that they require us to deal with the world through "charms" or fictions, but the kinds of charms required are different. Winter calls forth ritual activities: feasts, fires, love-making, prayers, poems, "and all recourses/Against the world huge and dead." These rites are both creative and protective. The "charms" of summer are those of "the shut head . . . Willing that its thought be all heat and hum,/That it not dream the time passes." These lines seem to imply a deliberate narrowing of the mental focus, a renunciation of the intellect, a consciously achieved oblivion—all aspects of an effort to respond appropriately to the summer season. (This response is perhaps what the speaker failed to achieve in "In the Elegy Season.") These two modes of dealing with winter and summer are epitomized later in the contrasting terms "tales or drowsing" (stanza four) and "rhyme or dreaming" (stanza seven). The "light buildings of summer" that "begin/To crumble" as fall comes on, "the air husky with blown tile," I take to be a metaphor for the summer vegetation. (Compare "green leaves building into the light" from "In the Elegy Season.") Winter is lived in "the shut houses"; summer, in "the shut head." Both seasons force the spirit to protect and to express itself by constructing "charms" or spells.

But fall and spring are unlike winter and summer: the April wind, like the dry wind of fall, "unhoused the spirit for awhile," enabling it to participate directly, without recourse to ritual or dream, in the natural process. The lines on spring recall "Lamarck Elaborated" (*Things*) in their paradoxical quality and in their manner:

Then there was no need by tales or drowsing
To make the thing that we were mothered by;
It was ourselves who melted in the mountains,
And the sun dove into every eye.

Our desires dwelt in the weather as fine as bomb-dust;
It was our sex that made the fountains yield;
Our flesh fought in the roots, and at last rested
Whole among cows in the risen field.

There is much more of interest in these brilliant lines than I have space to comment on. But clearly in the spring man and nature are identified in birth and growth; in the fall they are one again in death, as things dry up and blow away:

Now in its empty bed the truant river
Leaves but the perfect rumples of its flow;
The cottonwoods are spending gold like water;
Weeds in their light detachments go;

In a dry world more huge than rhyme or dreaming
We hear the sentences of straws and stones,
Stand in the wind and, bowing to this time,
Practise the candor of our bones.

This huge "dry world" is not to be "charmed." Once again, as in
April, our spirits "unhoused," we stand in the wind; but now it
speaks of the doom of all things. (But consider the ambiguities:
"sentences" are opinions pronounced on particular questions; or
judicial decisions determining punishment; or the punishment itself; or merely sayings, apothegms, maxims. Is it the wind that
pronounces the sentences—or the "straws and stones"?) Hearing
the "sentences," we acknowledge our mortality, of which our
bones will speak without evasion. A strange poem, full of unfamiliar and not always very convincing insights into what the
natural cycle means, it is rich and impressive all the same. It
exists not in the foreground of personal experience and recollection, but is grandly impersonal, at the height and distance of
myth.

Although "Advice to a Prophet" is less dense and austere in
style and structure, it resembles "Fall in Corrales" in its concern with the bonds between man and nature. "Advice to a
Prophet" is an attempt to imagine humanity without nature and
to measure the loss. The threat of the bomb is what starts the
poet thinking about earthless man and manless earth, but ultimately this threat is no more than a gambit for the introduction of Wilbur's oldest themes: What shall we make of the earth?
What has it made of us? How do we need each other? The voice
that speaks in the poem seems to be that of a spokesman for the
community, like the voice of the chorus in one of Sophocles'
tragedies. The voice addresses some lecturing scientist, likening
him to an ancient prophet; and it advises him how to touch the
imagination of the people when he comes to warn them about
the destructive power of modern weapons. He will reach them
only by building on their experience, says the spokesman. He is
not to speak of the weapons themselves, because men cannot
"fear what is too strange"; nor of "the death of the race," because
men cannot imagine the earth without human beings. Instead,
he is to "speak of the world's own change," for that men can
understand. Having experienced minor disasters that changed
the world, they can imagine this major one: the utter extinction
of animals and vegetation, the boiling away of rivers. They will

be moved, says the speaker, when they consider not what the
world would be without them, but what they would be without
the world:

> What should we be without
> The dolphin's arc, the dove's return,
>
> These things in which we have seen ourselves and spoken?
> Ask us, prophet, how we shall call
> Our natures forth when that live tongue is all
> Dispelled, that glass obscured or broken
>
> In which we have said the rose of our love and the clean
> Horse of our courage, in which beheld
> The singing locust of the soul unshelled,
> And all we mean or wish to mean.

The language is worth—indeed requires—the closest attention.
With characteristic tenacity Wilbur develops the point that not
only our image of ourselves but even our terms to describe ourselves come from the world outside us. The other creatures are
a "live tongue," a language by which alone we can "call our
natures forth"—think and act, express love, show courage, conceive of ourselves as human. These creatures are also a mirror
in which we see ourselves as we are or want to be. Our concep-
tions of human virtues like love and courage depend ultimately
on the qualities of the rose or of the horse, in which we have
glimpsed our own potentialities. The qualities of creatures are
perceived and named; their behavior is likened (and, no doubt,
contrasted) to our own; already in their gestures there exists a
language that we see and interpret; in our own terms for these
creatures and in their gestures we tell each other what we have
learned and what we want of ourselves. Without the world to
perceive and respond to in this way, we could not be human.
So goes the argument, logically complete at this point but
given further illustration in the final stanza:

> Ask us, ask us whether with the worldless rose
> Our hearts shall fail us; come demanding
> Whether there shall be lofty or long-standing
> When the bronze annals of the oak-tree close.

The "worldless rose" would be, I assume, our memory of the
rose, our conception of it, or our word for it. But "kept spirit is

corporate," as Wilbur said in "Lament" (*Ceremony*): without the objects, the things of this world, we shall not drink at "the spirit's right/Oasis, light incarnate." "The rose of our love" depends on the rose of the world, without which, perhaps, "Our hearts shall fail us"—meaning both that we shall lose our courage and that we shall be unable to love. The oddness of the phrase "whether there shall be lofty or long standing" wears off with familiarity. Shall there be qualities when there are no things? The implied answer is no. If we let the world, our language and our mirror, escape us, we may lose our humanity, our natures. This view of our intimate dependence on nature is striking; certainly in some sense it is true. Wilbur offers it wisely as a hypothesis, the last five stanzas being cast not as assertions but as questions by which the prophet may stir us to a consciousness of our true dependence on the world. It is like Wilbur to set this fancy gravely before us, to ask what human life would be like in a world utterly barren—as if there could be human life at all. But if, as he argues, this is the fancy that moves us, the practical prophet will be well advised to evoke it.

"Advice to a Prophet" is not a radically new poem, either in theme or in technique. It recalls Wilbur's earlier forays into the topic of our relationship, ideal and actual, with other things and creatures: the theme of man on earth. It gathers up from many earlier poems ("Objects," "Sunlight Is Imagination," "'A World Without Objects . . .,'" "Lamarck Elaborated," "Lament," "An Event," "A Voice from Under the Table," "Love Calls Us to the Things of This World," and others) Wilbur's hints that our attachment to this world is a matter of self-interest. In "Advice to a Prophet" Wilbur sees that his old question—what use do we have for the world?—is the one raised in a peculiarly dramatic way by the threat of the bomb. Those who don't raise it for themselves, as Wilbur has—out of philosophical curiosity, or mistrust of abstraction, or fear of asceticism—have it raised for them by the bomb's vast contempt for life. Some readers have found the style of this poem too oratorical for their taste, but the reviewers admired it almost without exception; and I imagine that it has appealed to many people who would not otherwise have been much interested in Wilbur's work. M. L. Rosenthal wrote, "I have seen at least one audience deeply moved by it, some to tears, when Mr. Wilbur read it aloud."[6]

II *Tensions and Apprehensions*

To many readers Wilbur seems the least tormented of poets, but I hope this study will help to make clear that the surface composure of his poems is often but the rein of a strict control over genuine and disruptive tensions of the spirit. In her review of *Advice,* Miss Deutsch put it, rather strongly, like this: "The book is, in effect, a dialogue between the poet, thirsting 'to drink creation whole,' and a man tormented because he cannot remain 'blind/To the damned universe.' "[7] Her quotations come from "The Aspen and the Stream," a fliting of opposite human types. The Aspen speaks first, addressing the Stream:

> Beholding element, in whose pure eye
> My boughs upon a ground of heaven lie—
> O deep surrendered mind, where cloud and stone
> Compose their beings and efface your own,
> Teach me, like you, to drink creation whole
> And, casting out my self, become a soul.

These are better couplets, I believe, than any other poet could write today. "Beholding element" is a strange and perfect opening: how well it reduces the Stream to what the Aspen is struck by. And how fine a word each is in its place, for each word has its own rich history, different and amusingly different, the first in the idiom of the Bible and the second in that of science. "Pure" is better than "clear" would be because the Aspen is admiring what it takes to be a perfect selflessness, and "pure" has the ambiguity needed here: its connotations being both physical and moral. "A ground of heaven" is equally witty, using the word "ground" to mean both background and the ground beneath our feet, depending on whether we envision the scene from the point of view of the Stream or from that of the Aspen. "Cloud and stone," heaven and earth, merge in the Stream, which drinks creation whole. The self is conceived of as the ego, the interested and assertive individual; and the Aspen assumes that self-effacement through total acceptance of the world is a saving discipline that might be learned.

Both the Aspen and the Stream want to cast out self and become souls, but they differ as to how to do it. Again, as in so many of Wilbur's poems, we have an old theme in a new guise: that of " 'A World Without Objects . . .' " or "Love Calls Us to the Things of This World" or "A Baroque Wall-Fountain . . ."—

a perfect acceptance of the world as against a perfect renunciation of it. The Stream hates the world that it sees and reflects so well:

> Why should the water drink,
> Blithering little tree?
> Think what you choose to think,
> But lisp no more at me.
>
> I seek an empty mind.
> Reflection is my curse.
> Oh, never have I been blind
> To the damned universe,
>
> Save when I rose in flood
> And in my lathered flight
> So fouled myself with mud
> As to be purged of sight.

"Purged," which normally means "flushed out and purified," is the happiest possible word here. What the Aspen sees as pure, the Stream sees as impure; the universe being damned, the Stream seeks to blot it out.

The Aspen's next speech surrenders to sheer fun in the middle of the developing drama. It develops nothing itself, though it characterizes the Aspen as a comic, well-meaning blunderer, indeed a "blithering little tree." Unlike the misanthropic stream, the tree leads a sociable life; it finds the motion of its own leaves (that is, of its mind) distracting and confusing:

> Your water livens me, but not your word,
> If what you spoke was what I thought I heard.
> But likely I mistook you. What with the claims
> Of crow and cricket teaching me their names,
> And all this flap and shifting in my head,
> I must have lost the drift of what you said.

But the Aspen, though it has admired the Stream's apparent serenity, is far closer to contentment than the Stream. If the tree lives fallibly, at least it lives in affectionate touch with other creatures and hates no one. If it has not "cast out self," at least it lives in the hurly-burly of life; and, though humble, it has no morbid self-contempt.

Asked to repeat and elucidate, the Stream instead explains what it wants to do in its search for an "empty mind." It is as eager as the Aspen was to cast out self and to "become a soul,"

but its method is the very opposite of the Aspen's yearning "to
drink creation whole":

> There may be rocks ahead
> Where, shivered into smoke
> And brawling in my bed,
> I'll shred this gaudy cloak;
>
> Then, dodging down a trough
> Into a rocky hole,
> I'll shake the daylight off
> And repossess my soul
>
> In blackness and in fall,
> Where self to self shall roar
> Till, deaf and blind to all,
> I shall be self no more.

The self is the will or the identity; the soul is something more
essential. Self-annihilation will enable the Stream to "repossess"
its soul. Its way is that of the extremist ascetic or Oriental mystic,
perhaps, who drives out of his mind all thought and all will, if
he can, to contemplate nothing. The Aspen finds the self an
obstacle to its love for the universe, but the Stream finds it an
obstacle to its hatred. The Aspen wants pure acceptance of
things; the Stream, pure renunciation. One is avid of experience;
the other hates its life and the world alike. The Aspen has the
final word:

> Out of your sullen flux I shall distil
> A gayer spirit and a clambering will,
> And reach toward all about me, and ensnare
> With roots the earth, with branches all the air—
> Even if that blind groping but achieves
> A darker head, a few more aspen-leaves.

Once again, as so many times before, Wilbur rejects solipsism
and asceticism in favor of a renewed commitment to life in the
world. Roots are a familiar symbol of the human capacity to dig
down firmly and deeply; branches, a symbol of the faculty for
exploration, for reaching out toward what warms, lights, and
interests—for developing in various directions at once. And since,
ultimately, the ends of life are uncertain, growth may be called
"blind groping." "A darker head" cannot be a more somber

spirit, for the Aspen has pledged itself to gaiety. Perhaps it is a head that sees or thinks less clearly as life presents its mysteries more fully and at length. At the very least the Aspen can be sure that its "blind groping" will bring "a few more aspen-leaves": the things done according to one's capacities, the fruit of "a clambering will," or the poems of a poet. One final thickening of the texture occurs as we notice that the hint in the Aspen's second speech ("Your water livens me, but not your word") is picked up and built on in its final speech: "Out of your sullen flux I shall distil/A gayer spirit and a clambering will. . . ." The Aspen turns the water of the Stream to its own ends, uses its "sullen flux" to "distil" its own opposing spirit, and makes of bitterness and self-contempt a strength to live by. The Aspen accepts the challenge of self-development with others in a damned universe; the Stream declines it.

The only other dialogue in the book, "Two Voices in a Meadow," also contrasts two character types; but, since there is no conflict, no resolution is needed. The milkweed and the stone simply exist side by side in the meadow with wholly different attitudes toward life, different ways of expressing themselves, different aims and purposes. The milkweed is ambitious; it wants power and gets it by yielding its innumerable seeds to the wind: "Shatter me, great wind:/I shall possess the field." The stone accepts its position in the field, a low one assigned by mere chance. Scornful of those who move from their places ("To move/Befits a light desire"), the stone feels that somehow the scheme of things rests on its own stolid immovability. And of course it does: we build on stone; obstinacy and sullen pride have their value, as flexibility has its value. The charm of the poem depends as usual on Wilbur's play with the several senses of certain words: "yield," "shatter," "possess" in the first speech; "light" and "aspire" in the second. But it depends also, I think, on our sense that these voices ironically carry the virtues of flexibility and steadfastness to the point where they approach opportunism and obstinacy.

The title of "Someone Talking to Himself" suggests that we need not take the "I" of the poem to be the poet; indeed, despite the unusual intensity of the lover's anguish, we might almost take him for all mankind. The lover says that even when he first fell in love, he was aware of forces indifferent to love, denying it, awaiting its end. Even in their ecstasy, the lovers "knew yet must deny" that their love was doomed. I cite the last and most

difficult stanza, in which the lover in his loss takes what consolation he can:

> Love is the greatest mercy,
> A volley of the sun
> That lashes all with shade,
> That the first day be mended;
> And yet, so soon undone,
> It is the lover's curse
> Till time be comprehended
> And the flawed heart unmade.
> What can I do but move
> From folly to defeat,
> And call that sorrow sweet
> That teaches us to see
> The final face of love
> In what we cannot be?

"Love is the greatest mercy" because it restores the weather of
the "first day" in Paradise. And yet it is "soon undone"—by
death or by the fading of passion in life? The images of the
"blind fishes" and the "recusant shark" in stanza one may, it
seems to me, suggest either. In stanza two, however, the image
of "the roaring course/That in the summer's drought/Slowly
would peter out/Into a dry marsh" suggests the diminishing of
love in this life. The lover is cursed, in any case, by his knowledge that love must end—cursed "Till time be comprehended/
And the flawed heart unmade." The meaning of "comprehended"
is not easy to determine. Perhaps over-ingeniously, I take it in
the obsolete senses (current before 1607, says the *Oxford English
Dictionary*) "to overtake, to attain to, to accomplish," suggesting
the end of the lover's time in death, when his heart is "unmade."
The heart is "flawed" either by its primal imperfection in fallen
man or by its experience in this life of love that has receded and
left the lover in despair. Then love is folly—even though it is
also "the greatest mercy"—because it ends in torment and defeat.
But we may call the sorrow of earthly love sweet if through it
we can come to conceive of ideal love, eternal love, God's love,
some perfect love. It is worth remembering that in the first
stage of their love, the lady's face "shadowed under its lashes/
Every earthly thing. . . ." "The final face of love," however, is
unearthly. The lover's progress is like that of Dante, through
love of a woman to love of God; but the last lines of the poem
are rueful, if not bitter.

Stanza two especially seems to me marvelously and characteristically rich in meaning, not only for its terms used in
two or even three senses ("fell," "bed," "current," "race")
but for the justice of the whole figure of the stream as a
symbol for the course of fated love. But I want to return to the
lines in stanza one about the lady's face, which "Shadowed under its lashes/Every earthly thing. . . ." "Shadowed" can mean
"shaded," "screened," "protected," "sheltered"; it can also mean
"stood for" or "represented faintly or prophetically"; it can even
mean "clouded," "cast a gloom over," for the poem is ultimately
about the transience of love as "the lover's curse"; it is an ode
on melancholy. The lover sees the world "shadowed" in this
way under her lashes. Rather oddly, the difficult third line of
stanza three echoes both these terms:

> Love is the greatest mercy,
> A volley of the sun
> That lashes all with shade,
> That the first day be mended. . . .

The only meanings of "lashes" that seem possible here are
"strikes" or "beats" and "binds" or "fastens down." Yet neither
of these meanings helps us to see how "love is the greatest
mercy." But this point might be made: that in his early work
Wilbur sometimes thought of shadows as emblems of the
mortality of things:

> they running reach
> On windy days
> To touch, to teach
> What stays
> Is changed, and shadows die into dying things.
> ("Sunlight Is Imagination")

In this poem from his first book the poet is not so much concerned with the sorrow of loss and change; although he gives full
recognition to the transiency of things, his mood is more cheer-
ful and hopeful, as in the early days of love. "Someone Talking
to Himself" is in a darker mood, one of the moods of experience,
in which a man can call love "folly" and loss "defeat" and con-
sole himself in his sorrow by thinking of what he has learned.
I do not think this mood has any true precedent in Wilbur's
earlier work; it must be counted among the new ventures of
Advice to a Prophet. I do not see how it could possibly be

thought that this handsome, heartfelt poem is an exercise or a trifle. It seems to me one of Wilbur's finest poems.

In "Another Voice" the poet, conscious of human suffering and wrongdoing, addresses himself to the "patient voice" of joy within himself and asks it to forgive him for curbing it. It would be more usual nowadays, at least among educated liberals, to ask one's conscientious and sympathetic side forgiveness for moments of spontaneous joy in this rotten world. There are those who do not find in Wilbur's poems enough evidence of his awareness of human misery. "Another Voice" insists on the "atrocious fact" without denying the soul's impulse to sing. The theme is one that Yeats treated greatly in "Lapis Lazuli" and other poems, and something of the manner of Yeats is recognizable in these spare three-stress lines:

> The sword bites for peace
> Yet how should that be said
> Now or in howling Greece
> Above the sorry dead?

Violence is sometimes employed in the world to prevent or to reduce violence, to re-establish a state of society in which violence is not necessary. A runaway force, producing its own problems, it may be adopted for the worst of reasons, or for a mixture of good and bad reasons, as well as for the best. The first line above assumes a situation in which violent measures are adopted to end violence. But then, says the poet, even if one believes that peace will result from the use of violence, or (by a slightly different reading of the line) that those who use violence genuinely desire peace, one cannot speak his mind to the victims of violence and their survivors. The reference to Corcyra recalls Thucydides' account of the siege that led to a disastrous civil war and a terrible demoralization of the Corcyrans. The "crows" will cry that violence rules the world and is never justified. In respect for the victims, those who believe that good is being accomplished through bloody means must remain silent: "The soul knows what it knows,/But may not make reply."

Stanza two repeats the point of stanza one in other terms: Violence is paid for by madness and bitterness. It is human to mourn this human damage, not to explain it away. "If soul in quiet sing,/Better not to explain." Why does the soul sing? Is it with hope of the good which it "knows" will result from human sacrifice? Is it rejoicing in its intuition of ultimate moral order in the universe? Presumably so, or perhaps it sings of an inner happiness that wells up spontaneously in healthy response to the sweetness and the comfort otherwise to be had in the world. "If soul in quiet sing," it must be in moments when it is not confronted by madness or malice, during its own quiet moments. Its quiet and its happiness will not be shattered forever, should not be, by its consciousness of human suffering; it should remain capable of quiet happiness, otherwise it too is a casualty, a damaged soul. It is a hard saying but a true one that unrelieved mourning is not required of all mankind, though many suffer.

In the third stanza Wilbur returns to the main argument, which is simply that the soul should be silent "before atrocious fact," that pain must be given its full measure of sympathy. "The giddy ghost" is a phrase that deprecates alike the singing of the poet's soul, the song of the martyrs, and the doctors' logic—all these responses to pain are light-minded or frivolous. And yet "the giddy ghost" has its own just claims:

> Forgive me, patient voice
> Whose word I little doubt,
> Who stubbornly rejoice
> When all but beaten out,
> If I equivocate,
> And will not yet unlearn
> Anxiety and hate,
> Sorrow and dear concern.

"Dear concern" may seem a bit weak after the nouns that precede it, but otherwise the diction of this stanza is marvelously just and happy and the lines very beautiful in their movement. One felicity is the double meaning of "beaten out"—by blows, by competition. "Equivocate" is perfect: to speak with two voices, now with one, now with another equally. The word flirts boldly with its secondary or derived meanings: to speak ambiguously or unclearly; to speak uncertainly or without determined or sure meaning; to speak misleadingly so as to deceive, prevaricate, or evade. This word is bold because Wilbur's first three stanzas may arouse the suspicion that he is not sufficiently sympathetic to those in distress: his soul continues to sing, and he must conceal its rejoicing from those who are suffering. As I have said, I think we may imagine that the soul sings in its own times of quiet, but the two final lines of each of the first two stanzas deliberately risk a great deal. Even in stanza three we may wonder why Wilbur speaks of the "anger, love, or tact" of others rather than of his own—as if he were not moved immediately to such feelings himself but were coolly choosing an example to follow. But, as I hope I have made clear, I think he comes free of our initial doubts in a powerful, frank, and responsible poem, one in which much of the excitement is generated by his rare honesty. The poem goes beyond any of his earlier poems in the direction of self-revelation.

III Myth and Allusion

It is a question whether "Stop" ought to be grouped with the poems of Section II, which concern themselves, however delicately, with some strain, disturbance, or conflict of the spirit. t is the only poem in Wilbur's whole output that records the ,ook and mood of a scene of such grim and cheerless desolation, but we respond to the scene without being chilled by it. Instead, we are strangely reconciled to it by the poet's finding in the "purple, glowering blue" of the baggage truck the color of Lethe or of "Queen Persephone's gaze/In the numb fields of the dark." We see that where we are is hell, but we perceive also that hell is of the eternal order of things. Something heroic and enduring in us is touched by the familiar reference; the hell of the Greeks is better than our modern emptiness. "Stop" and "Junk," other poems of this rather loosely definable group, can both be cited to test Theodore Holmes's idea that Wilbur's classical allusions are sometimes a mere "refuge." Of "Junk" Holmes says that it "would be a total poem did it not, as these poems so often do, take refuge in myth and allusion at the end."[8] Taking refuge would amount to evading the problem posed, shirking the resolution needed in the poem. Although, as I have said, the ending of "Stop" seems to strike a note that will bring comfort, if anything, to readers who know something about Persephone, I see no evasion in it. A grimmer ending is conceivable but not required.

"Junk" is headed by a quotation from the Anglo-Saxon poem "Waldere." Wilbur has a note on it as follows: "The epigraph, taken from a fragmentary Anglo-Saxon poem, concerns the legendary smith Wayland, and may roughly be translated: 'Truly, Wayland's handiwork—the sword Mimming which he made—will never fail any man who knows how to use it bravely.'" And the poem itself is written in an Anglo-Saxon form: each line is divided into halves by a heavy caesura; each half has from three to seven syllables, two of which bear heavy stresses; one of the stressed syllables in one half (no matter which syllable or which half) is alliterated with the two stressed syllables in the other half.

> An axe angles
> > from my neighbor's ashcan;
> It is hell's handiwork,
> > the wood not hickory,
> The flow of the grain
> > not faithfully followed.

This axe and some other badly made things have been put out to be carted away. It is painful to think of such junk and of the men who made it. But the poem ends with a vision of these things reverting to their original elements on the dump:

> Then burnt, bulldozed,
> > they shall all be buried
> To the depth of diamonds,
> > in the making dark
> Where halt Hephaestus
> > keeps his hammer
> And Wayland's work
> > is worn away.

The reference to Hephaestus carries us beyond the thought of the impersonal and protracted work of chemical forces that turn the separate objects into undifferentiated soil; it reminds us of the splendid craft and fury of the god who made gifts for his wife Aphrodite and armor for Achilles. The junk is not past the chance of redemption and glory; it may yet become the substance of some well-made object. If Wayland's work wears away, moreover, then any work will do so; and the junk is simply sharing the fate of all things, no matter how well made in the first place. The mythical references work to take the junk out of a narrow imaginative range, that of one's neighbor, last week and next week, and the city dump, and to put it into a broad perspective. As a result, we think of the honor in which all peoples have held good work. We are reminded thus more sharply of the boredom and guilt of the workman who barters his pride for a little money, of the ugliness of gimcrack objects, of their short, embarrassed lives. The myths are thus not a mere refuge; they recall a great tradition of craftsmanship. On the other hand, I find some banality in the details of the description; something forced and unconvincing in the efforts to suggest that the junk has its own honor, keeps "composure," improves through deterioration; some failure in the whole to rise above the mundane; some dullness or obviousness in the conception which is unredeemed by the language and the tone. To my taste, this earnest, detailed, and laborious poem is one of Wilbur's rare failures, but the mythical allusions are not responsible. Both "Stop" and "Junk" juxtapose a depressing urban spectacle with references to Greek myth. The results are better in "Stop," but the intent is the same in each poem and common enough in all poetry: to emphasize the meanness of the scene by contrast with the heroic Greek ideal—but also to suggest that it is all one world; that, if the Greeks could transfigure the mean and see it in the heroic light, so can we; and that we may gain strength by this transfiguration.

In 1950, in his contribution to Ciardi's *Mid-Century American Poets,* Wilbur had commented on the subject of poetic allusions. He said, "One does not, merely by referring to the dying god or what not, evoke a legitimate emotional response. The value of the reference must in every case be proven" ("The Genie in the Bottle," 4). Ten years later Wilbur returned to the subject in his lecture, "Round About a Poem of Housman's,"[9] in which he defended the value in modern poetry of echoes from other poets and of historical and mythical allusions. His own attitude he contrasted with that of Karl Shapiro, who had objected to poetry that "relates back to books, to other poetry, to names in the encyclopaedia. It is the poetry of the history-inhibited mind only, and as such it is meaningless to people who lack the training to read it." Wilbur argued for retaining the literary and historical past for reference: "It would not be worth it," he wrote, "to make poetry more generally usable at the cost of abridging the poet's consciousness." Housman's allusions in the poem he discussed ("Epitaph on an Army of Mercenaries") are not decorative but necessary. In good "referential" poems, Wilbur maintained, the echoes, though not essential to enjoyment and understanding, contribute meaning. Knowledge of the past, "a great index of human possibilities," is a guard against provinciality. The poet, through tact and talent, must make his knowledge of the past usable for his audience. In its theory—as in its demonstration—this lecture seems to me completely convincing.

Whether in particular poems Wilbur's own references, allusions, and echoes succeed in meeting his standards is another question.

In any case, the poems in *Advice* often do depend on mythical and historical references. As in "Stop" or "Junk," a unique event in time, once seen in the light of myth, becomes a timeless illustration of some essential human principle. Our attention is thus drawn to the archetypal aspect of this event, to its basic and recurrent pattern, rather than to what seems spontaneous and strange in it. But there is more than one kind of truth in poetry: there is the truth of the strange and the truth of the familiar. Any event embodies something of both, and a poet may keep the two in balance by turning from one to the other as a witness to their coexistence.

Several other poems in *Advice* are like those just discussed in relying to some degree on myth, but are different in being more detached and impersonal in tone. Even when they touch on some aspect of evil, they seem to refer not so much to the poet's as to everyone's experience, and the attitude they take is not so much moral as exploratory or appreciative. Two of these, "She" and "To Ishtar," concern themselves directly and primarily with mythical subjects. In "She," the poet maintains that man has never since Adam known woman as she is; he knows only the ideal forms in which she has appeared in response to his desire. He cannot guess what her beauty was in Eden, says the poet; but with the Fall she entered the world of laboring man and "in Time took on/The look of every labor and its fruits": harvest goddess, temple priestess, captive maiden, ship's figurehead—

> Tree, temple, valley, prow, gazelle, machine,
> More named and nameless than the morning star,
> Lovely in every shape, in all unseen,
> We dare not wish to find you as you are,
>
> Whose apparition, biding time until
> Desire decay and bring the latter age,
> Shall flourish in the ruins of our will
> And deck the broken stones like saxifrage.

These closing lines are characteristically witty and eloquent; but, like some lines in the earlier stanzas, they require a good deal of the reader. Perhaps we may take them to amount to this: "She," as "subject goddess of the dreams of men," has always taken the shape of their desires. When these decay and men's last age is upon them, what will "She" become? She will not cease to flourish, but will grace men's ruins. When they have ceased to value existence, she will help to destroy them, for "saxifrage," a flower that grows wild in the clefts of rocks, means literally "rock-breaker." The "apparition" of men's healthy desires, "She" must also be the emblem of their unhealthy ones. The reader who can assent to this interpretation will find a deeper meaning in such earlier lines as "A moonlike being truest in eclipse" and "We dare not wish to find you as you are." In style and theme, "She" is related to Wilbur's earlier poems about the power of the imagination to give form to desire.

Another fine poem in a style developed earlier is "Ballade for the Duke of Orléans," a title to which Wilbur appended the explanation, "who offered a prize at Blois, circa 1457, for the best ballade employing the line "Je meurs de soif auprès de la fontaine." It is pleasant to think that an American poet was interested enough to enter the Duke's contest, though five hundred years too late. The Duke's paradoxical, romantic line struck an old chord for Wilbur, who had already written poems in which thirst is an important motif ("Sunlight Is Imagination," "'A World Without Objects . . .,'" "Grasse: The Olive Trees," "A Voice from Under the Table"), along with many others whose theme is, more broadly, human yearning for the unattainable. While the whole project is an exercise (as it was in 1457), for Wilbur it is a particularly congenial one, not only in its theme but in its formal requirements; and there is a resurgence in the poem of his old high spirits and love of amusement. A ballade consists of three stanzas with an identical rhyme scheme followed by a shorter *envoi*, the same last line or refrain being used for each stanza and for the *envoi*. Wilbur's rhyme scheme is the most common one: *ababbcbc* and *bcbc*. Since the stanza has four *b* rhymes and the *envoi* two, he had to provide fourteen words on this rhyme. Despite the difficulty of finding rhyme words, the lines move easily and preserve their continuity and rhetorical fervor. They even have a quotable or epigrammatic quality, so skillfully has Wilbur surmounted the formal hurdles.

The first stanza tells with economy and vividness of a fisherman's battle with a fish till "he was caught,/Gasped in the net, lay still and stony-eyed." Then the fisherman sees that it wasn't the fish itself that he had wanted: fishing is a quest for something beyond the caster's reach. And he mourns, "It was no fading iris

I had sought./*I die of thirst, here at the fountain-side*." The second stanza is spoken by Odysseus after he has come home to Penelope and has seen that the irresponsible years with Calypso have cost him too much. Stanza three, a bit more complex, uses three sets of two lines and one single line before the refrain for four separate variations on the theme, a development that quickens the pace and increases the excitement in preparation for the resolution in the "Envoi":

> Where does that Plenty dwell, I'd like to know,
> Which fathered poor Desire, as Plato taught?
> Out on the real and endless waters go
> Conquistador and stubborn Argonaut.
> Where Buddha bathed, the golden bowl he brought
> Gilded the stream, but stalled its living tide.
> The sunlight withers as the verse is wrought.
> *I die of thirst, here at the fountain-side.*

And in the "Envoi," with a sudden turn back to the Duke who had offered the prize, the poet cries out:

> Duke, keep your coin. All men are born distraught,
> And will not for the world be satisfied.
> Whether we live in fact, or but in thought,
> *We die of thirst, here at the fountain-side.*

The poet sees that even winning the prize would not satisfy him. The word "distraught," with its several implications (diverted or turned aside, agitated by conflicting passions, perplexed or even crazed) has a brilliant justice, and the diction is rich in the lines that follow. Those who "live in fact" are either simply the living (like the poet but unlike the Duke) or those who live for facts or deeds, like the fisherman or "conquistador and stubborn Argonaut." Those who live "but in thought" are either the dead, like the Duke, who live only in the memory of the living, or those who, like the poet, live not for heroic action but for contemplation and for poetry. The second set of meanings recalls the poet's earlier lines in "A Voice from Under the Table":

> Groan in your cell; rape Troy with sword and flame;
> The end of thirst exceeds experience.
> A devil told me it was all the same
> Whether to fail by spirit or by sense.

The "Envoi" represents "all men" as "born distraught," with a thirst that is only human. But some unfortunate men suffer a special sinister kind of thirst described in "The Undead." Wilbur's note to the poem is as follows: *"The Standard Dictionary of Folklore, Mythology, and Legend* defines the vampire as 'One of the types of the undead; a living corpse or soulless body that comes from its burial place and drinks the blood of the living.'" "The Undead" resembles "Beasts" in style as in subject, but it makes a much clearer statement of its theme. In "The Undead" Wilbur attempts a whole life story and characterization of the vampire. As children, "Secret, unfriendly, pale, possessed/Of the one wish, the thirst for mere survival . . . ," they feared all that suggested dying. Now in their second lives, they rise with the moon and enter the town and the houses, invisible and intangible, subject to fits of their own peculiar madness, lust, and frenzy.

> Nevertheless, their pain is real,
> And requires our pity. Think how sad it must be
> To thirst always for a scorned elixir,
> The salt quotidian blood
>
> Which, if mistrusted, has no savor;
> To prey on life forever and not possess it,
> As rock-hollows, tide after tide,
> Glassily strand the sea.

The vampires, then, are those who "in utter self-concern" refuse or fear to enter life while on earth and who later thirst always for the blood they scorned or mistrusted. "To prey on life forever and not possess it" is the essential characteristic of those to whom the folk imagination has given black cloaks, bat-like shapes, and other dramatic features without losing sight of their fearful thirst. While Wilbur treats the vampires in the poem as if, during their lives as human beings, they were different from normal people, their thirst not for life but "for mere survival" is a disease of which most people perhaps have had a touch so that they know what it is and fear it. We can see in this poem a return to Wilbur's long concern with the importance of participating fully enough in the life of this world. Like many of the earlier poems, "The Undead" enjoins us, though indirectly, to live life and trust it—if we can.

In reading "To Ishtar" we ought to have in mind the outline of the story of the great mother-goddess of the Babylonian-Assyrian pantheon, the counterpart of the Phoenician Astarte, almost the personification of life itself:

She brings forth, she fertilizes the fields, she clothes nature in joy and gladness, but she also withdraws her favors and when she does so the fields wither, and men and animals cease to reproduce. . . . In myths symbolizing the change of seasons she is portrayed . . . as the life-giving and the life-depriving power. The most noteworthy of these myths describes her as passing through seven gates into the nether world. At each gate some of her clothing and her ornaments are removed until at the last gate she is entirely naked. While she remains in the nether world as a prisoner . . . all fertility ceases on earth, but the time comes when she again returns to earth, and as she passes each gate the watchman restores to her what she had left there until she is again clad in her full splendor, to the joy of mankind and of all nature. Closely allied with this myth and personifying another view of the change of seasons is the story of Ishtar's love for Tammuz—symbolizing the spring time—but as midsummer approaches her husband is slain and, according to one version, it is for the purpose of saving Tammuz from the clutches of the goddess of the nether world that she enters upon her journey to that region. . . .

(*Encyclopedia Britannica,* Eleventh Edition)

The poet addresses Ishtar at the moment when the snow has begun to melt but before the earliest flowers have appeared, imagining her back again at the "first gate," ready to re-enter the world. He asks the goddess's forgiveness for man's inability to worship her disinterestedly in the winter season:

> Forgive us, who cannot conceive you
> Elsewhere and maiden, but love you only
> Fallen among us in rut and furrow,
> In the shade of amassing leaves,
>
> Or scrawny in plucked harvest,
> Your losses having fattened the world . . .

All we can do in the winter is observe the cold and cheerless scene

> And in the desert heat
> Of vision force from rotten sticks
> Those pure and inconceivable blooms
> Which, rising, you bear beyond us.

In this difficult final stanza, where we are more than ever eager to seize the meaning, we encounter not one problem, but several.

The poet has said that we cannot conceive the goddess herself "elsewhere and maiden," but we can apparently conceive certain "blooms." So far we might follow the meaning if we take "blooms" as the salient detail of the dream or vision of spring which we can "force from rotten sticks" during the winter. But these blooms are "pure and inconceivable." We might take them as merely "conceptual," like those of "In the Elegy Season," or even as in some sense "accurst," like those desert visions of " 'A World Without Objects. . . .' " But how can we take them as "inconceivable"? Perhaps we may, without too much ingenuity, think of these winter visions as sterile seed—as false rather than true dreams. In this reading "inconceivable" takes on a biological meaning: to be incapable of "realization" in life on earth (that is, in Ishtar's womb). But the last line does not fall quietly into place. Even if Ishtar, on her return to earth in the spring, bears (carries) the false dreams "beyond us" by replacing them with present realities, a considerable residue of strain is felt. And the pun on "bear" is too much, for how can the inconceivable be borne in the biological sense of our speculation?

I must leave the stanza to better readers, but not without recording that, in spite of its difficulty, the poem seems to me one more searching exploration of the theme of the ideal and the actual so often encountered in Wilbur's poems. Basically, the poem turns on the distinction between the two, seen here as complementary rather than as irreconcilable. The connotations at each pole are delicately indicated but important in the action of the poem. A pure, disinterested worship of Ishtar would be a good thing; but, since men are not capable of it, they are guilty of less than perfect devotion. The poet asks the goddess's forgiveness for merely exploiting her in our sexual desire and in our greed for the harvest. Contrasting goddess and man, he speaks of her love (for Tammuz), for which she undergoes a death that is "perfect," but of "our itch/for defilement." An odor of human guilt is thus in the air in the last stanza, and I take it that the poem concerns itself with a yearning for life in a season of death that is somehow deserved. Ishtar figures in the poem not as a "refuge" from difficulty, but as a powerful symbol, long after the time of her fame on earth, of cyclical forces at work in every life and consciousness.

IV *Fools and Fainthearts*

It is possible to assemble from among the better poems in
Advice a group that, using the term rather loosely, may be called
satirical. Wilbur shows signs here and earlier of a dangerous
satirical firepower, though not many of his poems are satirical
in their main intent. The pair of classical epigrams entitled
"Gemini" (twins) represent something new in Wilbur's work.

I.

Because poor PUER's both unsure and vain,
Those who befriend him suffer his disdain,
While those who snub him gain his deference.
He loves his enemies, in a certain sense.

II.

It is the power of Heaven to withdraw
Which fills PUELLA with religious awe.
She worships the remoteness of a wraith.
If God should die for her, she'd lose her faith.

Puer and Puella are twins in their lack of self-respect, in their
way of admiring others precisely in the degree to which those
others despise or ignore them. This kind of poem depends for its
success on the shrewd recognition of a genuine weakness in
human nature, on compressed and powerful (often harsh) statement, and on a twist that induces the reader to laugh with the
satirist.

Like "Gemini," "Shame" is directed at those who despise themselves. It is just as clever as "Gemini," but its style and method
are very different—and different from anything else in Wilbur's
work. The rapid, prosy lines might be those of a witty spy in remote and little-known regions reporting back to his government:

It is a cramped little state with no foreign policy,
Save to be thought inoffensive. The grammar of the language
Has never been fathomed, owing to the national habit
Of allowing each sentence to trail off in confusion.

The observations on this "state" which follow are funny partly
because they are so penetrating. The extreme self-effacement of
the natives is not a healthy cultural trait but a symptom of
psychic imbalance, one caused, it seems, by a fear of having to

take responsibility in a world in which the struggle for power is a condition of life. So thoroughgoing is the natives' refusal to assert themselves that they respond to the census taker with a "flustered insistence/That they do not count" and with a "modest horror/Of letting one's sex be known in so many words." In all their behavior they maintain a colorless anonymity; yet "they lack the peace of mind of the truly humble."

Secretly these people are not interested in escaping notice; they only wish to be sought out and dominated. The guards leave their borders open to

> . . . the hoped-for invasion, at which time the happy people
> (Sniggering, ruddily naked, and shamelessly drunk)
> Will stun the foe by their overwhelming submission,
> Corrupt the generals, infiltrate the staff,
> Usurp the throne, proclaim themselves to be sun-gods,
> And bring about the collapse of the whole empire.

I do not understand what tactics the natives use to gain power; nor does it seem in character that they should adopt any deliberate policy; nor do I see why the invaders are so demoralized. The events suggest that the natives' self-effacement has concealed a yearning not exactly for power but for grandiose self-assertion. Instead of consolidating their gains and ruling, they proclaim their godhood and let the invaders' empire collapse. Thus once again, as before their victory, the satisfaction of their own neurotic hungers takes precedence over the maintenance of political order.

Considered as a type of personality, the "state" of shame is divided within itself between its fear of candid self-exposure and its thirst for the approval or admiration of others. "Shame" is incapable of taking initiative, but it unobtrusively invites conquest. Once its pent-up yearning is touched by the attentions of even the most purely self-seeking invader, it responds at once by abandoning all its reserves in an orgy of submissiveness. When nevertheless it comes into power, perhaps by flattery and intrigue, "Shame" throws off its excessive humility and makes its mad claim of being above humanity altogether and therefore of being entitled to be worshipped. Because it cannot live on equal terms with other personalities, but poses as deserving first less and later more esteem than the others, "Shame" is unfitted for the exercise of authority. This caricature is remarkably acute both in its analysis and in its clear representation of one of the varieties of human weakness, its symptoms and its successive phases. The countrymen of "Shame" thus take their place among Wilbur's other characters who are unfitted for a fully effective life in the world; the difference is that there is nothing in this poem of his usual sympathy for misfits. If the poem misses being satire, it is only because it is so easy to take "Shame" as a country of hopeless neurotics rather than of mere fools or fainthearts who might be capable of a healthy response to ridicule.

Although I shall discuss "Loves of the Puppets" with the satires, it is no easier than "Shame" to categorize. Reviewers pointed out that "Loves" recalls the idiom of John Crowe Ransom; some assumed that it was a deliberate imitation; others, an unconscious echo, of Ransom. The resemblances are of several kinds: in the witty, exact, yet stilted word-play; in the lovers' situation, which is a travesty of that of "The Equilibrists"; in the humorous detachment enforced by the prim, quaint diction. The poem concerns the efforts of two persons to achieve sexual satisfaction before they have learned to love each other. The manner of their failure is curiously and brilliantly described in language rich with puns and rich too in the imagery Wilbur finds to describe the spiritual isolation that accompanies their physical union, for these lovers "flew apart the more they came together." But finally, "exhausted yet unsated," they recognized that what was missing was love:

> . . . and they cried
> For want of love as if their souls would crack,
> Till, in despair of being satisfied,
> They vowed at least to share each other's lack.
>
> Then maladroitly they embraced once more,
> And hollow rang to hollow with a sound
> That tuned the brooks more sweetly than before,
> And made the birds explode for miles around.

The next-to-last stanza is one to tease us out of thought. Since what they lacked was love, what can it mean "to share each other's lack"? It is a crucial question, for only through their vow to do so do they attain to the blessed state of the final stanza, in which "hollow rang to hollow" as lack to lack. Is this a state of love or only a state in which love is no longer sought or expected? Could the joyous harmony of the final stanza be the consequence of an agreement to be content with the pleasures of the flesh? I think not—not because I assume any inherent incapacity for this arrangement in human psychology and not because the language of the next-to-last stanza provides any sure guide, but because the flesh alone is precisely what has failed the lovers earlier. "To share each other's lack," then, must be in some sense to feel a sympathy, at least to pity, perhaps to love. The landscape with brooks and birds described in the last two lines is prepared for subtly in the first two stanzas by references to April and "the gentle weather." The tuning of the brooks is a pleasant and intelligible conceit, but what shall we make of the surprising violence of the image of exploding birds in the last line? This violence goes beyond what seems required to suggest the violence of sexual transport; it seems to me to reflect a pervasive sense in the poem of the harshness of sexual desire and experience, of the ruthlessness of feeling it may arouse, of the exhaustion it may bring when things go wrong. The narrative implies this harshness, and it emerges too in the language of such a line as "Yielded their natures to insensate sense," where "insensate" means not only "without feeling" and "without wit," but also "without humane feeling" and thus harsh or brutal. The Ransomesque idiom stylizes and intellectualizes this harshness; but it makes its impression nonetheless, and it constitutes a new theme in Wilbur's work.

V From Daily Life

A final group of poems in *Advice* might be called "domestic" because they take their cue from some commonplace event or scene in daily life. These include some poems already discussed ("Stop" and "Junk") and several others: "A Summer Morning," "A Fire-Truck," "A Hole in the Floor," "In the Smoking-Car," and "Next Door." There is no avoidance in these poems, as there usually is in Wilbur, of the banal or vulgar details of life; on the other hand, these details are not mocked or used with disgust or comic effect. They are simply accepted, as if the poet were more tolerant of them than many serious poets are today. Except in "A Fire-Truck," the language of these poems seems more casual and relaxed, "lower," than that of most of Wilbur's work; its effectiveness depends in part on a special quietness, ease, or intimacy of tone; it takes fewer risks than usual and throws the attention off the texture, away from the local excitement of diction, imagery, and sound and onto the broader features of narrative and description. Neither the "low" style nor the mundane or domestic occasion is new in Wilbur (recall "Digging for China" or "The Mill"), nor is there in *Advice* any significant increase in the number of poems of this general type. That most of these poems appeared in *The New Yorker* proves nothing, since that is where at least half the poems of Wilbur's last three books have first been published; and yet something in their self-imposed limitations of subject, tone, and aspiration makes the poems of this "domestic" group seem particularly at home there. Clever as they are, these "domestic" poems have something about them of an urbane and comfortable slightness—a subtle air of confidence in the easy relationship between poet and audience—that is not the spirit of adventurous work in the arts. One may admire the poems and hope at the same time that Wilbur will avoid the danger they seem to represent.

"A Summer Morning" is one of his simplest poems in its language and in the immediate, familiar intelligibility of the feelings it conveys. Nothing could be more persuasive and yet more unobtrusive than the evocation in this poem of the look and sound of morning around the house as cook and gardener begin the day. The particular kind of pleasure they enjoy is not available to the young owners, modern and suburban, for whom the house is not so much the center of life. The last stanza makes the point:

> His young employers having got in late,
> He and the cook alone
> Receive the morning on their old estate,
> Possessing what the owners can but own.

The poem does not propose that servants are free of care or that a more expensive or sophisticated life is without its own pleasures. It presents a moment only, but a moment made authentic in the lovely details of the three middle stanzas. Dreams of peace are likely to be more lurid than this reality, like Walter Mitty's dreams of success or the seductive dream of "the grizzled, crew-cut head" of "In the Smoking-Car." If this latter poem be satire, it was seldom before so gentle, amused, compassionate—and, I am tempted to add, seldom so acute. The language of the poem is so easy that it may seem simpler, less varied and less brilliant, than it is: some lines parody the banal idiom of the sleeper himself; some elevate themselves mock-romantically, others neo-classically ("A sighing stream concurs in his repose"); in their inflated context, the flat last lines of stanzas three and four are little jewels of bathos.

In their power to give the look and feel and sound of violent or rapid movement, the first two stanzas of "A Fire-Truck," which show the truck on its way, recall "Juggler" and some other descriptive poems in the earlier books. But these stanzas are cunningly contrived to build up, not to a picture only, but to an idea or proposition suggested by the hurtling truck. The fitness of the idea to the scene, the suddenness with which it is introduced, its climactic position at the eighth line, and the cumulative weight of the description behind it give the quick shift to the abstract, when it comes, the brilliant justice of Wilbur's best passages:

> Right down the shocked street with a siren-blast
> That sends all else skittering to the curb,
> Redness, brass, ladders and hats hurl past,
> Blurring to sheer verb,
>
> Shift at the corner into uproarious gear
> And make it around the turn in a squall of traction,
> The headlong bell maintaining sure and clear,
> *Thought is degraded action!*

"Line 8," says Wilbur in a note, "echoes a notion entertained by Henry Adams in his 'Letter to American Teachers of History' (1910)." A lesser poet would have got only so far as to have the bell proclaim the glory of action, while he himself compared it cleverly with second-best thought. To give the bell the whole proposition is a characteristically bold and delightful stroke of wit.

The next lines are remarkable for the way they reflect the speaker's mood and carry it through stages that seem inevitable in their nature and their order. First shock, then emptiness and helplessness, expressed in the simplest possible fourth line:

> Beautiful, heavy, unweary, loud, obvious thing!
> I stand here purged of nuance, my mind a blank.
> All I was brooding upon has taken wing,
> And I have you to thank.

One reviewer wrote, "I know of no other poet who could get away with a descriptive line like 'Beautiful, heavy, unweary, loud, obvious thing' . . . and somehow make us *feel* that each of these overworked adjectives is freshly perfect for his purpose."[10] But no adjective is in itself overworked: it is only in particular contexts, to describe certain things, that it becomes overworked.

The cleverness and fitness of this line comes of its use at this particular moment in the narrative; it is the stunned recourse of the speaker's mind to the obvious which is the whole point of the line. We see that as we sense his mood, but he continues with an explanation: "I stand here purged of nuance, my mind a blank." The poem is dramatic, and momentarily blank minds must express themselves in obvious language.

If my reading is adequate, the final stanza seems to offer a less than usually firm resolution:

> As you howl beyond hearing I carry you into my mind,
> Ladders and brass and all, there to admire
> Your phoenix-red simplicity, enshrined
> In that not extinguished fire.

In entering the "not extinguished fire" of the poet's mind, the phoenix-vision of the fire-truck takes the place of the thought that formerly filled it and becomes a cherished image. It resembles a phoenix, then, in being capable of death and rebirth in the poet's memory. Has the proposition made by the fire-truck bell been abandoned? Or is the replacement of thought by image in the poet's mind meant to be an enactment of it? Either way, despite its ingenuity, the poem appears to lack a fully coherent development and therefore to remain a little disappointing.

One way to read "A Hole in the Floor" is to take it as a comment on the meaning and value of mythology for the poet. In the commonplace situation of the poem, which calls forth an immediate response from the speaker, and in the homely, unrhymed style of the opening lines, Wilbur seems to be trying for an unwonted spontaneity of effect. Beneath the familiar surface of things is "the buried strangeness" which is not merely there, only to be glimpsed in privileged moments, but "which nourishes the known," giving it meaning and value, restoring its power to amaze or even perhaps to frighten us, bringing the wonder of things to mind again, and showing existence as a mystery. The images in this final stanza are fittingly ambiguous and expressionistic, the new wildness of the lamplight reflecting the change in the mood and vision of the speaker. "That spring from which the floor-lamp/Drinks" is the spring of poetic inspiration, and the poem belongs in the line of "The Beautiful Changes," "Praise in Summer," "Juggler," and the others concerned with the poet's need to maintain his sense of wonder. The parallel with Schlie-

mann suggests that the poet too may dig up Troy and take the
myths to throw "a wilder bloom" on familiar things.

In "Next Door" the poet fancies that old people are constantly
making up just such myths as those of Troy. "The home for the
aged opens its windows in May," and the old people can be seen
and heard through the woods from the poet's house. But soon
the trees break into leaf, the birds sing, and the old are cut off
from his view and hearing. The poet speculates about their
thoughts and habitual talk. It may be, he says, that

> . . . they project
>   Upon a cloudy stage
>
> Gossip of strong-man, dancer, priest, and all
>   They knew who had the gift of life,
> Artisan, lover, soldier, orator,
>   · Wild bitch and happy wife,
>
> Lying the more as recollection fails,
>   Until for their enchanted souls
> The players are forgotten, and they see
>   Only such naked roles
>
> As David was, or Helen, and invent
>   Out of their fabulous memories
> Alcestis climbing home again, with big
>   Death-bullying Heracles.

This fancy is the more convincing because the first three stanzas
are full of counterbalancing details of a realistic order: "stale
voices," "dusty curtains," "every sigh or quaver," "the sick
cough." The language of the poem, having risen with the thought
to a visionary height as the speculation flourishes, lets itself down
with perfect tact and point in the final stanza:

> Is it like this? We have no way to know.
>   Our lawn is loud with girls and boys.
> The leaves are full and busy with the sun.
>   The birds make too much noise.

VI *"A Christmas Hymn"*

One more original poem, "A Christmas Hymn," represents
something entirely new in Wilbur. Its phrasing is consistent with
that of traditional hymns and of the Bible; its rhythms are strong

and regular; its lines three-stressed, with feminine endings in the first, third, and seventh lines of a stanza rhymed on the pattern *xaxaabxb*. The fourth and fifth lines of each of the four stanzas are identical: "And every stone shall cry," a line taken from St. Luke, xix, 40, where Jesus says to the Pharisees, "I will tell you that, if these [disciples] should hold their peace, the stones would immediately cry out." Wilbur quotes verses 39-40 as an epigraph to the poem. The hymn takes the form of a joyful prophecy of the nativity. It foretells the birth of Jesus, his triumphal ride through Jerusalem, and his crucifixion, and then returns in the final stanza to the rejoicing proper to the season:

> But now, as at the ending,
> The low is lifted high;
> The stars shall bend their voices,
> And every stone shall cry.
> And every stone shall cry
> In praises of the child
> By whose descent among us
> The worlds are reconciled.

Anyone familiar with Wilbur's poems and aware of their pre-occupation with the rival claims of two worlds, variously conceived and described, will feel that the Incarnation is an idea in which Wilbur could hardly fail to have a special interest. It might indeed strike such a poet as the crucial myth of myths. While a traditional hymn like this one has no room for distinctly personal thoughts or feelings, and while it sets more or less its own formal requirements, "A Christmas Hymn" is not an anonymous poem. Wilbur's signature may be read no less clearly in the choice of the subject than in the stylistic firmness, resonance, and dignity of the work itself.

CHAPTER **5**

Studies and Aversions

MOST OF THE POEMS of *Advice to a Prophet* that I have not discussed are translations: Jorge Guillén's "The Horses" and "Death, from a Distance," "Eight Riddles from Symphosius," Quasimodo's "The Agrigentum Road," Nerval's "Antéros," and Act I, Scene 4 from Molière's *Tartuffe*, the complete version of which appeared in book form in 1963. While these poems seem to me very good in Wilbur's English, I shall not take space to comment on them in detail. Instead, I turn to Wilbur's prose writings on two poets of the last century in whose views he has shown a special interest; follow this with some reflections on his position among his contemporaries; and conclude with an appraising glance at one of the most recent poems, which I take to be a significant experiment in the manner of Frost.

I "... the waiting past"

The first of the prose pieces is an essay on Poe, published in 1959 as an introduction to the complete poems of Poe in the Dell Laurel Poetry Series, of which Wilbur has been general editor for several years. He begins by conceding that Poe's poems after his twenty-first year "ceased to be efforts at full statement; they became in effect addenda to the prose pieces, embroideries, cryptic distillations" (7). For this reason one must go to the prose for an adequate understanding of the poems, and Wilbur does so in his essay. First, he points out that Poe drastically limited by his theories the scope and nature of poetry. Believing that "the scientific spirit and the universal prosaism which accompanies it have inherited the earth," Poe held that the poet's "sole present recourse is to repudiate all human and mundane subject-matter, all 'dull realities,' and to pursue visions of those

[*163*]

realms in which beauty was or is inviolate: the remote Earthly past, in which Naiad and Hamadryad went unchallenged, and the distant 'happier star' to which they now have flown" (9). The poet's object is "to get away from Earth and men" rather than to use in his poems a maximum of worldly experience. Wilbur remarks that in this respect Poe's ideas run counter to the aims of most poets today.

This is true, and ultimately Wilbur stands with most modern poets against Poe; but it is also true that Wilbur shares with Poe not only a mistrust of "the scientific spirit and the universal prosaism which accompanies it" but also that vivid sense of other realms for which Poe was ready to abandon the Earth. In "All These Birds," Wilbur gives some illustrations of the way in which, in the eye of creeping science, "the monsters of the sky/ Dwindle to habit, habitat, and song." His dismay is, I should think, very much in the spirit of Poe (as in that of most other poets from Blake to the present moment). But the counter-measures Wilbur proposes are entirely different. Instead of surrendering the Earth in despair to science and prose, he stakes everything on the power of the imagination to recover what has been lost; he urges that, even while we grant the validity of science within its province, we

> . . . tell the imagination it is wrong
> Till, lest it be undone,
> > it spin a lie
> So fresh, so pure, so rare
> As to possess the air.

Instead of seeking out ancient or unearthly or supernatural realms, the imagination, as "a natural thing" itself, should establish itself on earth and become a refuge for all natural things:

> Oh, let it climb wherever it can cling
> Like some great trumpet-vine, a natural thing
> To which all birds that fly
> > come natural.

The motive of the imagination as it does so will be very different from Poe's aversion to the natural world and different also from the disinterested curiosity of science that diminishes its objects as it studies them. The poem concludes

> Come, stranger, sister, dove:
> Put on the reins of love.

"The reins of love" do not constrain or diminish; they dignify and magnify objects through the power of the myth-making imagination. The poem is one of a number of Wilbur's poems that exalt the imagination over mere fact, but I think its thematic kinship with "Cigales," "In a Bird Sanctuary," "Objects," "Poplar, Sycamore," " 'A World Without Objects . . . ,' " "Merlin Enthralled," and "Love Calls Us to the Things of This World" is especially clear.

Poe and Wilbur both take for granted the conception of two worlds, one here and now, the other elsewhere and timeless. Poe regards this world as diseased and damned; Wilbur might share this view without ceasing to accept the world as the human estate and to strive for closer bonds with it. Poe never doubts the value of striving to enter the other world; Wilbur remembers that we can enter it only by—in some sense—dying. Poe's dream voyages are all "escapes from corrupt mundane consciousness into visionary wholeness and freedom" (23); more skeptical, Wilbur is aware of the danger of false dreams that may weaken our hold on life. "Poe," says Wilbur, "offered always the same account of the poetic process. Straining after a supernal beauty which might restore the unity of the diffused universe—and of his own shattered soul—the poet begins with earthly things (Rowena, Mary Chaworth, the City, the Sea), subverts their identities, and accomplishes their imaginative destruction. The supposition is that melodious and rhythmic destruction of the earthly must be heavenly" (19). Wilbur begins and ends by cleaving to the things of this world. But, as I have often insisted, the spiritual state reflected in his poems is not so simple as that. A good many of Wilbur's poems bear the marks, often "lightly hid," of a profound effort to resist the charm of some such ghostly siren as Poe's contempt for the world. He concludes his account of Poe's poetic purposes with a dictum that exactly reflects the ambivalence revealed in his own poems: "There has never been a grander conception of poetry, nor a more impoverished one" (39).

A reader who is familiar with Wilbur's poetry might reasonably gather from a lecture he gave at Amherst College, October 23, 1959,[1] that he owes a more grateful debt to Emily Dickinson than to Poe. From her, perhaps, he learned something of the active role of consciousness in coloring, shaping, or apprehending whatever we are conscious *of*. Emily Dickinson, says Wilbur, discovered personally in writing her psychological poems "that the aspect of the world is in no way constant, that the power of external things depends on our state of mind, that the soul selects its own society and may, if granted strength to do so, select a superior order and scope of consciousness which will render it finally invulnerable" (36). To act by these insights is not to destroy the world, like Poe, but through a discipline to make it serve our purposes. Wilbur's statement reminds us of the recurrent insistence in his poems on the power of mind or imagination to construct and to give value to reality.

Most of the lecture consists of an account of Emily Dickinson's "sumptuous destitution," the tactics she adopted in adjusting to her "sense of privation." In her outer and in her inner life "she came to keep the world's images, even the images of things passionately desired, at the remove which renunciation makes; and her poetry at its most mature continually proclaims that to lose or forego what we desire is somehow to gain" (39). Wilbur cites her poem "Undue Significance" as one with the moral: "Once an object has been magnified by desire, it cannot be wholly possessed by appetite." The moral recalls Wilbur's "A Voice from Under the Table," "Ballade for the Duke of Orléans," and a number of other poems. In "Success is counted sweetest," he says, it seems likely that Emily Dickinson "is arguing the *superiority* of defeat to victory, of frustration to satisfaction, and of anguished comprehension to mere possession . . . that food, or victory, or any other good thing is best comprehended by the eye of desire from the vantage of privation" (40-41).

How can desire define things? Wilbur asks the question and draws from Traherne a distinction between "the way of appetite and the way of desire. . . . The creature of appetite . . . pursues satisfaction, and strives to possess the object in itself; it cannot imagine the vaster economy of desire, in which the pain of abstinence is justified by moments of infinite joy, and the object is spiritually possessed, not merely for itself, but more truly as an index of the All. . . . Emily Dickinson elected the economy of desire, and called her privation good, rendering it positive by renunciation. And so she came to live in a huge world of delectable distances. . . . 'Heaven,' she said, 'is what I cannot reach'" (41-43). Poe abandoned the world as diseased and damned; but Emily Dickinson, equally desperate, we imagine, but not so drastic, looked past or through it as less than sufficient. Wilbur quotes a sentence from her correspondence: "Enough is of so vast a sweetness, I suppose it never occurs, only pathetic counterfeits"; and he comments that "The writer of that sentence could not invest her longings in any finite object" (43).

I do not mean to suggest that there is any very close correspondence between Wilbur's views and moods and those he attributes to Emily Dickinson. It is only that this lecture, like many of his poems, shows an unusually sympathetic understanding of the relationship between the thirst for perfection and a sense of the insufficiency of this world. It might be said that Wilbur characteristically strives in his own poems to record a moment of joy in which "the object is spiritually possessed, not merely for itself, but more truly as an index of the All." On the other hand, Wilbur is always on guard against an undervaluation of the finite object. This struggle between an inclination to unworldliness, moral and metaphysical, and a determination to give the world its due is, as I have argued earlier, perhaps the chief motive of his poems. Now and then, as in " 'A World Without Objects . . . ,' " "Love Calls Us to the Things of This World," and "A Christmas Hymn" in honor of "the child/By whose descent among us/The worlds are reconciled," he seems to have hinted at or adopted a Christian solution. But he is much more interested in the tension or paradox of the two worlds than in solutions, and he remains wary of ready-made patterns of thought and language. He begins his lecture on Emily Dickinson by saying that what he found most remarkable in her is that she would not let her inherited Calvinist vocabulary "write her poems for her." Instead, she forced it to "subserve her own sense of things" (35).

In Emily Dickinson, if not in Poe, the yearning for another mode of existence was matched and counterbalanced at times by an equally strong capacity for taking pleasure in the world around her; hence the humor, the happiness, and the vivid natural detail of many of her poems. The same balance is kept by Dante, by Milton, by Wordsworth, Keats, Hopkins, Yeats—all other-worldly poets who (as Wilbur says of his old people in "Next Door") "will not cheat the world of their regard,/Even as they let it go." Yeats struggled all his life with the problem posed by the rival claims of the ideal and the actual. When in Yeats's poem "Vacillation" the religious Soul advises, "Seek out reality, leave things that seem," the secular Heart replies: "What, be a singer born and lack a theme?" Rejecting Von Hügel's view that the way of the artist and the way of the Christian are the same,

Yeats chooses this world, saying "Homer is my example and his unchristened heart." This passage from "Vacillation" might be paraphrased to echo Wilbur: "Art calls us to the things of this world." It is true that Yeats in other moods can represent himself as turning away from this world with relief, as he does in "Sailing to Byzantium"; but Wilbur, though haunted by his own vision of "the dreamt land/Toward which all hungers leap, all pleasures pass," responds again and again to the injunction expressed in the happy slogan, "Love calls us to the things of this world."

The abstract pattern of this oscillation is that of the familiar doctrine of liberal Christianity in which the love of God implies a love of his creations and vice versa. In this view of things "The worlds are reconciled," and due honor can be done to both. But poets are not philosophers, even though they may, like Wilbur, have philosophical interests; in any case, even to mention the doctrine suggests the difficulty of holding it today as an article of faith. It will be better to keep our terms secular and to say only that, unlike many of his thoughtful contemporaries, Wilbur has managed to entertain his visions of perfection without paying the price of alienation from the "damned universe."

Wilbur's studies of Poe and Dickinson thus show something of his interest in keeping the two worlds of the ideal and the actual in balance, without withdrawal and without despair. They also illustrate his capacity for drawing sympathetically on the world of the past without getting out of touch with that of the present. The general aim and spirit of his study of earlier poets is well expressed in "Looking into History," where he promises himself that he will, if he can,

> . . . by some fervent fraud
> Father the waiting past
>
> Resembling at the last
> The self-established tree
> That draws all waters toward
> Its live formality.

The poet's "live formality" is not an isolated growth but the product of his active search for spiritual ancestors. Like Proteus, "by some fervent fraud," he takes the shape of his chosen dead and helps them to find their voices again. He does not relinquish his own individuality, which guides his choice of shapes and stands "self-established" in the end, but instead enriches it by entering at will into the minds and feelings of others. In the final image the poet-Proteus becomes a tree, and the voices become the nourishing waters of the tradition. The image of the tree is as important a clue to Wilbur's conception of the poet as is the image of Proteus. While every tree is an individual, it is not free to become anything it pleases; it is limited by its kind and by the soil and climate in which it finds itself. Unlike a tree, a poet can do something to choose his soil and climate (becoming in this sense "self-established") by seeking out the life-giving waters that flow from the past into the present. Wilbur is not afraid of academicism, of a poetry of echoes and allusions. Instead he conceives of the poet as one whose "live formality" depends on establishing, through the necessary effort of study, a significant relationship with older poets and with other great spirits of the past.

II   *The Present Moment*

But what about the poet's sense of his own time, with its own special experience, its own characteristic scenes and events, fears, desires, accents, and tempo? Most poets today are attentive students of the present moment, and many are concerned to bring into their poems something of the massive brutality and chaos of the past half-century. Some poets, and critics too, hold that a poetry which does not somehow take account of such disasters as our several wars, the concentration camps, systematic genocide, and the threat of nuclear annihilation is too remote from the characteristic horror of modern life. They are likely to insist also that external events such as these testify to corresponding horrors within us, for the outside world does not fail to reflect the worst of our private fears, desires, and impulses. A contemporary poet, they believe, must take a full look at the worst, both within and outside himself.

This argument has been given pungent expression recently by the English critic A. Alvarez in the Introduction to his anthology *The New Poetry* (1962). "What poetry needs," Alvarez argues, ". . . is a new seriousness." And he defines this seriousness "simply as the poet's ability and willingness to face the full range of his experience with his full intelligence." Thus he praises Robert Lowell and John Berryman for having learned in the 1940's how "to write poetry of immense skill and intelligence which coped openly with the quick of their experience, experience sometimes on the edge of disintegration and breakdown"

(24-25). Similarly, M. L. Rosenthal in *The Modern Poets* contrasts Wilbur, among others, with Lowell, Schwartz, Kunitz, and Roethke, who are linked together in his scheme by their interest in "the predicament and horror of the lost Self" and in a poetry of "therapeutic confession" (237). Elsewhere Rosenthal says that the advance "into the dangerous unknown territory of the 'crisis of personality' . . . seems to be our main poetic challenge at this time" (252).

The importance of facing the full range of one's experience without evasion must be freely granted. And yet, as Alvarez and Rosenthal are well aware, poets must choose their own subjects and present them as they can. No matter how determined a poet may be to make the effort Alvarez recommends, he may find that the full range of his experience is not available to him for poetry. Luckily for the poet, there are other themes that touch on human interests as profound and enduring as our interest in horror. Perhaps it is enough to ask that a poet be vividly aware of the horror, so that even though he does not represent it directly, it will lie behind or outside his poems and shadow or temper what does appear there. Wilbur's poems of his last collection especially show an effort to extend his range; they deal more openly than before with the strains and hardships of the inner life. And two poems, "Advice to a Prophet" and "Another Voice," take up the theme of violence explicitly. But in general he has not shown much interest in writing about those crises of spirit or conscience that seem specifically contemporary.

In technique also, as in the range of his subjects and themes, Wilbur has preferred to work so far within an established tradition rather than to break new ground. This tradition is what Donald Hall calls the "orthodoxy" that till about 1955 had ruled American poetry for thirty years. "It derived," he says, "from the authority of T. S. Eliot and the new critics; it exerted itself through the literary quarterlies and the universities. It asked for a poetry of symmetry, intellect, irony, and wit."[2] The only enduring alternative to the dominant orthodoxy of those years was "the colloquial, or the line of William Carlos Williams," for whom "the problem of native speech rhythm was of first importance" (21). Poets who took Williams' direction tended to go for experience to "the world outside" rather than to literature or to learning, to value such experience more than ideas or "civilization," to describe experience without comment, to improvise without reference to past poems, and to aim at "getting the tone right" rather than at turning their metaphors neatly or inventing new stanza patterns (22). Clearly this has not been Wilbur's direction.

Inside the "orthodoxy" Hall divides the chief poets into "those who admired the tough density of Donne, and those who preferred the wit of Marvell or the delicacy of Herrick" (19). These two strands culminated just after the war in Lowell's *Lord Weary's Castle* and in Wilbur's *The Beautiful Changes*. Since that time the "orthodoxy" has lost Eberhart, Roethke, Lowell, and others of its former members; but Wilbur, despite some signs of restlessness in his latest book, remains by and large within it. While Hall remarks that "there is no reason why a man should change if he doesn't feel like changing" (23), there are others who believe that Wilbur is working within too familiar a range of style and vision. Speaking of Wilbur and Elizabeth Bishop, M. L. Rosenthal says that "Although these two writers have done exquisite and richly suggestive work, they have touched the imagination of their generation very little. The reason seems to be that they remind us only of what we have already been taught to value: elegance, grace, precision, quiet intensity of phrasing."[3] And in his review of *Advice to a Prophet*, which appeared in 1962, a year or so after the publication of *The Modern Poets*, Rosenthal asked: "Why, with so much to go on and such depths of insight, can these poets [Wilbur and Ciardi] not strike out for the main chance and take the risk of 'making it new'?"[4] At the same time Rosenthal admitted that "Mr. Wilbur is perhaps the most quietly effective poet now writing in America." I think this estimate is perfectly sound, but one may ask why, if Wilbur is so successful within his chosen limits, he should be urged to move beyond them. There is no value in mere novelty, and from one point of view nothing matters in the end but good poems. If "making it new" will produce them, it then proves its value thereby; if not, it fails in the essential aim—though it may not fail to make conversation and even literary history.

There is, however, another point of view to consider, that of the poet; and it will not be quite the same as that of his readers. As Hall suggests, the poet's feeling about his work is all-important. Though a good poet would rather fail in a new venture than feel that he is merely imitating his own earlier poems, he cannot afford to let his readers decide when he has reached the end of a phase in his art. If his new work in his old style continues to interest him, if he knows that he is still learning what the old style is capable of, if the new poems are as fine as Wilbur's are, he will not want to abandon the old style. If he becomes interested in styles or subjects very different from anything he has used earlier, he may still prefer not to make a drastic break but to continue with what is familiar while he experiments with the unfamiliar. Most poets study the work of other poets, not only their contemporaries, in a constant effort to extend their resources of style and feeling. Though a poet cannot afford to yield too much to the influence of his masters, he must learn a great deal by example. A poet's experiments are often, if not always, inspired by another poet's achievement.

III *A Homely Influence*

I have already noted my impression—and that of others—that Wilbur's development through *Things of This World* was confident and triumphant, whereas *Advice to a Prophet* was more varied and experimental. I shall not record my guess as to whether Wilbur is likely in the future to renounce "elegance, grace, precision, quiet intensity of feeling" for something different—free verse or spontaneous effects, the most candid self-revelation or "free-floating images," "reporting the horror frankly" or whatever so far undreamed of. Instead, I shall reproduce one of Wilbur's recent poems, not only for its own merits as a fine poem, but for its value as an illustration of his interest in the idiom of an older poet whose typical style is homely rather than elegant. The poem will, I am sure, remind readers of Frost; and it would be a good guess that Frost is the one meant by the "R. F." of the dedication:

SEED LEAVES*

To R. F.

I

Here something stubborn comes,
Dislodging the earth crumbs
And making crusty rubble.
It comes up bending double
And looks like a green staple.
It could be seedling maple,
Or artichoke, or bean;
That remains to be seen.

* © 1964, The New Yorker Magazine, Inc.

II

Forced to make choice of ends,
The stalk in time unbends,
Shakes off the seedcase, heaves
Aloft, and spreads two leaves
Which still display no sure
And special signature.
Toothless and fat, they keep
The oval form of sleep.

III

This plant would like to grow
And yet be embryo;
Increase, and yet escape
The doom of taking shape;
Be vaguely vast, and climb
To the tip end of time
With all of space to fill,
Like boundless Yggdrasill
That has the stars for fruit.
But something at the root
More urgent than that urge
Bids two true leaves emerge,
And now the plant, resigned
To being self-defined
Before it can commerce
With the great universe,
Takes aim at all the sky
And starts to ramify.

Like so many of Frost's poems, "Seed Leaves" is a reflective narrative with moral implications, based on a firm sense of what must be. The poem is Frostian in its subject and occasion, in the homely ease and humor of its language, in the interest and exactness of its description, in the semantic richness of many of its words and phrases, and in the beautifully varied movement of its short-line couplets. It is Frostian also in its deliberate pace, in the gradual and unlabored emergence, as the poem proceeds, of the true parallel between the growth of the plant and the growth of a human personality. Frost would have enjoyed and approved of Wilbur's notice of the ineffable in this most common and yet most mysterious of phenomena: "But something at the root/More urgent than that urge/Bids two true leaves emerge. . . ."

What is surprising, after all this has been said, is that "Seed Leaves" is not a mere imitation; it is a marvelously good independent poem. In Wilbur's hands something of Frost's verbal idiom and something genuinely his own cooperate and retain their vitality. Frost could not have written "Toothless and fat, they keep/The oval form of sleep"—surely one of the finest couplets in the poem—nor would he have tried for just the tone of the high-flying passage about Yggdrasill. Actually, in all but the slightly laconic touches of Section I—and these are delightful —the poem is perfectly in accord with Wilbur's earlier work and quite characteristic of it. This resemblance suggests that all along, beneath their differences of tone and vocabulary, Wilbur's poems have been more like Frost's than one would have thought. But if "Seed Leaves" begins as an exercise which brings these similarities into view, it ends as an original poem which more than justifies itself by its excellence.

While the poem demonstrates by its success the value of a poet's studies of another poet, it provides in its argument a rationale for these studies. It does so by stressing the importance of those elements of personal growth and identity that are outside the reach of education. The poem is about the necessity of self-definition, of coming to display a "sure/And special signature," of "the doom of taking shape." It represents the growth of a plant as a struggle between the desire for amorphous expansion and the fundamental "urge" to become a thing of a certain kind. This latter urge, it says, is not to be denied—not by plants and, by analogy, not by human beings. The analogy implies a conception of personality as "something stubborn" that takes its own course toward a separate and distinct identity. If we can trust ourselves through all our experience to develop, like a plant, in accordance with an undeniable "something at the root," then a poet may learn by imitation without fearing that he will violate anything unique within himself. In fact, the stronger his sense of identity, the less he will hesitate to go to other poets for what he needs to know. The poet's strategy is that of any artist—the strategy, indeed, of anyone who wishes to make the most of his powers: to yield like the milkweed and to hold fast like a stone, to change and to remain the same.

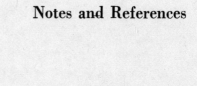

Notes and References

Notes and References

Chronology

1. Quoted directly from Wilbur by Stanley Kunitz (ed.), *Twentieth Century Authors,* First Supplement, p. 1080.
2. *Ibid.*
3. *How Does a Poem Mean?* (Boston, 1959), p. 664.

Chapter One

1. Quoted by Kunitz, p. 1080.
2. Introduction to *Contemporary American Poetry* (Baltimore, 1962), p. 17.
3. Edited by John Ciardi (New York, 1950), pp. 1-7.
4. Kunitz, p. 1080.
5. *Poetry and the Age* (New York, 1953), p. 229.
6. *Ibid.*
7. "The Meters of the Intermediate Poets," *Kenyon Review,* XIX (Winter, 1957), 48-50.
8. *New Yorker,* XXIII (November 15, 1947), 133.
9. *Poetry,* LXXI (January, 1948), 221-23.
10. *English Journal,* XLIII (February, 1954), 64.
11. New York *Herald Tribune* Books (March 21, 1948), 8.

Chapter Two

1. *Poetry and the Age,* p. 227.
2. *Hudson Review,* IV (Spring, 1951), 139-42.
3. *The Last Decade in Poetry: New Dilemmas and New Solutions* (Nashville, 1954).
4. Just such a figure appears in a published photograph, taken in 1952, of a corner of Giacometti's dark, rough-walled workroom in Paris. See Jacques Dupin and Ernst Scheiddegger, *Alberto Giacometti* (Paris, 1962), p. 246.
5. "The Poems of Richard Wilbur" in the film series *Of Poets and Poetry.*
6. *Poetry and the Age,* p. 228.
7. "The Poems of Richard Wilbur" in the film series *Of Poets and Poetry.*
8. Introduction to *Poe: Complete Poems* (New York, 1959), p. 19.
9. *The Last Decade in Poetry . . . ,* p. 39.
10. *World Review,* II (London, 1952), 6.
11. *Paris Review,* No. 3 (Autumn, 1953), 113-19.
12. *English Journal,* XLIII (February, 1954), 57-64.
13. *New World Writing,* No. 7 (New York, 1955), 231-47.

Chapter Three

1. New York: Harcourt Brace.
2. *Hudson Review*, IX (Summer, 1956), 286-88.
3. *New Yorker*, XXXII (December 15, 1956), 52.
4. New York *Times*, December 9, 1956, Section 2, p. 5.
5. "Some Younger American Poets," *Commentary*, XXIII (May, 1957), 457-59.
6. "The Poems of Richard Wilbur" in the film series *Of Poets and Poetry*.
7. When I heard Mr. Wilbur speak of this poem in his filmed interview as a poem about "pleasure," I had already written my commentary, in which I had found it to be a poem about two kinds of sainthood. The two interpretations are not, I think, quite concentric; but I have let mine stand because it seems to me to have some value even though it may see what it does see in a false perspective. The reader will take note of this warning and decide for himself. He will be interested, in any case, in Mr. Wilbur's account of the way the fountain assumed meaning for him. The poem, he says, "came out of a short stay of mine in Rome, a nine-months stay. I had a fellowship and felt obliged to turn out some work as well as enjoy myself. I used to pass the fountain of this poem every morning on my way to work and as I would whip myself to my study to begin an eight-hour day, I'd look regretfully at this very attractive fountain and I came to associate it with the idea of pleasure. And that's what this poem is about, really. It's a descriptive poem about this and other fountains, but my subject is pleasure and what place it has in life."
8. *Yale Review*, New Series XLVI (Winter 1957), 296.
9. *Hudson Review*, IX (Winter, 1956-57), 454.
10. In Anthony Ostroff (ed.), *The Contemporary Poet as Artist and Critic* (1964), p. 18. Although Wilbur does not give the exact reference in St. Augustine, he remarked in his film interview that the title comes from Augustine's commentary on the Psalms. The poem "Love Calls Us to the Things of This World" is well and fully discussed by the poets Richard Eberhart, Robert Horan, and May Swenson in Ostroff, pp. 2-16. These criticisms elicit from Wilbur some luminous remarks on the role of sound patterns in poetic meaning; on the work done by certain adjectives in "Love Calls Us . . .", on his conception of poetry as "a created object, an altar-cloth, Japanese garden or ship of death. Not a message or confession"; on the difficulty of judging whether or not one "is imparting a 'whole soul' to his poetry"; on the possibility that some of his poems are too "indirect" to convey the emotions intended; and on his recent attempts to express feeling less "through rhetoric or through hints embedded in an apparently objective description" and more through direct, dramatic means (pp. 17-21). He closes by quoting the first six drafts of the opening lines of "Love Calls Us . . ." to show "a gradual moving away from too much objective detail, and a liberation of the rhythm toward the abruptness of speech."
11. *Saturday Review*, XL (August 18, 1956), 19.

Chapter Four

1. New York *Times* Book Review (October 29, 1961), 16.
2. New York *Herald Tribune* Books (December 3, 1961), 4.
3. *Reporter*, XXVI (February 15, 1962), 48.
4. *Poetry*, C (April, 1962), 37-38.
5. *Kenyon Review*, XXIV (Spring, 1962), 376.
6. *Reporter*, XXVI (February 15, 1962), 51.
7. New York *Herald Tribune* Books (December 3, 1961), 4.
8. *Poetry*, C (April, 1962), 39.
9. In *The Moment of Poetry*, ed. Don Cameron Allen (Baltimore, 1962), pp. 73-98.
10. Samuel Hazo, *Commonweal*, LXXV (December 22, 1961), 346.

Chapter Five

1. In *Emily Dickinson: Three Views* (Amherst, Mass., 1960).
2. Introduction to *Contemporary American Poetry* (Baltimore, 1962), p. 17.
3. *The Modern Poets* (New York, 1960), pp. 252-53.
4. *Reporter*, XXVI (February 15, 1962), 51.

Selected Bibliography

Selected Bibliography

PRIMARY SOURCES

I. *Collections of poems*

The Beautiful Changes and other poems. New York: Harcourt, Brace, 1947.

Ceremony and other poems. New York: Harcourt, Brace, 1950.

Things of This World: Poems by Richard Wilbur. New York: Harcourt, Brace, 1956.

Poems 1943-1956. London: Faber and Faber, 1956.

Advice to a Prophet and other poems. New York: Harcourt, Brace and World, 1961.

The Poems of Richard Wilbur. New York: Harcourt, Brace and World, 1963.

II. *Translations*

The Misanthrope, by Molière. New York: Harcourt, Brace, 1955.

Tartuffe, by Molière. New York: Harcourt, Brace and World, 1963.

III. *Other works*

Review of *Poems 1943-1947,* by C. Day Lewis, *Poetry,* LXXIV (May, 1949), 114-17.

Review of *A Fountain in Kentucky and Other Poems,* by John Frederick Nims, *Poetry,* LXXVII (November, 1950), 105-7.

"The Genie in the Bottle," in *Mid-Century American Poets,* ed. John Ciardi. New York: Twayne Publishers, 1950.

"A Game of Catch," *New Yorker,* XXIX (July 18, 1953).

A Bestiary, with Alexander Calder's illustrations. New York: Pantheon Books, 1955.

Review of *Like a Bulwark,* by Marianne Moore, New York *Times* Book Review (November 11, 1956), 18.

Candide; a comic operetta on Voltaire's satire. Book by Lillian Hellman. Lyrics by Richard Wilbur and others. Vocal score. New York: G. Schirmer, 1958.

"The Poems of Richard Wilbur," in the film series *Of Poets and Poetry,* produced by the Metropolitan Educational Television Association in co-operation with The Poetry Center of the YM-YWHA, New York, for National Educational Television. (Internal evidence suggests that the production date was the winter of 1958-59.)

Introduction to *Poe: Complete Poems,* ed. Richard Wilbur. (Laurel Poetry Series.) New York: Dell Books, 1959.

"Sumptuous Destitution," in *Emily Dickinson; Three Views,* by Archibald MacLeish, Louise Bogan, and Richard Wilbur. Amherst: Amherst College Press, 1960.

"Round About a Poem of Housman's," in *The Moment of Poetry,* ed. Don Cameron Allen. Baltimore: Johns Hopkins Press, 1962.

Loudmouse, with Don Almquist's illustrations. New York: Crowell-Collier Press, 1963.

Comment on three critiques of "Love Calls Us to the Things of This World," in *The Contemporary Poet as Artist and Critic: Eight Symposia,* ed. Anthony Ostroff. Boston and Toronto: Little, Brown, 1964.

"On Robert Lowell's 'Skunk Hour,' " in *The Contemporary Poet as Artist and Critic: Eight Symposia,* ed. Anthony Ostroff. Boston and Toronto: Little, Brown, 1964.

SECONDARY SOURCES

I. *Reviews of Wilbur's books*

The Beautiful Changes

BOGAN, LOUISE. New Yorker, XXIII (November 15, 1947), 133.
EBERHART, RICHARD. New York *Times* Book Review (January 11, 1948), 4.
GOLFFING, F. C. *Poetry,* LXXI (January, 1948), 221.
ROSENTHAL, M. L. New York *Herald Tribune* Books (March 21, 1948), 8.

Ceremony

BENNETT, JOSEPH. *Hudson Review,* IV (Spring, 1951), 139.
BOGAN, LOUISE. New Yorker, XXVII (June 9, 1951), 113.
COLE, T. *Poetry,* LXXXII (April, 1953), 37.
DEUTSCH, BABETTE. New York *Times* Book Review (February 11, 1951), 12.

Things of This World

BOGAN, LOUISE. *New Yorker,* XXXII (October 6, 1956), 180.
BOGARDUS, EDGAR. *Kenyon Review,* XIX (Winter, 1957), 137.
CIARDI, JOHN. *Saturday Review,* XL (August 18, 1956), 18.
DEUTSCH, BABETTE. New York *Herald Tribune* Books (July 8, 1956), 2.
EBERHART, RICHARD. New York *Times* Book Review (June 5, 1956), 5.
GREGORY, HORACE. *Partisan Review,* XXIII (Fall, 1956), 545.
HALL, DONALD. *Poetry,* LXXXVIII (September, 1956), 398.
HECHT, ANTHONY. *Hudson Review,* IX (Winter, 1956-57), 454.
LOGAN, JOHN. *Commonweal,* LXIV (August 10, 1956), 474.
PLUTZIK, HYAM. *Yale Review,* New Series XLVI (Winter, 1957), 295.
ROSENTHAL, M. L. *Nation,* CLXXXIII (November 3, 1956), 372.

Candide

ATKINSON, BROOKS. New York *Times,* CV (December 9, 1956), sec. 2, p. 5.
GIBBS, WOLCOTT. *New Yorker,* XXXII (December 15, 1956), 52.

Advice to a Prophet and other poems

DEUTSCH, BABETTE. New York *Herald Tribune* Books (December 3, 1961), 4.
FITTS, DUDLEY. New York *Times* Book Review (October 29, 1961), 16.
FLINT, R. W. *Partisan Review,* XXIX (Winter, 1961-62), 147.
GUNN, THOM. *Yale Review,* LI (March, 1962), 482.
HAZO, SAMUEL. *Commonweal,* LXXV (December 22, 1961), 346.
HOLMES, THEODORE. *Poetry,* C (April, 1962), 37.

Selected Bibliography

MEREDITH, WILLIAM. *Poetry*, C (April, 1962), 40.

ROSENTHAL, M. L. *Reporter*, XXVI (February 15, 1962), 48.

WHITTEMORE, REED. *Kenyon Review*, XXIV (Spring, 1962), 372.

II. General criticism

CARGILL, OSCAR. "Poetry Since the Deluge," *English Journal*, XLIII (February 1954), 57-64. Speaks of Wilbur's "prestige"; calls his a "quiet poetry"; finds in his work a debt to Wallace Stevens; notes certain critics' hopes and fears for his future; grants that Wilbur must abandon certain mannerisms; and expects his "consistent philosophy" to "impart virility to his verse."

DAICHES, DAVID. "The Anglo-American Difference: Two Views," Part II, in *The Anchor Review*, Number One. Garden City, New York: Doubleday, 1955. Argues that younger American poets write in a distinctly American poetic idiom: assured, ironic, artful, wary and precise in its language, focusing the vision "quietly and steadily until idea is generated out of image." The English style is more open and discursive, more "poetic," more deliberately passionate; it is less sophisticated, deft, and mature. Americans quoted include Wilbur, Brinnin, Nims, Berryman, and Horan.

FLINT, R. W. "The Foolproof Style of American Poets," *Audience*, II (November 18, 1955), 1-5. Cites Lowell and Wilbur as examples in a refutation of the charge of "wit writing," made by Daiches in *The Anchor Review*.

FRASER, G. S. "Some Younger American Poets," *Commentary* XXIII (May, 1957), 457-59. Argues that American poets are concerned less than English ones with "the right basic attitude to life" and more with the shaping of a poem as a "luxury product." Uses Wilbur's "Piazza di Spagna, Early Morning" as an example.

HALL, DONALD. "American Poets Since the War," *World Review*, II (London, 1952). An appreciation of the poetry of major groups and individuals in which Roethke, Wilbur, and Lowell receive the most attention. Elegance, "the dominating theme of the younger poets in America," is represented by James Merrill, William Jay Smith, Peter Viereck, and Wilbur.

————. "The New Poetry: Notes on the Past Fifteen Years in America," *New World Writing*, Seventh Mentor Selection. New York: New American Library of World Literature, 1955. A closely informed and generous tribute to "the new poetry," which Hall calls "an extremely impressive body of work." Lowell the best, but Roethke, Wilbur, and others receive high praise, Wilbur for his lyrical elegance, artfulness, and intellectual subtlety. Hall sees in Wilbur's most recent work "a successful attempt to move away from the elegant pose."

————. Introduction to *Contemporary American Poetry*. Baltimore: Penguin Books, 1962. Describes the recent breakdown of the domination of T. S. Eliot and the new critics in American poetry. An orthodox poetry of "symmetry, intellect, irony, and wit" is giving way to a colloquial poetry in the line of Pound and Williams. Certain younger poets are writing with "a new kind of imagination," but Wilbur remains within the orthodoxy.

JARRELL, RANDALL. *Poetry and the Age.* New York: Vintage Books, 1953. Accuses Wilbur of being too "poetic," merely clever, too cautious, and too settled in style; but admires his verbal skill, wit, and delicacy and calls him after all "the best of the quite young poets writing in this country. . . ."

MILLS, RALPH J., JR. *Contemporary American Poetry.* New York: Random House, 1965. Wilbur "one of the most versatile and brilliant American poets to make his debut since World War II." Though Wilbur works well within "the tradition of English lyricism," he is "a very distinctive poet" with his own voice, "and his poetry has "a particular identity." One of the shrewdest appraisals yet written.

ROSENTHAL, M. L. *The Modern Poets: A Critical Introduction.* New York: Oxford University Press, 1960. Regards Wilbur and Elizabeth Bishop as "gifted exquisites" who "have touched the imagination of their generation very little" because "they remind us only of what we have already been taught to value: elegance, grace, precision, quiet intensity of phrasing." And yet they do marvelously good work within the established tradition, "their styles are more than the mere sums of their masters and they have something to say."

VIERECK, PETER. *The Last Decade in Poetry: New Dilemmas and New Solutions.* Nashville: Bureau of Publications, George Peabody College for Teachers, 1954. Roethke and Wilbur, "the two most original voices in the poetry of the decade," supplement each other: Roethke is Dionysian; Wilbur, Apollonian. Wilbur lacks a saving vulgarity, has "too serene a poise," but shows in *Ceremony* a "new capacity for a lurking ferocity."

Index

Index

The Practical Art of
Diagnostic Interviewing

The Practical Art of
Diagnostic Interviewing

Gerald Ross Pascal, Ph.D.

Diplomate, Clinical Psychology,
American Board of Examiners in Professional Psychology
Formerly Research Professor of Psychiatry
University of Mississippi School of Medicine

The Dorsey Professional Series

DOW JONES-IRWIN
Homewood, Illinois 60430

To Lalla, my wife, with love and gratitude
for her partnership in the writing of this book.

© DOW JONES-IRWIN, 1983

ISBN 0-87094-367-7
Library of Congress Catalog Card No. 82-73406

Printed in the United States of America

1 2 3 4 5 6 7 8 9 0 K 0 9 8 7 6 5 4 3

Preface

This book is written in response to an expressed need of mental health workers, people with whom I have worked during a long career as a consultant to mental hospitals and clinics.

The book has two main purposes. The first is to convince the worker of the validity and usefulness of information obtained in the diagnostic interview. So many workers feel that all they can get from the interview are the bare facts of the prospective patient's life, and then they question the validity of the information obtained.

The second purpose is to convey to the worker the *feel* of the interview. The symptoms or complaints of the patient are imbedded in the totality of the person. Acceptance of this concept enables the interviewer to grasp the significance of data obtained in the interview.

The book shows the mental health worker how to use interview data in treatment planning. Chapter 12 offers some guidelines for prognosis.

My thanks to Peggy Gainey, office manager, and Ann Janes, secretary, for typing and proofreading; to Professor Clifford Swensen for a helpful critical reading; and to colleagues Roy Darby, Ph.D., and John Nowlin, M.S.W., for their help.

Acknowledgment is made to the *Southern Medical Journal* for permission to reproduce Tables 1 and 3, also to *Psychosomatic Medicine* for permission to reproduce Tables 2 and 4.

Gerald Ross Pascal

Contents

1 | Introduction

Too often, in the mental health field, the diagnostic interview is a facet of training that is glossed over lightly. It is assumed that because of the previous training received in abnormal psychology and psychiatry, mental health workers know what they are doing and what they are looking for. My experience has been that however much you lecture the workers and however much reading you require, their first interview with a patient is one in which they feel awkward and somewhat bewildered.

Having taught workers in various mental health fields, I feel that we have failed to communicate to them the *import* of the diagnostic interview. Workers have a tendency to be overly concerned with getting information so that they can arrive at a correct book diagnosis. This tendency manifests itself in an easy acceptance of the patient's responses to questions and a failure to *consider* the patient in the light of what is known about the dynamics of human behavior. Thus, the worker is apt to miss nuances of behavior, contradictions, verbalizations indicative of tangential thinking, and so on. These deficiencies in data gathering become all too apparent when the worker's new case is brought to staff. When the patient's symptoms are clear-cut, the worker may come up with a correct book diagnosis but draw a blank when asked about the dynamics behind those symptoms in the individual patient. The worker has learned little about the patient as a unique human being.

The above statements are not made to downgrade the importance of the book diagnosis. This diagnosis is important for communication between practitioners, for statistical purposes, and for some research purposes. With the advent of DSM III (1980) the book diagnosis became even more important for research purposes. The clinician should have well in mind the guidelines

1

for diagnoses as set forth in DSM III but should not neglect the patient's dynamics stemming from life experiences or neglect careful observation of the patient's behaviors during the interview.

It is my contention that treatment plans for a patient cannot be efficiently formulated without specific knowledge of the dynamics of the individual patient. Thus, even in behavioral therapy, the treatment of a phobia imbedded in a lifelong history of fears has to be different from that for a circumscribed phobia dating from a single traumatic incident. In these days, with so many psychotherapeutic methods available, the practitioner has a choice of treatments to best fit the patient. Whatever the treatment, whether behavioral or dynamic, its efficient implementation depends on the specific dynamics of the patient under consideration. This is the *import* of the diagnostic interview. It is more than a knowledge of the patient's complaints. It is more than a knowledge of the environmental stimuli superficially associated with the complaints; it is a knowledge of the patient's life history so that judgment can be made of the patient's *perception* of the environment.

It is the intent of this book to involve the mental health worker in the diagnostic process of the interview. The book begins with a little bit of practically oriented theory. It brings behaviorism into alignment with modern cognitive behavioral approaches. Once this is done, it is easy for the worker to make the transition to dynamic psychiatry/psychology. The second chapter introduces a method of interviewing that helps obtain believable information. In the third chapter research data are presented that I hope will convince the worker the method is both reliable and valid.

Succeeding chapters present in intimate detail the practical aspects of the diagnostic interview, what to look for, how to get needed information, and what to do with it. Whenever possible, actual case material is used to point out the significance of obtained information. Throughout the book the assumption is made that the worker has the requisite knowledge of human behavior to follow the text.

It is not intended that the book stand alone as a guide to the diagnostic interview. It is intended that the book be a preparation for practical experience and further study as well as help prepare workers for their first patient encounters. Suggestions for further study will be found in Appendix III.

REFERENCES

American Psychiatric Association. *Diagnostic and statistical manual of mental disorders* (3rd ed.). 1980.

2 | The investigatory dyadic relationship

It might be profitable to speculate about a first contact between two strangers. Imagine one primitive man hiding behind a rock or tree, spying upon another. He observes the appearance and movements of the other. Unbeknownst to the man being spied upon, an interview is being conducted without benefit of words. Recorded in the brain of the observer are expressive movements and responses to stimulus situations which occur during the period of observation. If the spy reports his observations to a third person, he will, if he is objective, merely report what the person looks like and what he does in response to the observed stimulus situations. The predictive value of the spy's report will be limited to the stimuli observed.

Let us endow out primitive spy with insatiable curiosity, indefatigability, *and* invisibility. He returns to the rock and finds his subject. With his invisibility, he stays with the subject day and night. He watches the subject attack one man, bring food to another. The subject will cohabit with one woman, avoid another. He will exhibit grief when one man is killed, indifference at the death of another. The spy now switches his attention to another subject. He observes the second subject cohabit with a woman the first subject avoided, attack a man to whom the first subject brought food. The behaviors are incomprehensible to him. Although after observing several subjects he can predict the response of each subject to particular stimuli, he cannot generalize. He tries with great patience to catalogue characteristics of different stimuli but cannot predict what the response of a new subject will be to them. We leave him in the cave of his subjects still trying to classify the characteristics of the stimuli.

The primitive spy is, as you imagine, the early behaviorist. However much one describes and measures the physical aspects of a stimulus, the response-evoking potential for a particular person escapes us. For the stimulus situation is not only clothed with its physical attributes but with the past experiences of the responding organism to a similar stimulus situation. Definition of the evoking stimulus for a particular person is complicated also by the person's *perception* of the past experience. For instance, a child is frightened by a large, fierce, black dog. Later, he encounters another large, black dog. He responds to the second dog with fear even though the second dog is mild mannered. Another child with past positive experiences with large, black dogs is not frightened in the same situation. This child perceives large, black dogs as nonthreatening. The response-evoking potential of the large, black dog as a stimulus is related to the past experiences of the respondent, the child. Both children generalize from one dog to another but each child perceives the dog differently based on his past experience. Thus, although theoretically we can observe and describe stimulus-response (S-R) experiences throughout the history of the organism, we cannot know how these stimulus-response experiences are registered and stored in the brain.

One way to discover how an experience was perceived is to find out how it is remembered. This technique exposes us to all the well-known distortions connected with remembering past events. Yet at any given time after an experience, our best estimate of how it was perceived is the reported memory of it. The observance of the differential reaction of a young man to two equally pretty girls has no meaning to us unless we know that one of the girls is perceived as a cousin. The point is that the objective observation and description of S-R sequences omit the mediation of symbolic processes. By observing the S-R sequences we can, if we wish, indulge in speculations about what these symbolic processes might have been. If we observe a father angrily push away his son on several occasions, we can say the child must feel "not wanted." We cannot know, however, how these experiences registered in the child's brain until, after the experiences, we find out how the child perceives his father. It is our contention that valid prediction of the child's response to his father is based on knowledge of the child's perception of father, rather than descriptive knowledge of S-R sequences involving the father. It is our further contention that knowledge of how the child perceived the father is best obtained by the later reported memories of the child concerning the father.

The six-year-old boy who perceives his father as an unknown, rather fearful person may, in fact, have a father who loves his son, is concerned about the son, and works hard for the family; perhaps too hard with too little time to give to his son. Valid prediction of the boy's responses to his father lies not in the objective observation of S-R sequences involving father and son, but rather in the knowledge of the boy's perception of the father. Perception at the time of the S-R sequence is also related to the boy's adherence to the inculcations of his mother, who has had the most to do with the child's upbringing, and the mother's expressed or implicit attitude toward the father and other unknown factors. The registering and storing of the S-R sequence in the boy's brain may have little relation to what we might speculate from observation of behaviors. It is this process of registering and storing that we tap when, later on in life, we ask the boy for memories of his father.

Frank (1965), after a review of the literature for the past 40 years, concludes that no particular factors in the child-parent relationship seem to be related to later behavioral disorder. It is noteworthy that in his review, Frank did not include studies which reported the offspring's remembered behaviors of the parents. The studies reviewed are, for the most part, those that attempt to get at the accuracy of childhood experiences. In concluding his review Frank makes a very interesting comment: "Of course, it might well be that the reality of the family is not the important dimension in determining the child's reactions; rather, it might be the perception of the family members, and this might often have little or no relation to the people as they really are" (p. 201).

Psychoanalytic theory relating early familial experiences to adult behavior does not rest on objective observations of S-R sequences in the life of the child. Freud did not have a time machine whereby he could go back into the early life of his patients. What he obtained from his patients during interviews were memories of their childhood experiences. Psychological theories relating early life experiences to later deviancies of behavior for the most part, are based on information obtained by one person from another. This is a dyadic relationship. Data stemming from it contribute most importantly to the theories of psychogenesis.

In recent years many studies have yielded results which challenge the reliability and validity of data obtained in the dyadic relationship. We shall not quote the pertinent literature here but refer the worker to three articles: the one by Frank (1965), quoted previously, in which he reviews the literature on the role of the family in the development of psychopathology; another by Ulrich and Trumbo (1965) which presents a review of the selection interview since 1949; and, finally, a most pertinent review of Kintz, Delprato, Mette, Persons, and Schappe (1965) which presents studies bearing on the "experimenter effect"; that is, the effect of bias on the part of the investigator. Schofield and Balian (1959), after a comparative study of the personal histories of schizophrenic and nonpsychiatric patients, suggest the possibility of patterns of life events, rather than specific factors in the etiology of deviant behaviors. Frank (1965), as indicated above, suggests that the perception of events rather than their reality might be that which distinguished deviant populations with "emotional" problems from others.

The plain facts are that neither data about actual life experiences nor anamnestic data support psychogenesis. What then? Shall we give up on the conviction that people learn attitudes and feelings about themselves and others just as surely as they learn to walk and talk? Shall we disregard the daily clinical corroboration of the specific aspects of psychoanalytic theory that bear on psychogenesis? Or shall we question the data?

Acceptance of psychogenesis came after Freud (1923) convincingly presented his clinical data. The data he presented derived from a dyadic relationship. This relationship differed, however, from the relationship which obtains in the gathering of information from a diagnostic interview. Freud's relationship with his patients was an intimate one; one in which the patients had enough trust in him to reveal themselves. Their memories of their early experiences very often came out in a vivid emotional storm. The registration of these experiences and their consequent perception was reported to Freud in a "pure" form. They were not confused by later experiences and by intellectual concern about how they should have been. These *perceptions* of early life experiences seemed real to Freud and to all other clinicians who have lived through the transference relationship with a patient. We submit that there is a difference between the relationship between therapist and patient in the intensive psychotherapy relationship and that of the relationship which occurs between clinical investigator and patient. These two separate relationships produce different kinds of data.

Ask any man on the street if he loves his mother. The answer will invariably be yes. Yet in questioning the person you might find that the mother only lives one block away and that our subject only calls on her once every two months. The point of this observation is that there are perceptions which seem to be at variance with other data. Kahn and Cannell (1957) report on a study in which one of nine families on relief failed to report the fact that they were on relief when asked in an interview. In a questionnaire study, Pascal & Jenkins (1961) contrasted workhouse inmate alcoholics and college students; the latter reported *poorer* early relations with parents than did the alcoholics. For instance, in response to the question: "Did your father beat you more than he should have during your first 10 years?", 18 percent of college students answered yes while only 7 percent of alcoholics answered yes. In response to the question: "Did your father take good care of you?", 100 percent of alcoholics answered yes, and 87 percent of college students answered yes. Results were similar in response to questions concerning early relations with mother. These findings were in marked contrast to those obtained in a controlled study of the inmate workhouse alcoholics using intensive interview data (Pascal & Jenkins, 1960). The reader is referred to a study by Twiner and Barlow (1951) in which no differences were found in recall for pleasant and unpleasant material.

We do not wish to digress into perceptual theory but merely to cinch the argument that perceptions of the self and its relations to others obtained from interviews and questionnaires may differ depending upon the nature of the situation in which the data are obtained. This statement does not imply that the perceptual data thus obtained are not true of the respondent. The data are just different. Freud's data bearing on the perception of early life experiences differ from that obtained in many investigatory anamnestic interviews.

Let us go back to the man who said he loved his mother; in fact, has always loved his mother. When questioned about her, he expresses all the attitudes of a dutiful son. He remembers being cared for and loved by her as a child. We can get, in this manner, a man's perception of himself in relationship to mother. Is this a true perception? We don't know. There are, however, data which indicate that perceptions thus obtained have little predictive validity and little validity for differentiating between deviant and control populations (Frank, 1965).

The data that Freud obtained came from vividly described memories of actual events. The accuracy of these events as described by the patients has never been a consideration in psychoanalytic theory. The behavioral descriptions given by Freud's patients represent their perception of what happened. But so are the data obtained in anamnestic investigations with negative results. What are the differences between these two kinds of perceptual data?

Nearly everyone in clinical practice is familiar with the hospitalized paranoid patient who gives a beautiful, romantic history of his early life. Factual data and data from the Rorschach definitely contradict the patient's assertions. We are sure, for instance, that the patient has little use for men, doesn't trust them, is hostile and suspicious toward them. It doesn't make any clinical sense to believe that he had a wonderful relationship with his father. Yet, the paranoid patient, in question, will stoutly maintain he loved and received love from his father. He will tell about the good times they had together. Is the paranoid patient lying? I don't know. It seems to me that it is more parsimonious to believe that he is giving the Examiner the cultural norm as he sees it. We know from Bartlett's studies (1932) that memory will tend to conform to the cultural norm. This tendency is probably exaggerated in the paranoid but is most likely true of all of us. What we get when we interview a person about his early relations with his parents must be some combination of fact and fancy shaped by cultural norms. What we do not get, it seems to me, is the uncluttered perception of events as they register on the mind of the child. Freud seems to have obtained such perceptions. How can we, in the investigatory interview, procure similar data?

Astute interviewers of experience can get valid data from patients with minimal cooperation. The interviewers read as much into what is not said as into what is said. They are sensitive to nonverbal cues. They can come away from an interview with a good knowledge of the patient's psychological anatomy. Most workers, however, have difficulty even with cooperative patients. Examination of interview protocols reveals that they get very little information that can be described in stimulus-response terms. "Father *used to* take me fishing." There are no actual descriptions of what happened between the patient and father, as remembered by the patient. These activities that the patient tells about that *used to* occur between him and father tend to follow the cultural norms. It has even been observed that the student clinician cued the patient to respond with the cultural norm! It seemed to us that the student was not actually getting a memory. Certainly, he was not getting a memory of actual behavior on the part of the parent as it was perceived by the patient at the time.

Obviously, the response to "How do you get along with your father?" didn't help much. What we got mostly was a response based on the cultural expectancy that everybody loves his father. This set seemed to determine the rest of the responses about father. However, when we tried "When was the last time you saw your father?" and "What did you do?" our data came out differently. Two interviews on the same subject yielded different data. For instance, in obtaining data about early relations between a male subject and his father the usual clinical interview yielded a neutral first memory, a description of father as a "good" man and accounts of how his father took him to football games, fishing, and so on. The impression gained from this interview was that the subject did not have a negative relationship with father. When we interviewed the same subject and asked him for specific memories of his activities with father, we came out with a different conclusion. We discovered that the subject could only remember one time that father took him fishing. In the subject's S-R description of that event it came out that father criticized him for not being able to put a worm on a fishing hook. The subject could not remember any one time that father took him to a football game. To make a long story short, we found that the subject's frequency of contact with his father was less than might be expected for the status of the father. Father and son had few activities together. There was little in the way of affection expressed by the father toward the son. Physical punishment was frequent and vividly described.

It seemed to us that the difference between the two interviews was that in the one, the usual clinical interview, we allowed the subject's attitudes and opinions to bias the data. In the other, we did not ask for attitudes and opinions, rather we rejected them. We only accepted as data S-R descriptions of remembered events. When the subject said, "Father was good to me," we countered by asking if he could remember a specific event when father was "good." If the subject could, then we would ask what happened, who did what, and when. If the subject said, "Father used to take me fishing"; then we would ask, "Can you remember one time?" If the subject could, then we ask for the S-R sequences. If the subject could not remember specific events, then we considered we had no data.

Were these specifically described memories closer to Freud's data? We felt they were. If they were then they should have validity. The next chapter will consider the validity and reliability of these kinds of memories. It was found that structuring the interview in the way indicated also had other advantages. We knew when we had no data, which helped us with the experimenter bias problem; for example, no specific memories about father, and therefore, no notions about early relations with father and later behavior. We could tell when the subject was malingering. His memories just didn't "hang" together. Finally, the demand for specific memories prevented the investigatory interview from "degenerating" into a therapeutic one; something that the beginning clinical student was prone to do. We shall consider these advantages and others in a later section. The point to be made now is that these experiences In trying to teach the interviewer and the results of haphazard studies led us to attempt a systematic study of the interview.

Dr. William O. Jenkins, whose aid I enlisted at about this time, and I thought that what we actually wanted were remembered *behaviors*. If we could get a subject to describe a remembered event in specific stimulus-response terms, we could, hopefully, bypass his opinions and attitudes. This notion of obtaining accounts of actually observed behaviors was taken up by Dr. Hugh Davis, then one of our graduate students. Working on a psychiatric ward he had had difficulty in obtaining reliable data about patients when nurses and attendants were asked to use a simple rating scale of patients' behaviors. Instead of using the rating scale, Dr. Davis interviewed the nurses and attendants. His interview went something like this: "When was the last time you saw Patient X?" "What was he doing?" The interview then went on to specific stimulus-response sequences. This procedure elicited reliable data when the observations of two ward workers on the same patient were compared.

Davis's experience illustrates an important aspect of this approach to obtaining interview data. He found that in order to get reliability he had to ask the observers very specific questions about the stimulus situation. "Where was Patient X sitting?" "Who was sitting next to him?" It was found that the nurses and ward attendants had actually observed more than they thought they had. Now these were retrospective data just as are the data obtained in the anamnestic interview. True, in doing a clinical interview, we may be asking for data that goes back 20, 30, or 40 years, but the point is that we are apt to get more reliable data if we put the interviewees in the position of observers. They are put into that position when asked for specific events located in time and place and described in S-R terms.

What emerged was a unit of remembered observations called the behavioral incident (Pascal & Jenkins, 1961). It is a composite of Murray's episode (1938), Flanagan's critical incident (1954) and some of the techniques of Kinsey (1948). We defined a behavioral incident (BI) as "a stimulus-response sequence in gross human behavior which endures so long as there is no radical change in the stimulus situation as defined by the responses of the subject to it" (p. 44). The BI is intended to describe the interaction between the subject and a stimulus situation. BIs are then categorized into higher order variables such as displays of affection from father. For instance, suppose that we are interested in a specific aspect of the subject's early relations with father such as punishment by father. We might begin by asking who did the disciplining in the family when the interviewee was a child. If the reply is father then we inquire if the interviewee can remember any one time that father disciplined him. If the subject is prone to answer in generalities such as, "He used to whip me when . . . " talk about the kind of occasions in which father would whip the subject. The interviewer has to insist on a specific memory, the time, the place, the occasion, the father's behavior, and the subject's reaction to it. This report would constitute a BI. The interviewer would then have to continue and obtain other BIs about father's disciplining behavior in order to establish frequency, intensity, and duration of the BIs. From these BIs, and only from these BIs, a judgment is made concerning father's punishing behavior toward his offspring.

Other than demographic data such as age, education, vocation, the BIs form the units around which the investigatory dyadic relationship is structured. The BIs are intended to obtain from the subject verbal reports of specific memories as they were perceived at the time of their occurrence. The use of BIs helps the investigator to bypass culturally determined opinions and attitudes which tend to obscure individual differences. BIs are calculated to help the investigator avoid experimental bias. Broadly conceived they can be likened to psychological test results which also form the basis for clinical judgment. Thus a subject obtaining an information score of 11 and a comprehension score of 5 on the Wechsler Adult Intelligence Scale provides data upon which the clinician bases a judgment. Clinical judgment based on BIs is, unfortunately, more difficult than judgment based on psychological test results. The systematic normative data upon which to base judgment do not exist. Nevertheless, the use of BIs substitutes expert judgment for the opinions and attitudes of the subject. For instance, a patient is being interviewed about his physical condition. The Examiner inquires about the patient's sleep. The patient says he sleeps poorly, wakes up early. The Examiner asks when he went to bed last night, when he awakened. The Examiner inquires about the night previous to the last, and so on, in order to establish with reasonable consistency the hours the patient sleeps. The patient reports he actually sleeps eight hours a night. Whether or not insomnia is a problem for the patient is a judgment for the Examiner, not the patient. In all areas of the patient's functioning, throughout life, as reported by BIs, whether or not the patient's experiences and responses to them have been deviant, or within expectancy limits, is a judgment of the Examiner, not an opinion of the patient.

Asking subjects how they get along with their spouses is asking the subjects to make a diagnosis. It may be that the Examiner is interested in the subjects' opinions. BIs obtained about the interaction between wife and husband may, in the Examiner's judgment, be at variance with the spouse's opinion. For instance, it may be that the spouse is blaming the other spouse for difficulties which actually lie elsewhere. A few years ago the author was interviewing a male patient who complained that his sex life was "not right." He implied that his wife was at fault. In the systematic collection of BIs about the patient's daily life, it was discovered that the patient spent eight hours a day sitting on the toilet. Particularly, he sat on the toilet seat for the last four hours of the day, just prior to going to bed. He had to sit until he was "cleaned out" as he put it. This behavior got him to bed quite late. His wife, who had three children to get off to school in the morning, had already been sleeping for two or three hours. She was not very responsive to his sexual demands when he finally got to bed. BIs obtained from the husband yielded data about the wife which, in the Examiner's judgment, placed her behavior within normal expectancy limits. It was this judgment of the Examiner which led to further survey of the patient's behaviors which in turn led to the discovery of duration of sitting-on-the-toilet behavior. The point is, of course, that the Examiner did not accept the patient's diagnosis but rather arrived at his own conclusion based on the data. We do not wish to imply that the opinions and the attitudes of the patient are not important. They may be of first importance in the therapeutic process but we do wish to assert that they have little value in the diagnostic judgment.

Thus, a patient may say he is "unhappy"; he is not "interested in things anymore." You ask about wife, about children, about job, and so forth. "Everything is all right," he may answer, "It's just me." If you ask him for his opinion about what's bugging him, he may, if he has been in psychotherapy before, or if he has read a lot, regale you with his psychodynamics. When he is finished he does not know, nor do you, what stimulus situations are kicking off his behavior, let alone what actually deviant behaviors he is exhibiting. You will only know if you ask what happens in what situations. It is too much to ask that patients know their psychological environments. They cannot "see the forest for the trees." You will not know their psychological environments unless you can cut through intellectualizations, cultural postures, and defenses by getting BIs. The BI is a memory. It is a perception of an event. It is a window to the phenomenological world of the patient. It is the conscious intellectual counterpart of the data obtained by Freud when his patients reported memories under the storm of emotional abreaction.

It is important for the reader to realize that the BI approach to the diagnostic interview is quite different from the usual clinical approach. The worker does not need to approach patients hoping that they will talk easily and tell about their problems. The worker does not need to listen to long monologues by a patient. The clinician is not "stuck" when the patient will not willingly talk about himself. The clinician can get about as much data from a patient who does not talk except in response to questions as he can from a patient who likes to talk about himself. The BI interview is structured. It is systematic. The worker approaches the patient knowing what data are to be obtained in order to make a diagnosis. The clinician is not entirely dependent upon the patients' feeling sufficiently en rapport to reveal their innermost thoughts. The patients only have to remember specific events. The worker has the advantage in that most patients do not know what they are revealing about themselves in reported BIs. The very person who stoutly maintains that he had a happy childhood with his father will, with BIs, indicate lack of affection, neglect, and severe punishment from father. Of course, the patient may refuse to answer, an event so rare that it has never happened in the subjects we have interviewed. The patient may lie, in which case the worker will know it. The BIs given by the patient will not be plausible in the light of other data; for example, BIs obtained about the father and mother relationship indicate neglect of family by the father, when BIs about relationship between father and child indicate affection and many activities together.

The approach to the diagnostic interview presented in this chapter places responsibility for obtaining useful data upon the Examiner, where it belongs. With practice the clinician will find that the insistence on BIs does not interfere with the verbal interaction between Examiner and patient but rather is an aid. Although much of this chapter has been taken up by this very verbal interaction, the worker will find that nonverbal cues are not forgotten in our approach to the diagnostic interview. Direct observation of the patient's behavior during the diagnostic interview is a well-accepted method and renders believable data. The verbal data, however, have been suspect. In Chapter 3 we will consider the reliability and validity of such data.

REFERENCES

Bartlett, F. C. *Remembering.* Cambridge, Eng.: University Press, 1932.

Flanagan, J. C. The critical incident technique. *Psychological Bulletin,* 1954, *51,* 327-358.

Frank, G. A. The role of the family in the development of psychopathology. *Psychological Bulletin,* 1965, *64,* 191-205.

Freud, S. *Introductory lectures on psychoanalysis.* New York: Boni and Liveright, 1923.

Kahn, R. L., & Cannell, C. F. *The dynamics of interviewing.* New York: John Wiley & Sons, 1957.

Kinsey, A. C. et al. *Sexual behavior in the human male.* Philadelphia: W. B. Saunders, 1948.

Kintz, B. L., Delprato, D. J., Mettee, D. R., Persons, C. E., & Schappe, R. H. The experimenter effect. *Psychological Bulletin,* 1965, *63,* 223-232.

Murray, H. D. *Explorations in personality.* New York: Oxford University Press, 1938.

Pascal, G. R., & Jenkins, W. O. A study of the early environment of workhouse inmate alcoholics and its relationship to adult behavior. *Quarterly Journal of Studies on Alcohol,* 1960, *21,* 40-50.

Pascal, G. R., & Jenkins, W. O. *Systematic observation of gross human behavior.* New York: Grune & Stratton, 1961.

Schofield, W., & Balian, L. A comparative study of the personal histories of schizophrenics and non-psychiatric patients. *Journal of Abnormal and Social Psychology,* 1959, *59,* 216-225.

Twiner, R. H., & Barlow, J. H. Memory for pleasant and unpleasant experiences: Some methodological considerations. *Journal of Experimental Psychology,* 1951, *42,* 189-196.

Ulrich, L., & Trumbo, D. The selection interview since 1949. *Psychological Bulletin,* 1965, *63,* 100-116.

3 | On reliability and validity

It is not intended that this chapter be a review of the literature on the reliability and validity of the interview. There are a number of excellent reviews, Ulrich and Trumbo (1965), Frank (1965), Matarazzo, Wiens, and Saslow (1965), and Matarazzo (1965). Rather, in this chapter we will present studies which have been accumulating over the past several years, studies which have used the BI technique, and, therefore, bear most directly on our approach. Some of these studies have been published, others appear here for the first time.

The purpose of the chapter is to convince the mental health worker that the method of interviewing advocated is one that will yield reliable and valid data. Each patient has within him or her enough case history material to fill several volumes. From this almost limitless mass of material, workers must learn to extract that which is pertinent to their purpose; namely, the diagnosis of the patient's psychological/psychiatric disorder. The areas in which the workers seek information are the subject matter of this book but the method whereby they obtain information within the areas is the behavioral incident technique. All the studies presented below illustrate the usefulness of the method. They are presented here as the research backup for advocating the method.

Several years ago the author and Dr. William O. Jenkins were asked to help with a problem presented by Dr. James C. Thoroughman, chief of surgery at the Veterans Administration Hospital in Atlanta, Georgia. It seemed that some ulcer patients coming to surgery were classified as "intractable." These showed poor surgical results in 40 percent of cases as opposed to poor results in 10 percent of patients coming to surgery for perforation, bleeding, and obstruction (Thoroughman, 1963). The surgeon felt that there were important personality differences between the intractable patients and the others. An attempt to predict surgical outcome with the intractable patients, based on an estimate of personality by the surgeons, failed. At this point psychologists were asked to help.

The first approach to the problem was to study samples of patients with known surgical outcome, roughly matched for age, education, and vocation. All sorts of measures were tried in successive samples—measures such as IQ, age, education, duration, onset, socioeconomic status, and so forth. What emerged after the process of distillation was a 16-item interview guide, each item showing satisfactory reliability and validity against the criterion of surgical outcome. Table 3-1 shows this guide with the items briefly defined.

TABLE 3-1
Items of the deprivation scale

Item 1. *Employment:* Is the subject employed less than half time?
Item 2. *Income:* Does the subject have an income of less than $2,500 a year?
Item 3. *Debts:* Does the subject manifest undue concern over unpaid debts?
Item 4. *Job participation:* Does the subject show little interest in the job other than as a means of making a living?
Item 5. *Job status:* Does the subject feel superior to his job?
Item 6. *Other status:* Does the subject have a sense of status from a hobby or activity other than his job?
Item 7. *Education:* Does the subject have less than an eigth-grade education?
Item 8. *Residence:* Does the subject have a sense of pride in his house or neighborhood?
Item 9. *Church:* Does the subject attend church less than once a month?
Item 10. *Other organizations:* Does the subject belong to a club, organization, or church group in the community?
Item 11. *Friends:* Is the subject a relative isolate, with no warm friends?
Item 12. *Relatives:* Does the subject have close ties with any relatives?
Item 13. *Parents:* Does the subject feel that his parents are uninterested in him?
Item 14. *Wife:* Does the wife display a lack of nurturant behavior?
Item 15. *Children:* Is the subject without children or, if he has children, does he have little to do with them?
Item 16. *Fear:* Is the subject anxious and apprehensive about himself currently and about future plans?

Data were obtained from interviews of the patient about his life *prior* to hospitalization. The BI method was used in obtaining data wherever applicable. Thus, the patient was not asked how he got along with his wife, but rather, when did he see her last, what did they do, and so on. Based on the data obtained, the item was scored either 1 or 0, the score 1 indicating environmental impoverishment with respect to the particular item. Studies of reliability using the scale, called by now "the deprivation scale," showed coefficients in the 90s when two raters independently judge the same taped protocol. The repeat interview study of reliability made at this time yielded a correlation of .86 using total scores. For this study, 32 subjects were interviewed by two interviewers with a mean lapse of 29 months between interviews. All except two items, numbers 6 and 16, showed satisfactory reliabilities.

Forty-seven patients whose indications for surgery were intractability were administered the deprivation scale one week to one month after surgery. (The deprivation scale and manual for its use will be found in Appendix I.) Two years postoperatively these patients were medically evaluated as either good or poor surgical results. Deprivation scale scores were then compared to surgical outcome. When we used deprivation scale score cutoffs, which we had determined from previous studies, deprivation scales scores of 5 and below predicted the successes perfectly. Of the surgical failures falling into the deprivation scale score group of 10 and above, 14 out of 16 were predicted correctly (Thoroughman, Pascal, Jenkins, Crutcher, & Peoples, 1964). Table 3-2 shows the results of the study. It will be noted that for the middle group of deprivation scale scores (i.e., scores from 6 to 9 inclusive), the prediction is chance. A second truly predictive study, in which deprivation scales were administered prior to surgery and compared to medical evaluation two years postoperatively, yielded essentially the same results. Although deprivation scale scores of 5 and below and 10 and above predicted beautifully, good enough for individual measurement, the middle group of scores did no better than chance. It seems as if when an intractable duodenal ulcer patient is definitely environmentally impoverished, as this is estimated by the deprivation scale, he is a poor bet for surgery, and conversely, if he has a definitely satisfying environment, he is a good bet. The surgical outcome of the in-between patients is not predicted. We will return to the ulcer studies when we consider early life history variables. In the meantime we will continue with studies using the deprivation scale.

TABLE 3-2
Surgical outcome by grouped deprivation (scale scores)

Deprivation scale score	Outcome of surgery		Total
	Success	Failure	
5 or below	21	0	21
6-9	4	6	10
10 or above	2	14	16
Total	27	20	47

$x^2 = 29.8$; $P = .00007$.

The deprivation scale is an interview guide. Data to rate the items are obtained from interview of the subject. The accuracy of what the subject reports is not in question. What we get from interview data is a memory, even in a cross-sectional study, a perception, if you will. The reliability with which we can obtain such data has been shown in a number of studies using the deprivation scale. Two interviewers can get the same data from the same subject. The predictive power of such data has been illustrated with the ulcer study.

Interview data were also used in the study of alcoholics. Nineteen workhouse alcoholics were matched for age, education, and vocation with controls. The subjects were all males. We also studied a population of middle-class alcoholics, white-collar workers, business and professional men and matched these with controls. The details of these studies are reported elsewhere (Pascal & Jenkins, 1960, 1966). To measure alcoholism we used a scale developed by Jenkins and Davis (1957). The items of this scale, scored either "1" or "0", and administered by interview of the subject are as follows: amount consumed; variety of alcohol; rate of drinking; time between drinking periods; behavioral changes with onset of drinking; conditions of drinking; aftereffects of drinking and long-range consequences of drinking. Maximum score on this scale is 8, indicating an extreme in alcoholism. The usual precautions were observed in conducting the studies; that is, different interviewers were used for the two scales and insofar as possible interviewers were uninformed about the experimental or control status of the subject. For the workhouse alcoholics and controls we obtained nonoverlapping distributions. There was little overlap between middle-class alcoholics and controls. Workhouse alcoholics were significantly differentiated from middle-class alcoholics by deprivation scale scores. Table 3-3 shows the relationship between alcoholism scale scores and deprivation scale scores. The more the person is deprived of environmental satisfactions, as measured by the deprivation scale, the more alcoholic, as estimated by the alcoholism scale score.

Data for the study of the duodenal ulcer patients and the alcoholics were obtained from interview of the subject. For the two studies cited, the pre-

TABLE 3-3
Relationship between deprivation and alcoholism scale scores

	N	Mean alcoholism scale score	Mean deprivation scale score
Workhouse alcoholics	19	7.2	12.0
Middle-class alcoholics	20	5.7	7.4
Controls	39	.8	2.7

Note: For differences between column means $P \leqslant .001$.

dictive value of these data has been established. One might argue that these were cross-sectional studies; that is, that information was obtained about current behaviors and that such information might be more accurate than other types of interview data. As has been indicated previously, the accuracy of the data are not in question, only the reliability and validity of what the subject says in the interview. Nevertheless, one might still be more inclined to accept cross-sectional data than data from the anamnestic interview. We will, therefore, now go on to consider a number of studies which are truly anamnestic. All of the studies use the BI technique. All of the studies bear on early life experiences.

Over the years we have conducted a number of studies of subjects' reports of parental behavior toward them during childhood. Subjects were interviewed to obtain BIs about specific aspects of parental behavior. These variables are part of the Pascal-Jenkins (P-J) behavioral scales, and are more fully described elsewhere (Pascal & Jenkins, 1961). Table 3-4 gives the variables and a brief definition of them.

TABLE 3-4
P-J rated variables for parents

1.	Frequency of contact—How often is parent physically present?
2.	Activities—How much time did parent spend "doing things," playing, with subject?
3.	Displays of affection—How much physical affection given to subject by parent?
4.	Providing behavior—Did parent provide necessities such as food, clothing, and shelter for subject?
5.	Restraints—How much or how little restraining behavior displayed by parent?
6.	Physical punishment—How much actual physical punishment?
7.	Verbal punishment—How much verbal castigations by parent?
8.	Intellectual behavior—What did parent do that was intellectually stimulating?
9.	Status—What was parent's status among his peers?
10.	Social behavior—Was parent gregarious, socially participating?
11.	Religious behavior—Did parent attend church?
12.	Physical health—State of parent's health?
13.	Compatibility—What were behaviors of parents toward each other?
14.	Role—Did father and mother display behaviors appropriate for their sex?
15.	Variability of habitat—How often did parents move?
16.	Sexual behavior—Did parents sleep in same bed, and so on?
17.	Deviant behavior—Did parents display grossly deviant behavior; for example, drunken behavior, trouble with law, and so forth?

The interviews were conducted by skilled clinicians trained in the use of the BI technique. Each interviewer had in mind a set of expectancies for the behaviors of parents. The clinician obtained from the subject specific incidents of parent's behavior toward him as a child, below the age of 10. For each variable the interviewer collected BIs wherever feasible until he reached a point of subjective certainty about the rating to be given a variable. If unable to obtain BIs, the interviewer rated the variable ND (no data). If the subject's memories indicated that the behavior of the parent for a particular variable was within expectancy limits, it was rated 3. The rating 1 was given when, in the opinion of the interviewer, the reported behaviors of the parent was markedly deviant from expectancy. The rating 2 was used for intermediate behaviors.

At this point it might be pertinent to describe what is meant by expectancy. Since we are without statistical data on the specific behaviors which constitute the cultural norms of responding to stimuli we necessarily have to use our own judgment. Fortunately, as the data will show, we tend to judge behaviors similarly. Probably because we all belong to a similar culture, we each have within us a set of expectancies with which we view the behaviors of another. Thus, if a young adult tells us that he only sleeps two hours a day, we would agree that such sleeping behavior is a deviancy from what we would expect; similarly, if a man says he beats his wife every day, we would consider such behavior deviant. The expected behaviors of an individual are based on sex, age, education, socioeconomic status, and other considerations such as ethnic background and race. Thus, expectancy for a married couple with respect to communication between husband and wife in a couple from Appalachia would differ from that of a professional couple from New York City. In all of our studies it was found that the raters could agree perfectly on *extreme* deviancy from expectancy. There was almost perfect agreement in judging what was expected behavior. Difficulty was only encountered in judging behaviors that were not quite extremely deviant or were not quite normal, or expected. But, as you will see, the agreements between raters as to what was deviant and what was normal was so great that reliability and validity were not greatly affected by the disagreements as to what was rated intermediate.

We shall concern ourselves first with the reliability of these ratings. Later, we shall consider their validity. Reliability was measured in two ways, by comparing ratings of two independent judges using the same taped interview and by the repeat interview of the same subject by two independent interviewers. One of the first studies in which two independent judges rated the same protocol was done by Davis (1959). He computed rank correlations by the variable for five workhouse alcoholics and their matched controls. The 50 rhos computed ranged from .76 to .98 with a median of .88. The most usual way of computing reliability with the P-J scale variables has been to compare the percent agreement between judges. Table 3-5 summarizes a number of these studies. Not all of the P-J variables were used in these studies, some used only 10 variables, but all used independent judges and all took the usual precautions in attempting to conceal the status of the subject being rated. It will be noted that the modal percent complete agreement is 78. Disagreement by two points, on the three-point scale, is rare. Judges had little difficulty with the rating 1 markedly deviant from expectancy. Most of the

TABLE 3-5
Reliability of ratings on P-J scales percent agreement by independent judges

	Percent complete agreement	Percent differing by one point	Percent differing by two points	Number of ratings
Pascal and Jenkins (workhouse alcoholics) (1960)	78	18	4	544
Long (hypnosis study) (1968)	72	28	0	411
Edwards (homosexuals) (1963)	78	22	0	512
Horner (schizophrenics) (1964) . . .	82	17	1	240
Pascal and Jenkins (middle-class alcoholics) (1960)	78	21	1	600

disagreement by one point occurred between the rating 3 (expectancy) and 2 (intermediate). In the several thousand ratings reported in these studies *none of the judges disagreed by three points.*

Estimates of the reliability of interview data using the repeat interview are more convincing than those using two independent judges on the same protocol, but each of these ways has its advantages. Although the bias of the interviewer may be reflected in the data when two judges use the same protocol, the method has the advantage of being able to conceal the status of the subject from the judge. In the repeat interview the interviewer cannot help but know the status of the subject. The latter method does, however, have the advantage in that two separate interviewers can dip into the pool of data available on the subject. Within any given subject there is a vast amount of data available. The ability with which two interviewers can emerge with the same data is a direct estimate of the power of the method of interviewing. In Horner's study of schizophrenics (1964), two experimental and two control subjects were interviewed a second time. The time lapse between interviews ranged from 8 to 12 months. For 288 ratings the agreement between the two interviews was as follows: 77 percent perfect agreement, 22 percent disagreement by one point and 1 percent disagreement by two points. In another study (Pascal & Jenkins, 1966) of the repeat interview 12 duodenal ulcer patients were interviewed by a clinical psychologist and a psychiatrist. The mean time lapse between interviews was 40 months with a range of 15 to 70 months. Table 3-6 shows the results of this study. It will be noted that although there is variation between variables the mean percents compare quite well with those shown in Table 3-5.

The plain truth of the matter is that essential disagreement (by two points) between judges using the same protocol, and different interviewers interviewing the same subject, is rare, occurring on the average in less than 2 percent of the ratings for the three-point scale. These findings attest to the remark-

TABLE 3-6
Percent agreement by variable, two interviews of same patient by two different interviewers (total number of ratings 240)

	Percent complete agreement	Percent one point difference	Percent two points difference
Frequency of contact	81	13	6
Activities	60	40	0
Displays of affection	57	43	0
Restraints	87	13	0
Physical punishment	69	25	2
Religious behavior	81	0	19
Physical health	88	12	0
Compatibility of spouse	57	36	7
Role	75	13	12
Providing behavior	64	29	7
Mean percent	78	20	2

Note: Mean time between interviews—40 months; range 15-70 months.
Number Ss interviewed 12.

able consistency with which interview data can be obtained. We need now to concern ourselves with the validity of these data.

One of the first studies we undertook was with 19 male inmates of the county workhouse who had been arrested for drunkenness five or more times (Pascal & Jenkins, 1960). The alcoholics were matched, by pairs, for sex, age, education, IQ, and vocation. All subjects were interviewed using the alcoholism scale, the deprivation scale and the P-J scale. P-J variables were rated by persons other than the interviewer from verbatim transcriptions. In all cases, every effort was made to conceal the status of the subject from the rater. Ratings were compared by matched pairs, by the variable, using the binomial count to obtain *P* values. (See Pascal & Jenkins [1961] for a more detailed description of data analysis.) Ratings on mother and father were studied separately. The overall analysis, combining all variables, showed a significant difference in the ratings between alcoholics and controls (*P* equals .001). Of the 20 comparisons made between the skidrow (workhouse) alcoholics and controls, 15 are significant at the .05 level or less.

We repeated this study for a group of alcoholics of the middle, socioeconomic class. These were employed males, white-collar workers, businessmen and professional people. We carefully matched the 20 experimental subjects with controls from the community, subject by subject. The overall analysis, combining all variables, showed a significant difference between the ratings for controls and alcoholics (*P* less than .01). Table 3-7 shows the *P* values for the individual variables. Note that whereas we had obtained 15 significant variables for the skidrow alcoholics, we only obtained 7 for the middle-class alcoholics. The middle-class alcoholics report early parental behavior toward them as more "normal" which is what we would expect if there is a relationship between P-J ratings and alcoholism. To check out this hypothesis we arranged the mean, overall P-J ratings, alcoholism scale and deprivations scale scores as follows:

TABLE 3-7
Relationship between alcoholism, deprivation scale scores, and P-J ratings

	Mean alcoholic scale scores	Mean deprivation scale scores	Mean overall P-J ratings
Skidrow alcoholics	7.2	12.0	1.3
Middle-class alcoholics	5.7	7.4	2.2
Controls	.8	2.7	2.8

The differences between column means is significant at the .01 level or less for each comparison. We can consider the progression from controls to skidrow alcoholics as a prima facie intensity dimension of deviant behavior, correlated with alcoholism as measured by the alcoholism scale. We have previously shown the relationship between alcoholism and deprivation of environmental satisfactions as measured by the deprivation scale (Table 3-3). We now find a relationship between these measures and P-J ratings. The more a subject reports poor early relations with his parents, the more he reports he is environmentally deprived as an adult, the more he drinks! This study was partially supported by a grant from the Scientific Advisory Committee of the Licensed Beverages Industries.

We shall briefly report a number of studies using the P-J scales. In all these studies reliability was measured. All possible precautions were taken to conceal the status of the subject from the raters. In all of them, subjects were interviewed to obtain reported specific memories (BIs) about the behaviors of parents toward them in the first 10 years of the subjects' lives. These reported and recorded memories constitute the raw data from which P-J ratings are made.

Long (1968) measured 34 college students along a hypnotizability continuum. The parents of these subjects were rated on P-J variables. Ratings on P-J variables significantly discriminated between "high" and "low" hypnotizable subjects, the more hypnotizable subjects reporting less deviant behavior toward them by parents in the first 10 years of the subjects' lives.

Henderson (1962) studied 15 white unmarried mothers and 15 single, never pregnant controls, matching them by subject on age, education, verbal intelligence, religion, vocation, and parental vocation. Ratings on the parents discriminated between control and experimental subjects.

Clarke (1962) used as subjects 30 college students. He studied the relationship between ease of verbal conditioning and ratings on P-J variables on the parents of the subjects. He tested the hypothesis that subjects whose parents behaved toward them according to expectancy (as reported by the subjects) will show a higher degree of conditioning than subjects who have a poorer early relationship. He divided his subjects into high, middle and low groups on verbal conditioning. An analysis of variance revealed significant differences between groups on P-J variables.

Edwards (1963) matched 16 homosexuals with 16 control subjects for race, age, education, occupation, and IQ. Ratings on the parents for the P-J variables significantly differentiated the two groups. He writes, "the most consistent and significant finding in the present investigation was that the fathers of the homosexual males gave their sons few physical demonstrations of love and affection and did not engage in the usual play and childhood games with their sons" (p. 63).

In a careful study, Horner (1964) used the P-J scales with 10 hospitalized male schizophrenics and 10 controls matched for age, education, and socio-economic status by occupation. He contrasted patients and controls on the reported behaviors of grandparents, siblings, mother and father. Patients were not differentiated from controls on P-J ratings of grandparents and siblings. Ratings on mother and father differentiated the two groups at the .001 level. The study was replicated. Across both studies the variables, active play, displays of affection, and compatibility with spouse, significantly differentiated between patients and controls. These variables held up for both parents.

P-J variables have been used to predict surgical success or failure with intractable duodenal ulcer patients. In a study (Pascal, Thoroughman, Jarvis, & Jenkins, 1966), duodenal ulcer patients who had undergone surgery for intractability were interviewed. These patients, all male veterans, were medically evaluated two years postoperatively and a decision made as to whether they were surgical successes or failures. Each of these patients were interviewed with the P-J scales at about the time of surgery (give or take one month). Two years postoperatively 10 surgical successes were matched with 10 surgical failures for age, education, IQ, and vocation. P-J variables significantly differentiated between the successes and failures for ratings on parents. The study was replicated with similar results. When the parents were studied separately it was found that mothers were significantly differentiated across both experiments but fathers were not, a finding different from that obtained with alcoholics and schizophrenics. The one variable that held up at the P .01 level of significance across both studies was displays of affection from mother. This variable was tested with another sample of 24 surgical successes and 22 surgical failures and a P value of less than .001 was obtained. When ratings on this variable were applied to the sample in which the deprivation scale was used it was found that the patients in the middle group of deprivation scale scores (where prediction was chance) could be predicted. Ratings on displays of affection from mother correctly predicted 11 out of 12 patients falling in the middle group on deprivation scale scores. Description of the variable displays of affection from mother, and a manual for obtaining data to rate it will be found in Appendix II.

The purpose of a study by Baugh, Pascal, and Cottrell (1970) was to test the hypothesis that the reported perceptions of childhood experiences are related to the interview behavior of adults. Twenty-two college females were interviewed using the P-J scales for father and mother. Each subject was also interviewed by one of the investigators who had no knowledge of the P-J rating. This second interview was conducted over closed circuit television. The subject and the interviewer were in different rooms. In order to keep the interviewer in view, the subject was required to press a foot pedal at a prescribed rate. The number of presses per minute was one of three measures of interview behavior used. A second measure was the amount of time the subject avoided eye contact with the image of the interviewer on the television screen. The third measure was the number of words spoken by the subject during the interview.

The 30-minute interview was divided into three phases. The first phase of 10 minutes was rapport building. During this 10 minutes the subject was asked standard questions such as choice of career. At the end of this first phase, the subject was told that the next 15 minutes would be a test to find out how well she could communicate with another human being. During this second phase, the interviewer held a stopwatch in full view of the subject and remained silent. The third phase of five minutes was similar to the first phase. Subjects were categorized as mother positive or mother negative and father positive or father negative on the basis of a 50-50 split of rankings on the P-J scales.

The results indicate that the subjects who reported a good relationship with father duing the early years behaved differentially toward a male examiner during the stress interview as contrasted with subjects who reported a poor relationship with father during their early years. The reported early relationships with mother did not seem to affect their interview behavior.

We feel the evidence is quite conclusive that interview data can be reliable and valid. What, then, is the difference between the data we have so briefly presented and the data reviewed by Frank (1965)? In the first place the BI technique used in the P-J scales is not concerned with the accuracy of the interview data. Its chief concern is reliability of the interviewee's *perceptions.* Other investigators have noted that the child's perceptions of parents is of more relevance in discriminating schizophrenics from controls than the observed behaviors of the parents (Ausubel, 1948; Garmezy, Clark, & Stockner, 1961). Piety (1966) hypothesizes that "perceptual dissonance" may be a characteristic of maladjusted persons.

The use of the BI technique tends to give the interview structure. Ulrich and Trumbo (1965) report as a result of their review of the literature that "the bulk of the evidence favors the structured interview." Use of the BI technique tends to minimize experimenter bias (Kintz, Delprato, Mettee, Persons, & Schappe, 1965). Memories reported in stimulus-response terms by the interviewee preclude biasing statements by the interviewer.

The case history technique has a long and venerable history as a method of investigation. Of late years it has fallen into disrepute, particularly in the area of psychopathology. Cogent and reasonable arguments, based on data, have been used against the case history method. These have resulted in a tendency to discard the method, not in efforts to improve it. In our present state of knowledge, it has no peer as a method of clinical investigation.

The use of the case history method does, however, require knowledge, experience and skill. The use of the method has many pitfalls which trap even experienced interviewers. For instance, one hopelessly biasing parameter of measurement, which if one is unaware of it can lead to false conclusions, is that of experimenter bias. Take the case of a child of normal intelligence failing in school. There are clinicians with bias which leads them to consider family dynamics as the prime factor in the child's failure in school. Very often this bias will be such that the possibility of minimal brain damage in the child will be overlooked, although minimal brain damage in the child can lead to its own psychological problems. After all, one can always find some difficulty in any family if one is intent in that direction.

We have been at some length about the reliability and validity of interview data, particularly case history material. The subject's history taken from the subject is the vehicle which carries the diagnostic interview. The case formulation, that which forms the basis for decision making, stems from direct observations of the subject during interview *and* perceptual data given by the subject about himself and his environment. We have shown that it is not required that these perceptions be accurate as to objective fact, only that they be reliable and unbiased by cultural norms. Of course, the perceptions of the patient need to be imbedded in factual data such as presence or absence of parents, number of siblings, illnesses, and so on.

The use of the BI technique has been shown to yield not only reliable interview data but also data that can distinguish between degrees of deviancy. Early life history data obtained by the BI technique has been shown to be related to adult adjustment. The case history method is an invaluable diagnostic tool.

REFERENCES

Ausubel, D. T. *Theory and problem of child development.* New York: Grune & Stratton, 1948.

Baugh, J. R., Pascal, G. R., & Cottrell, T. E. The relationship of reported memories of early experiences with parent on interview behavior. *Journal of Consulting and Clinical Psychology*, 1970, *35*, 23-29.

Clarke, J. R. Operant verbal conditioning as a function of early history variables. Unpublished doctoral dissertation, University of Tennessee, 1962.

Davis, H. C. A comparative study of the experiential characteristics of a group of alcoholic and non-alcoholic subjects. Unpublished doctoral dissertation, University of Tennessee, 1959.

Edwards, H. E. The relationship between reported early life experiences with parents and adult male homosexuality. Unpublished doctoral dissertation, University of Tennessee, 1963.

Frank, G. A. The role of the family in the development of psychopathology. *Psychological Bulletin*, 1965, *64*, 191-205.

Garmezy, N., Clarke, A. P., & Stockner, C. Child rearing attitudes of mothers and fathers as reported by schizophrenic and normal patients. *Journal of Abnormal and Social Psychology*, 1961, *63*, 176.

Henderson, W. A. An investigation of the unwed mothers' relationships with important people in early life and cross-sectionally. Unpublished doctoral dissertation, University of Tennessee, 1962.

Horner, R. F. Important stimulus variables in the early family relationships of schizophrenic patients. *Journal of Clinical Psychology*, 1964, *20*, 344.

Jenkins, W. O., & Davis, H. C. On the behavioral definition of alcoholism. Unpublished master's thesis, University of Tennessee, 1957.

Kintz, B. O., Delprato, D. J., Mettee, D. R., Persons, C. E., & Schappe, R. H. The experimenter effect. *Psychological Bulletin*, 1965, *63*, 223.

Long, T. E. Some early-life stimulus correlates of hypnotizability. *International Journal of Clinical and Experimental Hypnosis*, 1968, *16*, 61-67.

Matarazzo, J. D. The interview. In B. B. Wolman (Ed.), *Handbook of clinical psychology*. New York: McGraw-Hill, 1965.

Matarazzo, J. D., Wiens, A. N., & Saslow, G. Studies in interview speech behavior. Chapter in L. Krasner and L. P. Ullmann (Eds.), *Research in behavior modifications: New developments and their clinical implications*. New York: Holt, Rinehart & Winston, 1965.

Pascal, G. R., & Jenkins, W. O. A study of the early environment of workhouse inmate alcoholics and its relationship to adult behavior. *Quarterly Journal of Studies on Alcohol*, 1963, *21*, 40.

Pascal, G. R., and Jenkins, W. O. *Systematic observation of gross human behavior*. New York: Grune & Stratton, 1961.

Pascal, G. R., & Jenkins, W. O. On the relationship between alcoholism and environmental satisfactions. *Southern Medical Journal*, 1966, *59*, 698.

Pascal, G. R., Thoroughman, J. C., Jarvis, J. R., & Jenkins, W. O. Early history variables in predicting surgical success for intractable duodenal ulcer patients. *Psychosomatic Medicine*, 1966, *28*, 207.

Piety, K. R. Perceptual dissonance and role learning. *Journal of Clinical Psychology*, 1966, *22*, 10.

Thoroughman, J. C. Surgery and the patient with intractable peptic ulcer. *American Journal of Surgery,* 1963, *105,* 334.

Thoroughman, J. C., Pascal, G. R., Jenkins, W. O., Crutcher, J. C., & Peoples, L. C. Psychological factors predictive of surgical success in patients with intractable duodenal ulcer: A study of male veterans. *Psychosomatic Medicine,* 1964, *26,* 618.

Ulrich, L., & Trumbo, D. The selection interview since 1949. *Psychological Bulletin,* 1965, *63,* 100-116.

4 | The nature of the diagnostic interview

Interviews come in various forms. On the directive, nondirective continuum they run from the directness of prisoner interrogation to the nondirective Rogerian first interview. On a continuum of subtlety they run from the simplicity of the pollster to the complexity of the psychoanalytic interview where "the red thread of the patient's unconscious" is followed (Deutsch & Murphy, 1960). In some approaches to the diagnostic interview it seems as if the patient is required to make his own diagnosis. The Examiner seeks knowledge from the patient about himself which he, the patient, does not have. This procedure is most often observed in the student interviewer. In other approaches to the interview, it seems as if by just getting the patient to talk, the Examiner, by some process of psychological osmosis, hopes to arrive at a diagnosis of the patient.

Many interviews are only concerned with the diagnostic label. Little attempt is made to get information which can make explicit the patient's basic problems and how these are related to his behavioral deviances. Overconcern with the diagnostic label leads the Examiner into a blind alley. We do not wish to imply that it is not important to know whether or not the patient can manage his own affairs; that is, whether he is psychotic or nonpsychotic; nor do we wish to imply that it is not important to know whether or not the patient is dangerous to himself or others. These are questions of intensity directly related to the nature of the patients' problems.

It cannot be too strongly emphasized that the interview we are proposing is diagnostic. It is to be sharply differentiated from, for instance, the nondirective first interview. The first interview is not meant to be therapeutic although the patients very often may feel that it is just that. Beginning workers often let the diagnostic interview degenerate into a "therapeutic" one by virtue of the fact that they get involved in the patients' feelings or become enthralled by the patients' account of their experiences. Allowing patients to talk at will may waste their time as well as the Examiner's. This procedure may be acceptable when the same therapeutic approach is applied to each patient regardless of his problems but is out of keeping with an approach that intends to approach treatment systematically and which depends on thorough knowledge of the patient before treatment is planned.

These remarks lead us to an important consideration for those who would conduct the diagnostic interview. Perhaps an analogy will make our intent clear. No one, in our culture, expects that a physical examination will be made by anyone but a physician. As a basis for conducting the examination, the physician has a thorough knowledge of the physical factors which may affect the patient. Similarly, the person conducting the diagnostic interview should have a thorough knowledge of the psychological factors which affect a person's behavior. A firm grasp of the principles of systematic psychology and its application to everyday human problems is a necessary background for the person conducting the diagnostic interview. The Examiner needs to be as familiar with "psychological anatomy" as does a surgeon with physical anatomy. It is this knowledge of the human body which makes it possible for the physician to approach physical examination with a confidence which is instilled in the patient. This same knowledgeability in the psychological Examiner is required before he can approach the diagnostic interview with confidence. It is this confidence which promotes the elicitation of data from the patient. It is this confidence which enables the patient, without embarrassment, to undress psychologically.

I am reminded of an incident which occurred while I was a psychologist on a psychiatric ward. At the time, we were videotaping intake and exit interviews from the ward patients. These interviews were viewed by me after the patient had been discharged after a stay of several weeks on the ward. The young resident was diffident and somewhat ill at east in his initial interview with a female patient, a middle-aged woman of college education. In the first interview, she tried to tell him something but we never found out what it was because each time the patient started to talk about sex the resident changed the subject. It was not until the exit interview that we found out what the patient had been trying to tell the resident. At the end of the interview she finally blurted out what she had been trying to say in her first interview and, evidently, during the weeks of her stay on the ward. She said that the thing that had been bothering her and why she got so upset that she had to come on the ward was that her husband had not, for the past several years, had normal sex relations with her. His idea of sex with her was for her to take his penis in her mouth. The story is a common one in terms of the relation between patient and student. The implication is that if the resident had been knowledgeable and confident, he would have been at ease and the patient would not have been embarrassed to tell him.

There is more concerning the attitude of the interviewer which has a direct bearing on the nature of the interview. In most instances the patient is having his first interview with a professional. It took a strong need and a real feeling of humility to come to that interview. The patient is confronted with a stranger. This stranger asks that the patient psychologically undress. To most people, this is a threat. It is much easier to physically undress oneself for a physician. Besides, a physician is a known quantity. To the average patient, the mental health worker is an omniscient person who can strip the patient of defenses and leave him a quivering, unintegrated blob. The patient is nervous and ill at ease. He needs reassurance. He needs to feel that the Examiner is an understanding and nonjudgmental person. This empathy for the patients and their problems is, for some people, difficult to come by. If a patient is brought in on a stretcher with two broken legs, we can look at this patient and say to ourselves "there but for the grace of God go I." On the other hand, if a patient is brought to emergency in a catatonic state, we do not have the same feeling. We tend to feel that the patient is alien to us. We could never be like him!

Dr. Gregory Zilboorg in his weekly lectures at Butler Hospital in Providence, Rhode Island, in the late 40s felt that this was one of the greatest problems that the new psychiatric resident had to overcome. As an example of this lack of empathy and understanding, he used to tell the following story. There was a young man who one day was discovered by his mother seemingly fishing in the washbowl. He had a stick, a string, and a bent pin which he held over a washbowl filled with water. His mother was alarmed and called the father. Father took one look and called the family physician. The family physician hurried over, looked, and called a psychiatrist. The psychiatrist came and immediately hospitalized the boy. The boy was placed on the ward. The next morning a young resident making his rounds discovered the boy with the rod in his hand holding the bent pin over the filled washbowl. The young resident rubbed his head and said, jovially, "How's the fishing this morning?" The boy took one scornful look at him and said, "Any damn fool would know you can't catch fish in a washbowl."

Those of us who have worked with rats know that rats behave differently with a handler who is afraid than one who is unafraid. The same is true of other animals such as horses and dogs. It almost seems as if the animals can smell fear. If animals are this sensitive then think of how sensitive the human being is. The patients know when they are feared. They know when they are disliked. They know when the interviewer feels superior. The answer to this sort of problem is, of course, that if you don't like or are afraid of people, and particularly people with problems, you ought either to get out of the field or do something about changing your basic attitude. To be critical of a person because he has a problem which manifests itself in a symptom you don't like or don't approve of is the same as if you were a physician and would have a critical attitude about a person who suffered a broken leg because of an accident.

It is the attitude of the interviewer that determines the nature of the interview and has a direct and powerful bearing on the amount of data that can be obtained from the interviewee. I have spoken only of the more obvious attitudes. There are a number of subtle attitudes that determine how the interview goes. For instance, if you "don't like" homosexuals as patients, it may well be that you are reacting to your own fear of homosexuality. What is your inferiority that you feel superior to the "weak" alcoholic? Perhaps, it is these considerations which have made the interview a neglected tool for data gathering for both clinical and research purposes. The lack of awareness of considerations such as these has introduced tremendous variation in the measuring instrument, the clinician.

The validity and reliability of interview data are enhanced, not only if the clinician is a person who by his knowledge of "psychological anatomy" inspires confidence in a patient and who is a person sufficiently at ease with himself so that rapport is easily established, but also reliability and validity vary directly as a function of the clinician's knowledge of the kind and amount of data he wishes to obtain from the patient. The efficiency of the interview depends to a large extent on the clinician's knowledge of what kind of information he wants to obtain from the patient. Obviously, he doesn't have the time, and he may not even be interested, in all the data that can be obtained from a patient. A thorough history of the patient's life would fill a volume. It is all too true that students of the interview are often inclined to obtain inconsequential data such as where the patient lived at different times in his life and other boring demographic data ad infinitum. The clinician must necessarily be selective in the data obtained from the patient.

Naturally, the nature of the data obtained varies with the bias of the interviewer. This author has seen a sexually frustrated young male interviewer obtain very complete accounts of the sexual history of a female patient with a relative neglect of all other aspects of the patient's life. All the data obtained have to contribute to the ultimate case formulation upon which clinical decisions are based. The question becomes: How much data are sufficient to make a clinical decision as the result of an hour-long diagnostic interview? There is no really good answer to that question. We can only present what we consider guidelines for obtaining what are deemed basic data. From this basis, the individual clinician has to branch out according to his own needs and predelictions.

We shall briefly present a systematic approach. For details of this approach, the worker is referred to previous publications (Pascal, 1959; Pascal & Jenkins, 1961). Basic to this approach is the conviction that behavior is "the payoff." Behaviors observed during the interview or reported daily behaviors become the dependent variables. We are immediately concerned with how the patients behave toward us in the interview and how they behave in response to typical and daily life situations. We bring to these observations of the patients a set of expectancies. Unfortunately, these expectancies do not, for the most part, have a quantitative basis. We do not have, for instance, data on how much time, on the average, a person of a given status spends in bed sleeping. Without normative data, we do not have a quantitative basis for making a statement that a person differs significantly from expectancy. Nevertheless, most of us can roughly agree on expectancy for hours of sleep in any given person. If an adult person sleeps only 2 hours a day or as much as 20, most would agree that either one of these figures represents a significant deviancy from expectancy. In the absence of any specific data, therefore, we can only make a rough estimate about deviancies of behavior. Our judgment has to depend on derived knowledge and personal experience with people. We are somewhat better off when we are estimating children, because we do have some data. An instrument such as the Gesell and Amatruda developmental scale (Gesell & Amatruda, 1962) is a big help. None of these scales, however, cover all the areas in which we might be interested.

The plain fact of the matter is when we accept behavior as our dependent variable, we are stuck with very crude measures. Nevertheless, as shown in Chapter 3, the data that can be obtained are both reliable and valid.

If you think that behavior in response to life situations is a crude variable, then pause a moment and think about the alternatives. We should, at this point, let the reader know that we have no quarrel with test data. These data are important for a total evaluation of the psychological state of the individual, but they are different. They do not give the same kind of information that can be obtained in the interview. The chief alternative to behavior as a dependent variable that we shall consider is that which comes under the realm of feeling. We do not say that feelings are unimportant, but only that they have no status as a dependent variable.

A patient may say he feels that he would like to kill another person. The credibility that we give to such a statement depends on a number of factors most important of which, it is asserted, are behavioral manifestations. If such a statement is accompanied by nervous manifestations, snarling, and behaviors in the environment indicative of loss of judgment and control, we are apt to take it seriously. If, on the other hand, the statement is made mildly by a person who exhibits in interview and in life no other behavioral manifestations, we are apt to take it as a simple expression of negative feeling toward the other person. The extent to which a person is "disordered," the extent to which he is deviant, is estimated by *behavioral* deviancy. If he sleeps a reasonable number of hours, gets out of bed active, goes about his morning ablutions, smiles some, eats a hearty breakfast, kisses his wife, pats his children, and goes off to work, we would say that for a person of given status his behavior is not deviant. For the time over which we observed him we would say that his behavior was within expectancy limits. On the other hand, if we questioned him about his feelings, we may find he had all sorts of feelings, such as being irritated and angry with his wife because his toothbrush was not in its right place and so forth. He also may have had a number of aberrant thoughts. Without behavioral manifestations, these thoughts and feelings are of little concern to us in this stage of our investigation.

Hopefully, it has become apparent to the reader that what we are insisting is that the dependent variable be observable and communicable. With respect to interview data we have very little choice in this matter. The only objective data that we can obtain are behaviors. Even here, when it comes to the behaviors in response to typical life situations, behaviors that we cannot directly observe, we are dependent upon the report of the patient or information obtained from collaterals who have observed the patient. The extent to which a person deviates from expectancy and the degree of the disorder can only be judged by behavior. In the last analysis, objective criteria can only be applied to observable behaviors.

So far, we have been concerned with the dependent variable, observable behavior. Now we need to consider independent variables that covary with observable behaviors. It is an unfortunate fact that however rough our estimates of the dependent variables are, we cannot do nearly as well with the independent variables. Therefore, this becomes an equation that more or less works backward. The estimates of the dependent variable, behavior, will help to estimate the strength of independent variables. Perhaps an example will make clear what we are saying. Let us say a young man is avoidant in response to stimuli consisting of his male peers. Our judgment is that he spends less time with them than would be normally expected. When he is in their company he does not verbalize as much as we would expect. The patient has reported to us that he exhibited fearful behaviors in response to his father. We hypothesize a relationship between these fearful responses to father and his deviant behaviors in response to male peers in the current environment. The degree of deviancy in response to male peers in the current environment helps us to estimate the extent to which the patient exhibited fearful behaviors in response to father. This estimate is important in psychotherapy. The patient very often asks: How long will psychotherapy take? The answer to that question is difficult. Part of the reason for this difficulty, it seems to me, is because there is no good way, other than the way indicated, to estimate the amount of early learning that has taken place. In other words, how many learning trials did the patient have with his father? What was the reinforcement schedule? We simply do not know the answer to such questions in a given patient. We can only make a very crude estimate based on the knowledge of current behavioral deviancies.

The approach to getting data for independent variables consists of information that the patient has obtained from others or that the Examiner can obtain from others, and that which the patient remembers. Obviously, prenatal data and data about the first two years of life have to come from someone other than the patient. Other than these data, one depends almost completely upon the patient's memory, if he is in contact. Otherwise, one necessarily has to depend upon the memories of some other person. Essentially, what one does is to take cross-sectional slices at different stages in the patient's development. The first slice is taken from the patient's memory of experiences in response to specified stimuli from earliest memory to the age of approximately six. We attempt to obtain behavioral incidents involving important persons in the patient's life. The next slice is taken from the patient's memory during early school years, ages 6 to 12, and then for the high school years. Thereafter, a cross-sectional study is made of young adulthood, say during college or an equivalent. These cross-sectional studies enable us to postulate, or if you will, anthropomorphize, about habits and attitudes acquired by the patient.

At this point we ought to stop and consider what we mean by a cross-sectional study. I must say I am not quite sure what it does mean. I suppose we might say that we are interested in certain phases of a person's life. For instance, we might be interested in his current life. We commonly call such a study cross-sectional. However, we are not quite sure about the time over which the cross-sectional study extends. If we are studying a young adult who has been two years out of college, we would most likely consider a cross-sectional study to be concerned with everything he has done since college. The college years represent another phase of his life. This leads to the speculation that we encompass in a cross-sectional study a period of life during which there have been no important environmental changes. Admittedly, the cross-sectional studies of a person's life that we have been talking about are somewhat fuzzy around the edges.

Perhaps it would be better if we back up just a little bit and approach the problem from the point of view of the kind of data we are looking for. What kind of stresses both physical and psychological were experienced by the individual? In the patient's prenatal life, did the mother experience an illness that might have affected the patient? Was there a possibility of an anoxia or head trauma at birth? What about severe illnesses, accidents, an early injury, and so on? From the data that can be obtained, what were the implications for the type of mothering received by the patient? In this manner we go on to the early years of the patient's life searching for independent variables. From the early experiences reported by the patient (or someone else) a judgment is made about the impact of the experience on the patient. A judgment is made about what the patient has learned. Particular attention is paid to the early formative years because we believe that attitudes acquired about the self and others during these years are particularly tenacious. Because a child cannot differentiate between stimuli as well as an adult, response patterns acquired during these early years are cued to many stimulus situations. There is evidence, at least from animal studies, that response patterns acquired very early in life may sometimes be irreversible. Careful study of early life experiences, therefore, may help in the prognosis for behavioral change in the adult.

At this point, it will undoubtedly occur to some readers that there is much data concerning the fallibility of memory. We are aware of these data and they are undoubtedly to be trusted. We hope that when a person tells us that he is an only child that he gives us accurate information. When he says that his father died when he was about four-years-old, we also hope that that is approximately accurate. There is no way of really knowing. True, these data are used, but we are not completely dependent upon them. The primary concern is for the patient's perception, not the accuracy of memory. The behavioral incidents that were discussed in Chapter 2 are only a means of arriving at a patient's perception about the important people in his history. Our data have shown that these perceptions as obtained by behavioral incidents can validly differentiate between patient populations. As indicated previously, the data do not stand alone. The work of Ausubel (1948) and Garmezy, Clarke, and Stockner (1961) indicate the same kind of validity. A paper by Piety (1966) makes the same point. Yes, we are interested when the patient broke his leg; or when, for instance, the patient was apprehended for delinquent behavior. But we are most interested in the reported memories of his relations with people. And it is exactly in this area that previous studies have shown that the patient's perceptions of parents have direct bearing on current behavior.

There are two aspects, then, of early memories. We are concerned with demographic data. These data can be obtained either from the patient or from collaterals who know of the patient's early life. We feel that it is important to know if the patient is the first of nine siblings. It is important to know if the patient is an only child. If the patient's mother died at birth, it makes a difference in our thinking about the current attitudes of the patient. Obviously, there are a great number of factual data that might have a direct bearing on the patient's current behavior. The point to make here is that there are any number of circumstances that might have a direct bearing on what stimuli the subject has been exposed to and what he has learned. For instance, we only need to mention the sequelae of poliomyelitis and the deprivation experienced by the patient as a result of such an affliction. Careful attention has to be paid to the factual data as related by the patients, factual data, mind you, which have to do with the events of their lives. Sometimes these events can be verified by another person. However, most of the time they are not. There is always the question as to whether or not the patients are telling the truth about these so-called factual events in their lives. When it comes to evaluating the truth of such a recounting of events, we are not completely without recourse.

Almost every clinician has had the experience of listening to a hospitalized paranoid patient who gives him a glowing account of his early life. In listening to such a patient, if we believe him, we are led to wonder how it came to be that the patient we are observing is suspicious of people, angry with the world, and in general, just doesn't like people. Obviously, the history that was obtained doesn't make any sense. Somewhere along the line the patient learned not to like people. Nevertheless, we are stuck with the data obtained from the patient and very often there is no other way to obtain data about the events of the person's life. It is precisely at this point that we become dependent on the patient's perceptions. This is the other aspect of early memories.

It is not what the patient said his father "used to do." Rather, it is whether or not the patient can remember specific incidents, described in stimulus-response terms, of his father's behavior toward him. Similarly, we seek behavioral incidents concerning "the important people in the patient's early life." The patient may say that his father always used to take him to the ball game yet cannot remember one specific time. The patient may say that his father "used to" beat him with a wooden club twice a week and yet cannot remember any specific occasion. Data have to "hang together." Subsequently, the father was said to be an alcoholic who got drunk every weekend; this reported behavior of the father is not consistent with going to the ball game every weekend.

It may seem to the reader that we are trying to force the data into a pattern to fit our theory. It is true that we do believe that attitudes affecting the responses to current stimuli are learned. We are bound, therefore, to look for the kind of experiences which fostered such learning.

It cannot be said too emphatically that the events and perceptions in which we are interested have to have a direct bearing on current behavior. How do we know this? We infer this connection from our knowledge of human behavior. The principle of generalization is a pervasive one in all of human behavior. People tend to respond similarly to similar stimulus situations. If the child is avoidant of father, he will tend, also, to be avoidant of other older men. If a young lady sits before us with her legs twisted like a pretzel and avoids looking at us and then tells us that she had a very happy relationship throughout her life with her father and other important men in her life, we are very skeptical of what she says. The behavior we observe and the reports of her early experiences do not jibe.

The diagnostic interview is part of the psychological/psychiatric examination of the person. (The other part is psychological testing.) The data obtained in the interview are directly related to a number of variables. Some of these can be identified. We have already written of the biases and training of the interviewer. There are some less apparent factors that are worthy of consideration. Take, for instance, the first contact. The interviewee is taken to the Examiner's office or the Examiner goes to a waiting room where the prospective patient (the interviewee) is waiting. (I prefer this latter procedure.) This first contact is important. It sets the stage for the relationship.

The dress and the manner of the Examiner make an impact on the patient.

If the Examiner is barefooted and dressed in shorts, obviously, deviant from the establishment, the effect on the waiting patient is, to say the least, a readjustment, not to mention a most probable loss of confidence. The patient comes in for help. He expects to encounter a person at peace with himself and the world he lives in. The manner and dress of the Examiner must reflect this security. It is communicated to the patient. A courteous greeting, with the name of the patient, a warm handshake, help the patient make the transition from the waiting to the consulting room.

Consider the consulting room. The Examiner can sit behind a large and imposing desk and interpose this desk between himself and the patient—an effective physical and psychological barrier. He may have one of those cozy rooms with a "this is just entre-nous" atmosphere. The consulting room should be businesslike, but not harsh; comfortable, if it can be afforded. In any case, it should be just as comfortable for the patient as the Examiner. If one has a hard chair the other should. The seating arrangement should be such that there is no obstruction between patient and Examiner. If the Examiner sits behind a desk then the patient should sit *beside* the Examiner, not across the desk from him. The patient should be seated at a distance from the Examiner consonant with the mores of the culture, not too far, not too close. There are a number of studies which relate distance and attitudes in communication (Duncan, 1969). In general, the farther away the patient from the Examiner the more the expectation of negative attitudes. The patient should be asked to sit at an appropriate distance from the Examiner. See Figure 4-1.

The stage is set. We bring together a professional person, the Examiner, and a patient. The purpose of the meeting is a psychological examination. The meeting is conducted by the Examiner. The tactics of the encounter

FIGURE 4-1
Proxemics of the dyadic relationship

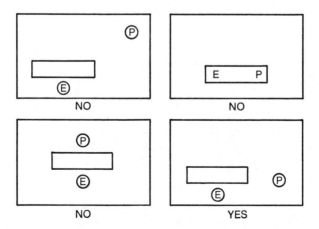

are those of the Examiner. This is not a democratic relationship. The Examiner has a job to do. The patient is seated in the consulting room. The Examiner proceeds to conduct the examination. The details of the procedure are the subjects of the next few chapters.

REFERENCES

Ausubel, D. T. *Theory and problem of child development.* New York: Grune & Stratton, 1948.

Deutsch, F., & Murphy, W. F. *The clinical interview,* Vol. One: *Diagnosis.* New York: International University Press, 1960, p. 11.

Duncan, S., Jr. Nonverbal communication. *Psychological Bulletin,* 1969, *72,* 118-137.

Garmezy, N., Clarke, A. P., & Stockner, C. Child rearing attitudes of mothers and fathers as reported by schizophrenic and normal patients. *Journal of Abnormal and Social Psychology,* 1961, *63,* 176.

Gesell, A., & Amatruda, C. *Developmental diagnosis.* New York: Paul B. Hoeber, 1962.

Pascal, G. R. *Behavioral change in the clinic—A systematic approach.* New York: Grune & Stratton, 1959.

Pascal, G. R., & Jenkins, W. O. *Systematic observation of human behavior.* New York: Grune & Stratton, 1961.

Piety, K. R. Perceptual dissonance and role learning. *Journal of Clinical Psychology,* 1966, *22,* 10.

5 | Direct observation

The purpose of this chapter is to bring to the clinician's attention those aspects of the interview that are not directly related to the verbal responses of the patient. We hear what the patient says but we also hear how he says it and we *see* how he behaves *when* he says it. We see what manner of person it is who is doing the saying. In this chapter we will consider nonlanguage communication. We are fortunate in having at hand four reviews of the literature by Mehrabian (1969), Duncan (1969), Siegman and Pope (1972), and Harper, Wiens, and Matarazzo (1978). George Mahl was kind enough to send us a working copy of his studies in "Gestures and Body Movements in Interviews" (1966).

The first and most obvious thing for the Examiner to do is to look at the patient. This statement may seem frivolous to you; yet, I have known Examiners who have been so busy writing what the patient says that they have had little time to observe the patient. Of course, we may need to write some things such as demographic facts but for the most part we must give the patient our undivided attention. The Examiner also needs to develop a "third ear" (Reik, 1948) so as to catch the nuances of verbal behavior. What to look for and what to listen for other than verbal responses form the content of this chapter. It is by learning to see and hear beyond the content of the patient's report that one develops the sixth sense of the good clinician.

You will, as a result of the diagnostic interview, be able to form an educated, clinical opinion about the emotional state of the patient. You will know whether or not he can be an outpatient. You will know how to plan for his treatment. How the patient dresses, his size, his behaviors during the inter-

39

view, and what he says will help you form your opinion. Let us begin with how the patient dresses.

One day, a few years ago, I went to the waiting room to see a young man, a new patient. All I knew about him before seeing him was obtained from the "intake form" filled out by the receptionist. He was 21, a college student, referred by Dr. X. I opened the waiting room door. There was a stench—an unwashed body odor. I shook hands with the young man. He was unshaven. Greasy, blond hair hung about his ears. His open shirt and trousers were soiled. He wore old moccasins with no socks. Was I prejudiced? I suppose I was. We had to spray the waiting room to get rid of the odor, and I later told him not to come back unless he got rid of the offensive odor. (Yes, he did wash and he did come back.) The only point in relating the incident is that the young man's appearance registered on me, became part of the data I used to come to a diagnostic conclusion. What registered? Was it aversion? Did I think he had contempt for me or no respect for himself? At the time I did not know but it became part of the interview to find out. As you probably have already guessed, his appearance was part of his rebellion. "You are to accept me no matter how dirty or how bad I smell."

In contrast to the young man cited above we have the person who is meticulously dressed. Is it compulsiveness? Is it to hide? I have known many alcoholics who, after three or four before breakfast drinks, dress to perfection. These are people who hide bottles around their living quarters. For each person you have a set of expectations as to dress and appearance based on the demographic data given. All deviations from these expectancies become considerations which are part of your diagnostic conclusions. This is *not* to say that you are to form a bias because of a person's appearance. Quite the contrary! You are to observe and keep an open mind but you must ask yourself why. Perhaps you don't like 60-year-old women with blond hair, high style, and much makeup, particularly if they have brassy voices. Your job is to find out, in the course of the interview, why they dress that way. The knowledge may have an important bearing on your clinical opinion.

It is quite common to find young clinicians who tend to disregard the datum of dress, either because they are not careful observers or because they feel that how a person dresses is of no consequence. In my experience how a person dresses is always a datum, even the nuances. The painstaking adherence or the flamboyant disregard for cultural norms in dress are too apparent, but how about the grown woman with the girlish hairdo, the slightly effeminate dress of the young man, or the overemphasis on masculinity such as wearing cowboy boots? A person's manner of dressing may have an important relationship to attitude-forming early experiences. It may not. In any case it surely may be related to the impression made on other people.

The human organism sitting in our consulting room is a specimen. He is a person offering himself for examination. It is our duty to observe what manner of specimen is being offered. In the human organism, compounded of heterogenous strains, appearance is an important variable. We have been at some length considering dress. What of the body that wears the clothing?

Body size is an inevitable factor in our relations with other people. It influences the course of our lives. Any youngster, male or female, who is markedly deviant from the norm in height, is a target. The undersized child struggles to compete with larger companions. The child overcompensates or withdraws from the physical arena, defeated. The struggle or the withdrawal leaves an indelible mark on the psyche which becomes a part of the admixture of the adult.

A former graduate student, now a colleague, is almost six feet, seven inches tall. When I first saw him I was struck by his posture. He stooped like a very old man. It was as if he were apologizing for his height. As a youngster he had been subjected to much ridicule for being outsized. He had the inferiority feelings to prove it. It was not until after psychotherapy that he was able to stand straight and enjoy the advantages of his height.

Marked deviation in height is a datum in the observation of the patient. The undersized man who says it made no difference in his life experiences is either repressive or suppressive. You know his height had something to do with his conception of self and his attitudes toward others. Do I need to go into the effects on a girl? Girls deviant in height, particularly very tall girls, are the objects of much ridicule from other girls.

What about body size, the very thin or very fat child? The appellations "skinny or fatso" are not exactly compliments. Body size, however, differs from height. It can be changed. Thus, the clinical judgment will depend on whether or not the person has a lifelong history of over- or underweight. If the deviation in body size has fluctuated then you will be concerned with factors related to these fluctuations. For instance, a young woman gets a divorce and then becomes fat. This reaction is depressive. It may imply she has given up being heterosexually acceptable.

A girl, a college student, sits before me in my consulting room. She has a pretty face but is grossly overweight. She tells me her problems—can't concentrate, poor grades. She admits she has few friends, no dates. Not one word about being overweight! It is as if a person with one leg would tell his problems without reference to his most obvious defect. What's with such a person?

What about the fat, jolly, ho-ho person? "Don't really look at me. I'm hiding here behind this layer of fat and I will not be discovered." Sometimes, with people like that I get the feeling that there is a small person peeking at me from behind a shield, looking to see how dangerous I am, ready to vanish at the slightest doubt. I have to remind myself to be *very* gentle.

Then there was the pretty girl with one eye. She wore an obvious prosthetic device where the eye should have been. She lost her eye at the age of six. Her parents and her doctor, she said, had taught her to adjust to the loss of her eye. It had made no difference in her life. Yet, she complained, she couldn't seem to get dates like other girls. She didn't feel as if she were accepted by her peer group. She wept.

Now, what had happened to this girl? She learned to feel accepted if she *behaved* as if she had *two* eyes. The scar on the psyche caused by the loss of the eye was covered. It did not heal. It continued to affect her behavior. The treatment for this girl was to uncover the layer of defenses over the scar. The scar had to be brought into the open to heal. The girl had to learn to accept herself as a person with one eye—that having only one eye *had* made her different but *not* unacceptable.

There is a reaction in people called psychomotor. It means that with every thought or feeling there is a corresponding motor reaction. This reaction is maximized in infants, diminishes with age, and is minimal with adults. Nevertheless, this reaction exists in adults to a greater or lesser degree. It manifests itself in facial expressions, movement of appendages, and in other more subtle ways such as flushing. The psychomotor reaction is, of course, the basis of the flare-up of interest in body language. In the diagnostic interview this body language is exhibited by the patient for the clinician to observe. It is a primary datum.

A young lady sits before me. Her legs are twisted around each other like a pretzel. She is stooped, her head close to her knees, her face averted from me. What is her body language telling me? If I were a casual observer I'd say she is obviously "uptight." To the clinician, however, she is telling much more.

Her overall posture approaches the fetal. Is she reaching for the womb? Most likely. Withdrawn and very depressed would be my opinion. Her legs are twisted around and holding onto each other. Are they held there to keep her from running away from me? What about her averted face? Yes, she fears me and wants to get away. She feels I am judging her negatively.

I, an old man, am the stimulus. She is reacting to me! Obviously, she doesn't see me, a kindly old man, not at all dangerous. I *have* to be a symbol of what—another old man, or all men? I don't know. What I *do* know is that reality testing in her is poor. Very poor! Her perception of me is based almost entirely on her past experiences with similar figures. Reality has little to do with her perception. But that is what a psychotic does! In her reaction to me, then, she is psychotic. Whether she is as far removed from reality in other stimulus situations remains to be determined.

Eye avoidance is a frequent reaction in patients. The least you can say about that reaction is that it is a movement away from the clinician—with the eyes. In my experience, eye avoidance is often related to feelings by the patient, that he is being adversely judged by the Examiner. Sometimes these feelings are accompanied by fear, sometimes by hostility.

In contrast to the eye-avoidant patient is the patient who will not take his eyes off of the Examiner. This reaction is often associated with paranoid alertness, and sometimes with deception (Sitton & Griffin, 1981). I had one lady patient who kept looking at me even when lying on the couch. She was afraid. She wanted to anticipate any sudden movement on my part, and, as she said, to see my reactions to what she was saying. Another patient, a schizoid man, stared at me during an entire interview. He was nonresponsive, verbally; he just stared.

The eye-avoidant patient and the one who stares at the Examiner represent significant deviations in the dyadic relationship. All body movements are noteworthy. Some are related to reactions to the clinician. Some are related to the patient's other problems, a tic for instance, or a woman slipping her wedding ring on and off her finger. Body language "talks" to the clinician whether it be the absence of movement in the psychomotor retardation of the psychotic depressive or the histrionic gestures of the hysteric.

Direct observation is also concerned with verbal behavior—such aspects as pitch, loudness, frequency, and appropriateness. The verbal behaviors dealt with in this chapter differ from verbalizations which *report* memories or experiences. Reported experiences are not directly observable by the Examiner but the *manner* in which they are reported *is*. Thus, a patient might say, "I killed my brother." Was the manner in which it was said appropriate to the content?

Sometimes we become so involved with the content of verbal behavior that we forget to observe accompanying behavior. I remember one graduate student who was interviewing a World War II veteran. The student became so enthralled by the veteran's war experiences that he was unaware that he was being taken on a diverting hayride.

Verbal content is the facade which can sometimes obscure verbal behavior. Content is important and the clinician needs to pay attention to it, but must also remain alert to its behavioral concommitants. Why is this patient talking so rapidly? Why is this one hesitant and searching for words? Why is another slurring his speech? Sometimes patients speak so softly that we have to strain to hear them. Others talk too loudly. All these deviations raise questions that need to be answered by more data.

Especially important is the logicalness of content. Obvious non sequiturs are easy to catch. Thus, if in response to "How are you?" the patient replies, "I'm 5 feet 10," the clinician's attention is easily aroused. More difficult are verbalizations indicating tangential thinking, suggestive of thought distortion. For instance, a patient is saying, "I lived with my mother all those years. Even though she sewed well I never had a tear in my pants." The patient then goes on to talk more about life with his mother.

Some patients seem logical in their verbal content. For the most part they stay with the topic under discussion. Every once in a while, however, their talk strays for just a short time to an unrelated topic. Then they come back to the original topic. Now, the clinician may hear this verbal disconnectedness but not pay attention to it or, really, disbelieve what he hears. Yet this sort of verbal behavior may be indicative of a psychosis the patient is trying to cover.

One important aspect of verbal behavior that needs to be observed is the affect displayed by the patient. Even the prototype of the "he-man," the strong, silent westerner showed *some* emotion, a tight smile, for instance. I know because as a child I watched silent films of the Old West. The point is that we *all* display emotion, however slightly. And, our display is appropriate to the verbal content, a happy mien with joyous content, and sad with sad content.

One of the most easily observed deviations in affective display is inappropriateness. Recently I interviewed a married woman who talked about her years of unhappiness with her marriage and about her husband's peccadilloes. She laughed frequently when talking about her husband's boyish behaviors. Of course I reacted, and when I did she wept. I was glad for her because if she had persisted with her laughing I would have judged her seriously disturbed, either possibly psychotic or a dangerous, smiling depressive.

In the initial interview we, as clinicians, have the responsibility of determining whether or not the patient is potentially dangerous to self or to others. A case in point is the smiling depressive. We interview a recently divorced man. He looks at us and matter of factly tells us his wife left, taking the children. He now lives in an apartment, spends his evenings and weekends alone. He loves his wife and children. He doesn't blame his wife. He is working every day. He feels fine except he is suffering from insomnia. He smiles reassuringly at the Examiner. Occasionally, he grips the arms of the chair. We try to elicit emotions, by suggesting he must be lonely, and so on. He denies this, smiling. All he wants is help with his sleeping. No, no dreams. No, no alcohol. Does he go to church? Not anymore. What the hell are all these questions about? The flare-up of anger is followed by a reassuring smile. He's OK, just can't sleep.

So what? you say. Can a man not have the fortitude to bear his grief in silence? Of course, he can. He can channel the repressed emotions into work, physical illness, religion, even the social treadmill or, a psychosis. But the emotions have to go *somewhere!* And here is where the clinician needs to hang onto his knowledge of human nature. The clinician must not be deceived by the patient's apparent behavior. We *know* the human organism reacts to profound stimulus change.

Here is a man who, before his wife left him, enjoyed family life, socialized, and went to church. Now he lives alone, no wife, no children, no social life. He just works eight hours a day. Is he reacting? We know it, no matter what he says. He not only says he's fine but he smiles about it! This is inappropriate affect. There is also tension, revealed by the tight grip on the chair arms. There is also the flare-up of unreasonable anger. Is this man potentially dangerous to himself or others? We think so. There are enough indications of the possibility to warrant immediate treatment.

Affective display can also be inappropriate by its absence or by being "flattened." The expression "flattened affect" refers to a minimal affective display. Thus, a paranoid psychotic might tell how he cut someone's throat in a matter-of-fact voice. No affect. Flattened affect is often displayed by depressives. Tragic experiences are related in a monotone, showing little change in loudness and pitch.

The classical "belle indifference" of the conversion hysteric is rarely seen these days. (I had one about 20 years ago, a piano player who calmly announced that his hands were paralyzed.) What we do see, however, are cases of heightened affect. The patient is overreactive with fluctuating loudness and pitch and other histrionic behaviors. These behaviors are characteristic of hysterics and other overemotional individuals.

We have discussed the topic of affective display at some length because of its diagnostic importance. If there is one observation in the diagnostic interview that can be likened, by analogy, to a vital sign in medicine, it is the observation of affect. But there are others. One of these psychological "vital signs" is the reality contact of the patient. We have mentioned this topic in discussing the logicalness of verbal response but now we shall examine it more specifically.

It is not enough to know that a patient is oriented for time, place, and person, that is, knows when, where, and what he or she is. A person comes or is sent for consultation about a personal problem. The patient refuses to answer personal questions. Not very realistic, is it? It is like going to a physician for a complete physical and refusing to take off your clothes. It is also unrealistic for a young man who is five feet, six inches tall to say he is going to be a professional basketball player. What about a 13-year-old girl who refuses to sleep alone because she sees men peering into her window?

Such observations are judged to indicate emotional disturbance, the severity of the disturbance being tempered by other considerations. For instance, in the case of the 13-year-old girl, we discover that her mother double locks all doors, has a burglar alarm, and won't stay by herself at night. This information plus the girl's expressed hostility toward her mother tempers our judgment about the presence of hallucinations.

However, when a middle-aged lady, a bookkeeper, tells us with the utmost seriousness that her telephone is tapped and that she is under constant surveillance by the police despite repeated protests to the FBI, we are immediately concerned. When we ask questions trying to establish the reasonableness of her assertions, she persists in her allegations against the police. In fact, she perseverates. We conclude she has a delusionary system, indicative of a paranoid state. The key, here, is the manner in which she perseverated. She was given many opportunities to accept the possibility that she might be wrong. She would admit of no reality except that of her convictions.

The person afflicted with a hand-washing compulsion is also not very realistic. The difference between this person and a psychotic is that he will admit that it doesn't make sense to wash his hands as often as he does. In obsessed patients there is often a thin line between psychosis and neurosis. A patient I had ruminated constantly on his inadequacy as a male, focused on the size of his penis. He believed that girls avoided him because they knew he was inadequate. Yet, he could admit that this belief might be a projection of his own feelings about himself. If he were convinced that girls *did* know about his inadequacy, then he would be verging on psychosis. I have seen psychotic patients with hypochondriasis as a primary symptom. For these patients, the physical symptom is real. No amount of medical evidence will convince them that it is not.

A case I had comes to mind. A woman was a reputable, physical scientist in a famous national laboratory. She reported to the medical division with the complaint that she was losing energy. She felt that her loss of energy was related to the chemicals being used in her lab. A thorough medical examination could reveal no organic basis for her complaints. She was sent to me. I found her essentially psychotic, although other than her physical complaint her behavior was not deviant.

My diagnosis was partially based on the fact that she would not admit the possibility of any reality other than her conviction about her illness. I recommended psychotherapy. But, against my advice, a team of physicians presented their medical findings to the patient in detail, appealing to her objectivity as a scientist. She accepted their findings and she cracked. Her psychosis became full blown. She was committed to a mental hospital.

Yes, the determination of whether or not a patient is reality oriented has many facets. Everyone tends to distort reality somewhat. The perception of the real world outside ourselves can be thought of as a continuum running from the complete denial of reality exhibited by a hebephrenic to the objectivity of the observations of a physical scientist in his laboratory. All of us are encapsulated in our emotional past. The translucence of the capsule varies with a number of factors such as stress and physical trauma. For most people, however, the capsule remains reasonably clear so that we can see the outside world. It is when the capsule becomes opaque that one considers the person divorced from reality, and psychotic.

What has been discussed in this chapter, is what you will be observing with your eyes and ears while conducting the interview. You do not ask questions about these observations. You do not, for instance, ask the patient about his affect or reality contact. You *do* ask him about his complaints, physical health, contacts with others, and other pertinent areas. It is while the patient is responding to your inquiries that you observe him.

The judgments you form on the basis of direct observations of behaviors discussed in this chapter are a measure of the patient.

I remember when I first went to the east Tennessee area. My students took practicum at the Veterans Administration Outpatient Psychiatric Clinic and I was the consultant. I was puzzled by the fact that we were diagnosing so many simple schizophrenics. It was not until I consulted a professor of sociology at the University of Tennessee that I discovered that the behaviors displayed by the mountain people whom I had diagnosed as simple schizos were part of their cultural heritage. They always acted that way with "furriners."

The point is that we judge *all* people on the basis of our own background and knowledge of the culture of those we are judging. In this chapter, I have tried to make explicit these judgments; and to point out in what areas it is necessary, that we carefully observe behaviors if we are to make valid diagnoses.

In reflecting on the contents of this chapter think of yourself in a courtroom where you are required to testify about a patient with no knowledge of the patient except that which you have obtained in the interview. You are not allowed to testify about what the patient said he did or didn't do. That is called heresay. You can only testify as to what you have directly observed. That, and that only, can be the basis on which you formed your clinical opinion.

To summarize: You first looked at the patient, observing dress, height, weight, and visible body defects. You watched body movements, interpreting body language. You listened to verbal behavior for loudness, pitch, and fluctuations. You took particular notice of the patient's display of affect. Was it appropriate? Was it absent or flattened? Finally, you judged whether the overall nonverbal behavior and verbal behavior were indicative of good or poor reality contact.

REFERENCES

Duncan, S., Jr. Nonverbal communication. *Psychological Bulletin*, 1969, *72*, 118-137.

Harper, R. G., Wiens, A. N., & Matarazzo, J. D. *Nonverbal communication: The state of the art.* New York: John Wiley & Sons, 1978.

Mahl, G. F. Gestures and body movements in interviews. Paper prepared for Third Research in Psychotherapy Conference, Chicago, June 1-4, 1966.

Mehrabian, A. Significance of posture and position in the communication of attitude and status relationships. *Psychological Bulletin*, 1969, *71*, 359-372.

Reik, T. *Listening with the third ear.* New York: Farrar & Straus, 1948.

Siegman, A. W., & Pope, B. (Eds.). *Studies in dyadic communication.* Elmsford, N.Y.: Pergamon Press, 1972.

Sitton, S. C. & Griffin, S. I. Detection of deception from client's eye contact patterns. *Journal of Counseling Psychology*, 1981, *28*, 269-271.

6 | Current behaviors

The patient eats, sleeps, works, reacts to situations and people. Are his behaviors within expectancy limits, or does the patient deviate? If the patient does deviate, where? Bear in mind that the expectancy limits are within you. *You* are the measuring instrument. The more you are part of the larger world around you, the more knowledgeable you are about religious and social subcultures, the better your judgments. Thus, if you belong to a religious subculture that believes masturbation is a sin and your expectancies derive solely from your religious beliefs then you will be wrong about most people. You get my point. This is not the place to bring up, again, the characteristics of the Examiner, but I cannot help but feel that it is important enough to wear it down to the point of redundancy.

Now the interview begins. Some patients need no prompting but begin immediately with their complaints. Others are hesitant and need help. You could, for instance, say, "What brings you in to see me?" or, "How have you been?" Usually, that little bit of prompting will start them. Some patients have difficulty in talking. In such cases, you can ask if they mind being questioned. In such a situation I usually begin with their physical health, an area that is not threatening to most people.

Your attitude is one of a dispassionate observer, constantly judging what you see and hear. The patient is an organism. His environment impinges upon him. What is the nature of that environment and how does the patient react to it? The why of the subject's reactions come later in the interview—from early history data.

As indicated above, we begin with an area that most people do not mind talking about, their physical health. The topic of physical health is not only easy for the patient to talk about, it is also of first importance to the Examiner. It may be, as the Examiner should know, that the patient's psychological problems stem from an organic base. This knowledge needs to be acquired before undertaking the diagnostic interview.

The patient is asked about his last physical examination—when, by whom, and how thorough? Need I add that if the patient has never had a physical or not had one recently, that he should be referred for a complete physical? Do it! No telling, for instance, how many "psychasthenic" patients have merely been suffering from hypothyroidism.[1]

This seems the place to tell of the experience of one of my former teachers, a well-known psychoanalyst, now deceased. He had a very famous person in analysis. Unbeknownst to the analyst or his patient, the patient's symptoms derived from a brain tumor from which the patient died, while undergoing analysis.

In this chapter we are trying to find out how the patient is operating in his environmental milieu. I could outline the topics we will cover but I won't. I feel that the worker should know the areas he needs to cover so well, that he naturally will obtain the necessary information. Think of these first behaviors we are interested in as operant. In fact, in a previous book (Pascal & Jenkins, 1961), I did so label these behaviors. These behaviors occur without readily apparent stimuli. In order to remember these behaviors think of yourself, your own "operant" behaviors. You eat, sleep, drink, smoke, and so forth.

So you have asked the patient how he feels. He has either responded with an account of his psychological or physical problems. After you have listened to the complaints, you proceed with inquiries concerning health. You ask about aches and pains, headaches, gastrointestinal upsets, and so on. With women you inquire about menstrual cramps. In asking these questions, you are obviously displaying an interest in the patient—a concern. You are "establishing rapport," a rapport you will need when you get to more sensitive areas.

It's a natural transition to go from aches and pains to questions about appetite and typical diet. Nowadays with much ado about the effects of nutrition on human well-being, with megavitamin treatment, and even the specificity of vitamin lack and psychological symptoms, we need to find out about the patient's food intake. There is a good deal of evidence (Fredericks, 1976) which indicates that malnutrition and subsequent psychological symptoms can occur even with ample food intake.

As long as you're in the oral area it is easy to inquire concerning smoking and drinking habits. What and how much? In this area you will also be concerned with drug intake. Is there addiction? I remember a middle-aged secre-

---

[1] For the reader unfamiliar with psychosomatic medicine, Chapter 9 by Saslow and Matarazzo, in Berg and Pennington (Eds.), *An Introduction to Clinical Psychology,* provides a good summary (Saslow & Matarazzo, 1966). For a more recent and thorough coverage, see Christie and Mellet (1981).

tary who came in with vague complaints. I discovered that she was taking 100 aspirins a day! If you don't ask, you'll never know. If it seems to you that this is a sensitive area for the patient, a good approach is to ask what the patient takes when he feels a cold coming, gets a stomach upset, or just feels nervous.

You have at this point satisfied yourself about oral intake. You now ask about sleeping habits. Does the patient sleep well? How long, on the average? Anything peculiar about the conditions under which sleeping occurs such as preconditions? I once had a patient who had to be sure his bowels were completely empty before he could go to sleep, even if it took two hours! It is not only rituals you are interested in but also sleeping aids.

While you are on the topic of sleep you ask about dreams. At this point, you don't know enough about the patient to interpret properly, but many dreams are easily interpreted, and very revealing. Thus, there are any number of anxiety dreams, such as dreams of falling off of a high place. Dreams of frustration, helplessness, and fear are common—attempting to get somewhere and never making it, fighting someone without impact on the foe, a girl with dreams of threatening snakes. All dreams are of some significance. Recurring dreams are of particular significance. The Examiner needs to have knowledge of dream interpretation.

So far we have covered physical health, oral intake, and sleeping behavior. We now proceed to a quick rundown of daily activities including weekends— more "operant" behaviors. What does the patient do after getting out of bed in the morning? Does the patient have to have a cup of coffee before he can move? Then what? Setting up activities? Morning ablutions? Breakfast? Work or whatever? Let the patient tell you. How does he spend his evenings, weekends? Is he an active person, sedentary? At this point in the interview, we are trying to get some notion of the person's activity level, not only physical but also psychosocial. How involved is he in the life about him? What does he do on his own, when no demands are made? How can I make it clear? You want to get a feel for the patient's *èlan vital:* you are not really interested in the specifics of his behaviors at this time but rather you want some notion of the patient's *life force,* his adaptive capacity. Does the patient do only what is necessary to stay alive? How much more does he put into his life?

Up to this point we have been concerned with behaviors for which there are no readily apparent stimuli. We now go on to investigate the stimulus situations encountered and the patient's responses to them. We begin with the patient's main occupation.

You don't begin by asking the person how he likes his job. If you do you will most likely get the culturally expected response—"Just fine." Keep in mind the admonitions in Chapter 2. You want to know if his main occupation is a source of support, a life satisfaction, an ego builder, or is it the reverse? You might say, "So you're a civil engineer?" and wait for the response. If it is noncommittal then you might say, "What hours do you put in?" or "Can you tell me what you do on the job?" The point is to get the patient talking about work, the people involved, working conditions and satisfactions, including remuneration.

This is an area too often easily dismissed by the inexperienced Examiner. Contrast the professional person who willingly gives to his work and enjoys it, with the worker who grudgingly gives as little as possible. The first has identity, pride, a reason for being. The second has little sense of worth, no feeling of belonging from his work. A person who has no vocation and no vocational goals is adrift in our work-ethic society, a misfit, a focus for opprobrium. Even the housewife and mother who would rather be doing some other kind of work dare not downgrade her job. If you ask, "How do you like your job?" you will get "Fine!" So, don't ask that. Just get the person talking about work and find out how he feels about it. From these feelings you judge whether work is supportive or stressful. Sometimes it is a means to an end; for instance, the man who works so that he can afford to go fishing.

It is surprising how often the unemployed person is quite content with the things he does instead of a regular job. With some unemployed, it seems as if not working at a job is a vocation in itself. Most, however, will give the impression that they subscribe to the work ethic and want to work, if they could get a job or are able to work.

Not long ago I had referred to me a man complaining of back pains. He had suffered an injury to his back several months ago and now couldn't work. Physical findings were negative. The man used crutches. He was angry at being sent for a psychological examination, protesting that he wanted to go back to work as soon as he was able. When I got him to tell me how he liked "not working," I got the impression very quickly that a wife who had been demanding was now made to wait on him "hand and foot." Need I say more?

Then there was the case of the single girl in her 20s who came in because she couldn't stand her job any longer. It was a good paying job in work she liked and she couldn't afford to quit. I found out that her previous superior had been a kindly, fatherly figure in whom she could confide. He was replaced by a cool, efficient young man. This young lady was really distressed, couldn't sleep, cried a lot, felt life was not worth living. She had no boyfriends, few women friends; she worked and went to her apartment. She had lived in the warmth and acceptance of the older man superior who was now gone. She grieved for her father figure now lost to her. Of course, she didn't know that; she just hated her job.

The point in the examples is to illustrate the importance of going beyond the facts of employment, or unemployment. In so doing the Examiner easily can go on to obtain information about avocational activities. Sometimes a person gets very little satisfaction from the work he does to earn a living. His satisfaction, his pride and identity are in his avocation. The avocation can be in any area, just so long as the person is emotionally involved.

A government inspector tells of his work, giving the impression that it is prosaic, dull. When he talks of his hobby, woodworking, his eyes light up. Every night, after supper, he retreats to his shop and stays there until bedtime! (Meanwhile, his bored wife is watching TV.) A sport can qualify if it is more than a source of exercise and companionship. Thus, a golfer who practices in his spare time, who enters tournaments, whose sense of belonging is with other golfers, has a satisfying avocation. The idea, of course, is to find out if the avocation is an environmental support, particularly in those people who get no satisfaction from their jobs, or who are unemployed.

We go on now with other possible activities of the patient. Our studies have shown (Chapter 3), that church attendance can be an important source of environmental support. We are not concerned here with the religious aspect of church attendance, but rather the social implications. It means little if the patient's church attendance is perfunctory, something he does every Sunday morning. It can mean much to him if he participates in the church's activities, finds his friends and a sense of belonging in the church. The same is true, but to a lesser extent, of other organizational activities, social and civic. Does the housewife sit and watch soap operas all day or does she have coffee with friends and neighbors, belong to a bridge club, garden club, and so on? Does the man belong to and contribute to the social life about him or, as our friend cited above, does he escape to his workshop? The same sort of information is obtained from unmarried working people and students.

Thus far, we have only casually touched upon the patient's relations with people. Hopefully, by this time rapport has been established and we are in a better position to proceed to more sensitive areas of behavior. We want to know about the people in the patient's environment and his reactions to them. We begin with peripheral people; that is, casual friends, and then go on to people more intimately associated with our patient, his wife, for instance.

If you ask the patient, "Do you have any friends?" you will get the culturally correct answer, yes. Instead, you ask about people he sees often. What do they do together? How often? You want to find out if the patient feels accepted, gets emotional support from others. This information is particularly important for a single individual living away from family or without family. Has he anyone with whom he can relate, confide in?

The family comes next. I have found it convenient at this point to inquire about living arrangements. Who is living with the patient and their relationships? What are sleeping arrangements? In this way I found out, almost casually, that a 15-year-old boy was still sleeping with his mother! Are mother and father alive? Where do they live? What is the frequency of contact? What happens on contact? The same information is obtained about siblings and other important relatives.

At the risk of being redundant, I again call your attention to the method of interviewing. Remember, you want behavioral incidents, enough to make up your own mind about a particular relationship. Too often Examiners accept the patient's judgment. That is what you are doing when, for instance, you ask the patient how he is getting along with his mother. You do not ask such leading questions. Instead, you find out where the mother lives. When did the patient see her last? What happened? How did they greet each other? What was said, and so on. Then go on to previous contacts with the mother, eliciting the same kind of data until you are satisfied to pass judgment on the nature of the relationship.

If a person is married and has children, the relationship between them and the patient is an important area of inquiry. Are the children a source of environmental satisfaction or stress? I remember a case, a new mother who was brought in because she had a phobia about her kitchen. She panicked in the kitchen. Especially, she could not go near where the knives were kept. She went on at length about her newborn, about how she would let no one else take care of the baby, about how she rejected time out, and so on. It was too much! As you've already surmised, she hated the baby and the knives were connected with her unconscious desire to do away with the baby. Yes, children have a profound impact on the parents and are an important area of inquiry.

We come now to a sensitive topic—the heterosexual relationship. By this time I hope you have grasped the method of interviewing well enough so that you would not ask, "How do you get along with your spouse?" I have used something like, "What is your spouse like?" I remember a patient, a married man, to whom I put that question. He responded with a glowing account of his wife, what a lovely, upstanding person she was, and so forth. If I had been satisfied with his response I would have been left with the impression that he and his wife had a beautiful relationship. Instead, I proceeded with questions about daily behaviors, such as what happened when he got home at night, how did they greet each other. I found that the man thought his wife self-indulgent, neglectful of him, and that he carried a lot of unexpressed resentment toward her. In fact, he had a paramour about whom he was very serious.

For married persons, the spouse is, in most cases, the most important stimulus in the environment. In thinking back over my practice through the years I can't remember a single case in which an emotionally disturbed married person had a satisfying relationship with his spouse. Now, that statement is not to imply cause and effect, rather it is meant to illustrate how important and how sensitive is the relationship between husband and wife. A good relationship can be very supportive just as a poor relationship can be emotionally destructive. The keys to the relationship are in the nuances of behavior. Is there standing up affection? Is affection only shown when the couple are lying down preparatory to sex? Is there communication, a mutual exchange of each others' activities and thought, or does one burden the other with daily problems? Is there a sharing of household duties and concern? Who leads whom?

Sex relations are of particular concern. It is surprising how often this area is neglected by the student Examiner, yet no area is more sensitive to the relationship between husband and wife. Also surprising is how difficult it is for most couples to discuss their feelings in this area. Even seemingly sophisticated couples have difficulty in talking about sex to each other. We know how susceptible the sexual response is to emotional influences. Thus the man with contained hostility toward his wife may become impotent. The wife who feels unappreciated and gets no affection in the daytime may not be very responsive in bed. It is necessary for the Examiner to inquire into the details of the sex act, the foreplay, the responses and feelings before, during, and after.

I am reminded of a case involving a physician and his wife, a former nurse. They had two children, had been married 10 years. The wife had recently been hospitalized for a variety of symptoms: extreme nervousness, inability to sit still, insomnia, irritability, impatience with the children, frequent uncontrollable emotional outbursts. No physical bases for her condition could be found. She had had psychiatric care. On examination by me she painted a picture of a loving husband and general satisfaction with her life. She had no complaints except her irritability and lack of patience with things and people. To make a long story short, it was not until I began to probe into the details of her sex life that I discovered that this poor woman had been pretending orgasm for 10 years! There was little foreplay in the sex act. A couple of kisses and her husband began. He was soon finished and she was left—frustrated. This procedure went on two or three times a week. This had to be what Freud, somewhere in his works, called the true neurosis. In any case, with the aid of her husband she was easily treated and made symptom free.

Yes, careful inquiry into the details of the sex relationship is important. Unmarried adults (and nowadays, teenagers) are also subjected to the same questioning. You will want to know if the single person is capable of a satisfying heterosexual relationship. The successful sex act does not, in itself, imply a satisfying heterosexual relationship. It takes more—companionship, ability to communicate, mutual respect, and tolerance. In my experience so many unmarried females easily trade sex for a little affection and acceptance. So many unmarried men seek solace for the unrequited need for succorance from a female in the sexual act. It takes more than mere sex to qualify for a satisfactory heterosexual relationship.

Inquiry needs to be made concerning masturbation. It is a natural activity practiced by practically all men and most women. If masturbation is a form of self-love, then more men seem to love themselves than women. I suppose this difference has its roots in our cultural upbringing but it is revealing to observe how many women feel negatively about their genitalia. They become indignant or act repulsed by the suggestion that they might masturbate. So often women who have never masturbated have sex problems. They seem to have a deep-seated rejection of their sexuality. What does the person think about during masturbation? I once had a male patient who thought of being dressed in girl's clothing during the act. Are the thoughts heterosexual? How frequent is masturbation? In some patients masturbation becomes addictive, analogous to compensatory overeating.

There is one final area of sexual behavior that needs to be investigated. It is a topic about which many interviewers are hesitant. Yet, it is necessary to find out if the patient is a homosexual or homosexually inclined. Although we are presently discussing current behavior this particular topic is often best approached from past history. The patient can be reminded that children often play "doctor" and investigate each other sexually. Something can also be said about how common it is for children to display some form of homosexual behavior. Then the Examiner can go on to inquire about other instances of homosexual behavior, leading up to the present.

There are varieties of homosexual behavior. There is the man who under conditions of extreme sexual deprivation will allow fellatio to be practiced on him. Such a man is most often heterosexual. Then there are men who can be bisexual. Very often they indulge in mutual fellatio. Probably at the extreme of this continuum is the homosexual queen who uses his anus as a substitute vagina. The prognosis for change from homosexual to heterosexual behavior with psychotherapy is probably related to this continuum. In females, too, there is most likely such a continuum ranging from the mutual stimulation of girls deprived of males to that of a "male-female" type relationship in which one female assumes the role of the male.

Now is the time to stop your interviewing. Go over in your mind all the areas of daily living. Have you covered health, eating, drinking, sleeping, dreaming, and all the other activities for which the stimuli are not so apparent? What about job, leisure activities, organizations, important people? Do you have a good grasp of how the person is functioning in his environments?

The important goal in the interview is to cover the areas. The sequence in which these areas are covered is not, in itself, of great moment. I have indicated that it is most often less threatening for the patient if matters of health and other "operants" are investigated first, the interviewer then proceeding to more sensitive areas. What is more important than sequence, however, is the free flow of the interview. If the interviewer rigidly follows an interview guide the session is apt to degenerate into a question and answer one. Within the limitations of the need to obtain the data, the Examiner gives the patient his "head," gently, so to speak, leading him into the areas of interest. Because the interview most often does not follow the sequence here presented, the Examiner at this point needs to check over the areas in his mind to determine if he has indeed secured the information he needs to make clinical judgments.

An interview guide is provided in Appendix II. The worker may, at first, need to check off the areas in order to avoid omissions. Very shortly, however, he will find that the topics of the guide are easily remembered. All one has to do is relate these to one's own daily activities. Another word about Appendix II, I have included an abbreviated manual for the interview. It was developed for sociology graduate students who were doing a survey of the adjustment of individuals on a house-to-house basis. In statistical use of the guide they marked the items of the guide plus or minus, counted and then rank ordered. What they did compared very favorably with the judgments of experienced clinicians using the same interview data.

Let us get back to the end of this part of the total diagnostic interview. This final part of current behavior is more subjective in the sense that we are not concerned here with behavioral incidents. Rather, the patient is asked to express his feelings. How does he perceive the future? What happens from here on out? Does he have any plans? Are the plans realistic? Will he take charge of himself or others? What are his apprehensions? What worries him most? How does he view his problems? Any insight? The patient has told you how he is getting along in the world. Would he like to do differently? What and how? Does he want the environment changed or himself?

A certain amount of depression accompanies almost all deviant behavior. What we are concerned with, of course, are suicidal tendencies. How does the patient feel about his life? Does he feel that it is worth living? How do these feelings compare with what he has told you previously?

In the next chapter, we will consider what you do with the information thus far obtained. In essence, we have concluded with what is often called the intake interview. It is usually after this interview that a decision is made about whether or not the patient can be treated on an outpatient basis, whether or not he should be hospitalized, or he should be referred for physical examination and/or a neurological.

REFERENCES

Christie, M. J., & Mellett, P. (Eds.). *Foundations of psychosomatics.* New York: John Wiley & Sons, 1981.

Fredericks, C. *Psycho-nutrition.* New York: Grosset & Dunlap, 1976.

Matarazzo, J. D. The interview. In B. B. Wolman (Ed.) *Handbook of clinical psychology* (Chap. 17). New York: McGraw-Hill, 1965.

Pascal, G. R., & Jenkins, W. O. *Systematic observation of gross human behavior.* New York: Grune & Stratton, 1961.

Saslow, G., & Matarazzo, J. D. Psychosomatic phenomena. In I. A. Berg, & L. A. Pennington, (Eds.), *An introduction to clinical psychology* (Chap. 9). New York: Ronald Press, 1966.

7 | Decisions

You now should have sufficient data to make some decisions about the person you have been interviewing. Can the person manage his own affairs? Does he need to be hospitalized? Is he dangerous to himself or others? Does he need to be referred to another discipline; for example, internal medicine, neurology? Can he be treated by you? And, finally, is further study required before you can make these determinations?

At this point in our study of the person, we are not interested particularly in specific diagnostic categories such as paranoid schizophrenia or hysterical neurosis. Rather, we are concerned with very practical matters. If you are in private practice or doing an intake in an outpatient clinic, can you safely treat the patient as an outpatient? Is medication indicated? If the patient is a candidate for admission to a hospital, decisions also have to be made. Is emergency treatment required? What placement? What temporary regimen?

Whatever diagnosis is made at this point should be provisional and descriptive. It should communicate your impressions and have provisional implications for treatment and prognosis. (Only further study will suggest the "best-fit" diagnosis.) For instance, a provisional diagnosis of depressive neurosis-suicidal will indicate the necessary immediate care for the patient. If you write as your provisional diagnosis "hysterical manifestations in a basically paranoid personality" it also will communicate. All I am suggesting is a summary in diagnostic jargon that will be meaningful to you and other professionals.

Before going on to the specifics of the decision-making process I would like to present some basic principles I have found helpful. This part of the diagnostic procedure is concerned with practical considerations such as what do we do right now. In order to answer this question we need to have a grasp of the nature and seriousness of the patient's disorder.

I can think of three basic continua: (1) the depressive, danger to self; (2) the paranoid, danger to others; and (3) the manic-depressive, manic, danger to property. Whether or not characteristics of the person eventuate into dangerously deviant behavior depends on the seriousness of the disorder.

How then, do we determine the seriousness of the disorder? Obviously, since the diagnostic impressions are subjective, the Examiner has to gain experience with himself as the measuring rod. But experience has to start somewhere. In thinking it over it seems to me that the best way to start is to take a quantitative approach, the greater the number of deviations the more serious the disorder.

Everybody has problems. The "crazy" people in mental hospitals have the same type of problems we so-called normals have. Why not? They are people. Everybody gets depressed sometimes, suspicious, and maybe slightly paranoid. Under certain circumstances we may get euphoric and impulsive. What's the difference between us and the psychotics? Stress seems to account for most of the difference, stress internal or external. For internal stress count alcohol, other drugs, and tissue change through disease or trauma. For external stress count enforced fatigue; for example, battle fatigue, brainwashing procedures, and "voluntary" isolation with internalization of problems.

From interview data how do we measure the effects of these possible "causes" on the individual patient? All we have are our observations of the patient and our judgment. Let us begin with the mental status observations.

It's easy to agree on the extremes. When a person is "way out" on every observation we have no trouble making a decision about the seriousness of his disorder. Behaviorally, as an example of an extreme, I think of the mute catatonic, his masklife facies, often displaying waxy flexibility. Verbally, the delusions of a paranoid told with utmost seriousness come to mind. These extremes cause us little trouble in arriving at a provisional diagnosis. Nor do we have too much trouble with people who "tell it all." They tell us quite readily how they have thought of suicide or maybe how they have thought of committing murder. They ask for help. They want to know what is wrong with them and what they should do about it.

The people who cause us trouble are those who cannot help being defensive. Even if they come in for help they put up a good front. They can't quite bring themselves to admit weaknesses. I remember a case that is pertinent here. A man in his early 40s, a business executive, said his wife had persuaded him to see me. He was a likable person. He talked easily and logically. He was oriented. Affect was appropriate. There was evidence of some tension manifested in finger movements but I, at the time, attributed it to interview-stress. There was also a quick, mirthless deprecating laugh when he was telling some things about himself but, again, I did not make too much of it. Outside of a confessed nervousness about all the plane trips he had to make in his business, I could find little wrong with him. It was this "nervousness" that his wife was reacting to, and, he said, she was making too much of it. I must confess that at the time I was at a loss. I knew that he was somehow "not right." He was making light of himself. In a sense, for a man who was taking the time and spending the money to submit to a psychological examination he was too cavalier.

At about that time he produced a cigarette. He was reaching in his pocket when I produced my lighter and held it out to him. He refused it and produced a packet of paper matches. With a smile he explained to me that there were 20 cigarettes in a pack and 20 matches in the packet. He used one packet of paper matches per pack of cigarettes. No more and no less! I just looked at him. He was serious! It came over me. This man had done a fine "snow job" on me. Then I confronted him, accusing him of concealing his true feelings. When I did that, he broke down, revealing the panic he felt about airplane travel, how his wife had had to accompany him on his last several trips, how depressed he had been, and how this had affected his sexual potency!

With the case just cited I mean to illustrate that sometimes minor deviancies add up to an impression that something is wrong. Another case comes to mind. In this one I want to show how the mental status indicators (affect, logic, and so on) can cluster around one area and lead to a diagnostic impression. The man was a dentist. Again, he was a person who said he came in to please his wife. Suffice it to say that he checked out well in all areas except on one topic. He believed that he could learn the Bible, verbatim, by listening to tapes while he slept. That, in itself, was not so far out. There *had* been some publicized research in the area. It was the inappropriate intensity of affect with which he told me of his efforts in that direction. He stared. He gripped the arms of his chair. Then suddenly he lapsed back into his easy affability. To make a long story short, this man had been sniffing nitrous oxide each day after his last patient. His wife had urged him to come in after noticing a personality change.

By far the most frequent type of case is the one where the person wants help but doesn't know what is bothering him. The medical doctor can find nothing wrong with him. All the patient knows is that he feels depressed, tired, can't sleep, or whatever. Now, here is where the quantitative approach I am suggesting really helps.

How is the person functioning in interactions between himself and his job, family, friends, and the community in which he lives? Is he responding "normally"? What is he missing of the environmental satisfactions that we all need? In Chapter 3 I cited studies indicating a direct relationship between seriousness of disorder and environmental deprivation. The extreme, of course, is the person with no job, no family, no friend, no activities except those centered around his own survival needs. (In some extreme cases even this last is missing.) At the other extreme is the person who, in spite of complaints, seems to be well-adjusted to his job, family, and community. If he is functioning that well in his community, then what? Either his complaints are due to something physical or there is something else to be uncovered.

You must remember that emotional problems *do* manifest themselves in the behavior of the organism, either overtly or covertly. If the manifestation is overt, then deviancies in behavior in the interactions with the environment will emerge; for example, deviancies in response to job demands, wife, friends. At what we have called the operant level, deviancies in personal cleanliness, eating, sleeping, and so on can be detected. Less specifically, overt deviancies can be observed in nonverbal behaviors during the interview. Although these nonverbal acts may not pinpoint problem areas, noted deviancies can lead the Examiner to more specific overt behavior. This was the case with the obsessive-compulsive behavior of the man who matched paper matches and cigarettes. Noted deviancies in all aspects of the interview, however small, add to something wrong. In cases where the patient is not revealing, the astuteness of the Examiner is put to test. He must tick off, in his mind, the number and areas of minor deviancies. Very often, personality disorders can only be detected in this way.

By covert responses I mean to imply those responses to emotional problems not visually observable without instrumentation. Most often these responses are somatic, but not always. Sometimes, even a psychological reaction can only be detected with an instrument such as the Rorschach test. Fortunately most somatic disorders have their behavioral counterparts, even if no more than going-to-the-doctor, or drug-taking behavior. But, again, not always!

I am reminded of another case where vague complaints of the patient led nowhere as far as detectable deviancies of behavior were concerned. Neurological examination, however, led to the discovery of a growing midbrain tumor. This example leads into a point I wish to emphasize. If careful study by you, via interview, does not uncover *any* behavioral deviancies, then referral to another discipline should be considered.

Of course, as I indicated above, most somatic disorders have their behavioral manifestations. Of particular concern to us are those somatic disorders related to brain function. This is the area of the neurologist. However, it is, unfortunately, the type of disorder frequently missed in routine medical examinations. Again, severe organic brain disorder is easily observed. Thus, the severe mental defective leaves little doubt in the Examiner's mind. This is not the place to discuss differential diagnosis, but I must remind the Examiner that in children, especially, mental deficiency and psychosis are often confused. To get back to easily observed deviations in the behavior of organic brain disorders, aphasias come to mind. Gross disturbances in motor movements, speech, memory, and thought processes are also obvious. It is the nuances that are difficult to catch.

Some principles are known which can be helpful. One of the first is that which we can call dynamic coherence. An example is: a man comes in complaining of headaches, general irritability, and a depressed feeling. We find that he likes his job, loves his wife and children. His favorite child is his daughter. He spends little time with his sons. He sees his mother, who lives in a nearby town, *every* week. His wife makes all the decisions about the children, what the family does, and so on. In short, he is a female-dependent man. He has been happy with this situation but lately his wife has become "pretty bossy." He gives examples of this bossiness. We also find out from him that she is menopausal. She hasn't been as attentive to him as she used to be. We detect a good deal of hostility in him, a feeling of being neglected by his wife. His hostility is unexpressed. He has never been able to express it. *Now,* this man's dynamics "hang together," even to the point that he is uncomfortable with his male peers—has no male friends. We diagnose his headaches as due to tension resulting from suppressed hostility. He has, of course, reported negative medical findings.

It all makes sense. We have on our hands a mamma's boy, an insecure male, a passive-aggressive person. The symptoms make psychological sense. We know what to do about it. Suppose that, instead of the patient described above, we found our patient to be an upright male with no external stress and with the same symptoms? Then the symptoms might not make psychological sense. There would not be dynamic coherence. Even with further study we cannot get a psychological handle on his symptoms. Then we are forced to the conclusion that there may not be a psychological basis for his symptoms. We refer to a neurologist for a complete neurological with EEG, even if the patient has been referred to you as "medically clean."

We will notice that in discussing the notion of dynamic coherence I brought in the external stress factor. External stress is not always readily discernible. This does not mean that there is none, only that it is not readily apparent with the data we have obtained. A psychasthenic person cannot tell us about any specific factors of the environment that are bothering him. It's the whole world! The study of life history variables which will be discussed in later chapters may enable us to identify environmental stimuli that are stressful. (This is what was meant by the further study referred to above.) When even this sort of further study does not reveal any external stress, then we are forced to the conclusion that the source of stress may be internal and the problem belongs to another discipline.

Two factors have been mentioned that are helpful in the diagnosis of possible organic brain disorder, lack of dynamic coherence, and lack of external stress. There is another factor worth discussing. Call it sudden onset, although it might not be all that sudden. It was this consideration that led me to suspect the dentist who had been taking nitrous oxide. You see, I could find no behavioral aberrations until the time he started listening to tape recordings of the Bible while he slept. And this is what is meant by sudden onset—a marked change in behavior without external stress. Of course, with the dentist it was the drug but it could be anything not apparent from the interview data; for instance, a brain tumor.

At this point you could say the same about the onset of psychosis. I once knew an elderly lady in whom the onset of psychotic behavior seemed to follow the death of her cat. Not satisfied with that explanation the Examiner continued the diagnostic investigation and it resulted in a diagnosis of a cerebro-vascular disorder whose insidious effects were evident prior to the onset of blatant psychotic behavior. Another case in which deviant behavior seemed to occur in the absence of external stress: a man suddenly began giving away money in a grandiose manner. There seemed to be no sudden change in the environment. Further investigation, however, revealed that he had previously incurred large debts he couldn't possibly hope to repay in order to increase his collection of antiques. Additionally, prior to the onset of his psychotic behavior he had been threatened with divorce by his wife. He was diagnosed manic-depressive.

You must be careful before excluding external stress. What seems to be a sudden onset in the absence of external stress may be preceded by minor deviancies in behavior or stresses that the patient is not admitting. One answer is to interview collaterals. Another is to obtain life history data, which will be discussed in succeeding chapters.

Your decision, then, after the intake interview rests on your provisional diagnosis. This diagnosis, in turn, evolves from what you have observed and what you have learned from the patient. Serious deviancies of behavior, either observed or reported, cause no difficulty. To relatively minor deviancies you apply the quantitative approach, adding their number in your mind. A pattern will emerge. Keep in mind the principle of dynamic coherence. The deviancies from expected behavior should "fit" the psychological or physical stresses being experienced by the patient; for example, prolonged physical and psychological stress, as in combat, can lead to "nervous exhaustion" and mental and physical collapse as in an acute psychosis. Thus, death of a loved one may lead to depression but death of a cat should not lead to psychotic depression. If, at this point, you cannot find psychogenic factors that logically can be related to the manifested deviancies then diagnosis is deferred and the patient is held for further study.

8 | The importance of life history variables in diagnosis

In this chapter the effects of early environmental experiences as they relate to later behavior will be discussed. Moreover, interest will be directed to these effects insofar as they help identify the current stimuli evoking deviant behavior.

Very often in the diagnostic interview we are at a loss to account for the noted deviancies of behavior. At this point I can hear those behavioral therapists, those who are unsophisticated in behavioral science. "Why do we have to identify the stimulus?" They declaim, sometimes very loudly, that the observed deviant behavior is behavior in the repertoire of the organism and as such can be manipulated. This simpleminded approach has many faults, both theoretical and practical. The theoretical we shall leave but the practical is of concern to us in this discussion.

In the first place the above approach can only deal with a limited number of clinical problems. Surely, there are a number of ways to deal with a circumscribed phobia. I remember, way back during World War II, when knowing very little, I was thrust into clinical psychology, which as a discipline, did not exist. The case was a WAC who was referred because each time a bird flew over she broke formation. It turned out she had always been afraid of birds, had never eaten fowl. Thank heavens, I had been exposed to hypnosis and, also, that the girl was hypnotizable. Under hypnosis I regressed her back to an incident in her early childhood when a bantam hen, one of her mother's pets almost suffocated her while she was asleep. The traumatic experience was relived, and thereafter she was "cured"! I performed a miracle. I was so excited about it that I reported it (Pascal, 1947).

Cases such as the above don't come along often in day-to-day clinical practice. Most often we are faced with vague complaints, fears, suicidal behaviors and thoughts. We can teach a shy person self-assertive behavior and it seems to work, but under certain unknown stimulus conditions the former behavior will return. This will always be so, if the eliciting stimulus is not identified.

Let me illustrate what I mean. Given a patient whose chief symptom is shyness with strange people, we identify the stimulus as strange people. We put the patient into a group with strange people. Then by dint of practice, persuasion or whatever, we elicit responses from the patient that we can reinforce and that are self-reinforcing. Fine. We have changed the response to strange people. Shortly thereafter the patient applies for a job. She finds herself in a one-to-one relationship with a questioning, stern-looking older man. The patient clams up. The old symptom is back, full force. What happened? The older man was on a generalization gradient with an overbearing, rejecting father, the eliciting stimulus that should have been identified in the first place (Pascal, 1959, p. 85).

It is this failure to identify the eliciting stimulus that not only leads to variable results but also to failure. At present, the only practical way in which we have a chance to identify the stimulus is by acquiring data on the patient's life history. But sometimes, however painstakingly we conduct the diagnostic interview, we still cannot grasp the subtleties of the patient's early environment that might account for present behavior. In such a case we have to defer the diagnosis of dynamics. Fortunately, such occasions are rare.

Let me cite a case in which the diagnostic interview did not reveal stimuli which might plausibly account for the observed behavior. The patient was a 28-year-old school teacher. She had been divorced for five years. No children. Her chief complaint was that she was obsessed with thoughts of committing suicide when she was alone. As she lived alone and did very little socializing she had these thoughts most of the time when she was not working. I couldn't get a handle on her problem, was not sure what was kicking off the thoughts and the isolation. This state of affairs I explained to the patient. She accepted my reassurance that her dynamics would most likely emerge and we began. "With sitting-up" therapy she improved. Suicidal thoughts went away. She began to accept dates. A new symptom, insomnia, appeared. I could get nowhere with hypnosis. Her cooperative physician prescribed sleeping pills and she was relieved of insomnia. Of course, through all this her self-doubts and distrust of others remained, but she seemed to be handling those problems quite well.

At this point I still was not sure and I discussed the matter with the patient. She was still dissatisfied with her feelings and wanted to go on. I put her on the couch and remained silent. After several sessions her behavior toward me began to change. She became increasingly hostile. She said she couldn't stand me, hated me, said I was making her worse; and, in truth, she began "acting out." She dropped her boyfriend, rejected dates, and the sleeping pills no longer worked. All this time, you understand, she was keeping up normal relations with her mother and her father whom she admired. I felt I had it! The important stimulus was the rejecting father. I could now proceed with confidence, and it worked!

Now, let's see what happened. By putting the patient on the couch, darkening the room and sitting out of her line of vision and keeping quiet I enabled the patient to project her own feelings. She moved me up the generalization gradient until I was close to father. When I got there all the repressed feelings she had toward father emerged. (It could have been the mother.) For the patient the process was painful, but for me it meant my diagnosis was complete and I could get on with definitive psychotherapy.

But, you say, that is like psychoanalysis! No doubt. Yet in certain cases this ultimate approach to the diagnostic interview must be attempted to help the patient. In advocating this approach I am very conscious of its potential dangers. Consider this. By promoting generalization you have the patient so that he projects onto you feelings and behavior appropriate for a child toward a parent. In other words, the patient has regressed. His behavior in the consulting room is irrational-psychotic. Good, you say? But suppose, instead of confining this behavior to the consulting room the patient carries on with it in life on the "outside?" Then you will have created a full-blown psychosis. It behooves us, therefore, to know to whom we can and to whom we cannot apply this approach to diagnosis.

Obviously, you would not take steps to promote generalization with one who is already there, so to speak. Thus, if a patient is hostile toward you during the diagnostic interview, he is already projecting his feelings for someone in his past onto you. Such a person needs to be taught discrimination, not helped to generalize. Therefore, you would not apply this approach to a very disturbed patient. Further, you would look for what has been called ego-strength. In this case, it means the wherewithal to withstand the effects of generalization without "acting out"; that is, can the patient confine his regressive behavior to the consulting room. To estimate this capacity you look to the patient's adjustment to his environment. Is he meeting his obligations? Are his deviancies, although many, small so that they are not grossly observable to people? What have been his reactions to stress in his past? By observations such as these the clinician comes to a decision as to whether or not he can attempt the diagnosis by promoting generalization. It is the sort of decision concerning which the beginner would be wise to consult an experienced clinician.

Admittedly we have, in the case just cited, gone far beyond what the beginner should do, but not what he should know. First, the case illustrates the importance of life history data. Second, it shows how early history data can be obtained by means other than the ordinary diagnostic interview. Third, I hope I have demonstrated to the worker that when he reaches a point of impasse with a patient he should seek a consult with an experienced clinician. This point was reached with the school teacher when she had to have sleeping pills for her insomnia. Fourth, the worker, if tempted to try the "couch procedure" I have outlined, should be aware of the danger to the patient involved. The possibility of a frank psychotic break was very real.

Even an experienced clinician can make a mistake or, sometimes, in desperation take a calculated risk. It is necessary to keep a close watch for the first signs of acting-out. The patient needs to be carefully questioned about his behavior in the environment for irrational behavior. At the first sign of it the procedure needs to be reversed. The patient is put back in the vis-à-vis situation. The clinician needs to speak up, promote cognitive awareness by the patient. In this manner the clinician becomes discriminated from a parental figure and the patient regains the controls he had before the procedure started.

In this discussion of the extension of the diagnostic interview by promoting generalization it may seem to the worker that I have drifted into the area of psychotherapy. I have not. I conceive of the promotion of generalization as a legitimate tool for diagnosis, sometimes the only one left to us. From the point of view of an approach to diagnosis that insists on the identification of eliciting stimuli it is a necessary tool which, hopefully, does not have to be used too often. It is my contention that definitive psychotherapy cannot be accomplished without such identification.

Whatever the approach to treatment, the diagnostician tries to identify the stimulus situations that elicit deviant behavior. Sometimes the stimulus is identified as a "high place" or strange people, or water. Such identification may be correct and efficient, as is very often the case with a phobia resulting from a traumatic experience; for example, fear of water stemming from a near drowning accident in childhood. Most often, however, the eliciting stimulus is more subtle.

I had a patient a long time ago, a surgeon, who came to me at just about the point of immobilization. He had gotten so that, after surgery, he just wasn't sure how many stitches were enough and kept adding them to the point where it distressed the surgical nurse and embarrassed him. The surgeon also had a number of other symptoms. Each night before leaving the hospital he carefully tidied up the men's rest room, picking paper towels off the floor, and wiping the washbowls. He drove home each night by exactly the same route, parking his car in exactly the same spot. There were other compulsive symptoms too numerous to bother with here. Also, he had many superstitions revolving around good and evil. Yes, he was classic.

Now, I ask you: What were the eliciting stimuli—the surgical incision, the men's rest rooms? Only careful study of this man's life history could reveal the overprotectiveness of his mother, his consequent ambivalence toward her, and his fear of father. All of his life this man was plagued by feelings of masculine inadequacy which affected his behavior toward men and women. He said, at one time, that even when he was grown, a qualified surgeon, he felt like a small boy with his male peers. The key to understanding this man was in his self-doubts as a male, his fear responses in the presence of male peers. His symptoms began right after puberty—just at the time society began expecting "maleness" from him. It was then that he tried for security by compulsive behaviors.

What to do? As a behaviorist I sought to elicit and extinguish the fear responses to me as a male stimulus. At the same time when different responses emerged toward me, I reinforced those that were positive. This is a much oversimplified account of what happened in over four years of psychotherapy, twice a week, but it is the essence. This is behaviorism; this is Freudianism. It is an approach with which both Freud and Skinner (Skinner, 1976) could agree.

In going over this chapter I cannot help but feel that I have beaten this topic to death. This overkill has, I guess, been my response to exposure to young behavioral therapists who strongly deny that they have to have any truck with the patient's past—which brings us to the problem of definitive psychotherapy! This approach to psychotherapy requires that the original stimuli that elicited responses to be changed be identified. Then it requires that the original stimuli be re-created and the responses extinguished. Of course, in practice, this re-creation of the original stimulus can only be approximated. Thus, the therapist, however much generalization occurs, can never *be* father, he can only approach father on the generalization gradient by way of the patient's projection. Nevertheless, when generalization is achieved and the responses extinguished, all the maladaptive defenses based on these responses are undermined and disappear. In the case of our obsessive-compulsive, for instance, his compulsions, obsessive self-doubts, and superstitions were sloughed off. They were no longer needed.

Without definitive psychotherapy the deviant behavior will recur whenever the patient encounters a stimulus situation which approximates the original. Definitive psychotherapy as I have described it cannot always be achieved, nor is it always feasible or practical. However, when it is not done, the diagnostician and the therapist need to be aware of those situations that can elicit the deviant behavior. This awareness needs to be communicated to the patient so that, with this knowledge, he may be taught either to avoid such stimuli or, in many cases, to learn alternate responses. The important thing is that whenever definitive psychotherapy cannot be prescribed, the limitations of whatever other psychotherapy is prescribed be known.

It follows from the above discussion that if this approach to diagnosis is to be used, case history material is essential. The diagnostic process must reveal the patient's history. When I was younger and more idealistic, I used to fantasize a whole series of standard stimulus situations. All we would have to do would be to observe and measure the patient's responses to these situations. No questions! Truly a behaviorist's dream! As it is, we are stuck with the diagnostic interview.

In the next chapter we will consider how to go about obtaining data on the experiential background of the patient. In so doing we will learn about the psychological anatomy of the patient—knowledge that our ethics require us to have if we are to "operate" on the patient.

REFERENCES

Pascal, G. R. The use of relaxation in short-term psychotherapy. *Journal of Abnormal and Social Psychology*, 1947, *42*, 226-242.

Pascal, G. R. *Behavioral change in the clinic*. New York: Grune & Stratton, 1959.

Skinner, B. F. *About behaviorism*. New York: Vintage Books, 1976.

9 | Life history data

In this chapter we will consider life history data as it is obtained from the patient. Data obtained from collaterals will be discussed in succeeding chapters. Data obtained from the patient has always been suspect. Such data, it has been said, has little validity. (See Chapter 3.) We need to consider this matter at the outset.

Our business is unlike any other. A lawyer has to have facts. In getting a medical history a physician has to have facts; not so, the diagnostic interviewer. The facts referred to are those concerned with the relationships with people. Obviously, the interviewer needs to know objective data about the patient's life; for example, constitution of the patient's family, history of physical illnesses, school history, and so on. More about these matters later. Primarily, however, in case history material we are interested in feelings. The problem is to get at true feelings, not what the patients think they should feel, nor what the patients think are the socially acceptable feelings they should have. How many times have I listened to a hospitalized mentally ill patient, give a glowing account of his wonderful childhood! Then there are those who have repressed unpleasant memories; and there are others, in a way the most deceptive, who overwhelm us with how they have suffered.

What we want are data that we can believe in. In a sense we want to be able to "anthropomorphize" about the feelings that must have been instilled into the child; that is, project our own feelings about how the child must have reacted to the environment. Let me give you an example. The patient is a 20-year-old girl. We are satisfied that all she has known from her mother has been criticism and physical punishment. Whatever emotional nourishment she received came from a Casper Milquetoast but kindly father. We hypothesize that the child must have felt rejection, fear, and hatred toward her mother; that all her needs for emotional succorance were directed toward her father. Once we have done that, we are in a position to hypothesize about the feelings underlying her behaviors toward men and women in her current life.

Other than direct observation of a person throughout life, there is no perfect way to get the data we need; but there is a way to get data in which we can believe (Pascal & Jenkins, 1961). The essence of this approach to case history material lies in an attempt to bypass culturally formed opinions and deceptions. Thus, the patient is never asked, "How did you get along with your mother as a child?" Instead of such questions, which beg for a culturally determined response, the patient is asked for early memories of his mother.

Let us get down to the specifics of the procedure. First I try to get a feel for the kind of family into which the patient was born. Where was the patient born? What were the mother's and the father's vocations at the time of the child's birth? What siblings, if any? Spacing between siblings? Was the father a sharecropper, traveling salesman or businessman? Was the environment rural or urban? Was the patient an only male child with three older sisters? Was the patient 1 of 10 siblings? Obviously, this sort of information gives some notions about the effects of the patient's early environment.

These basic facts are rarely falsified, at least not in my experience. Besides they can be easily verified. Once these facts about the early environment are obtained we are no longer concerned about accuracy except where feelings are involved. Let me make my meaning clearer by an example. Suppose that our patient, a young man, remembers his early relations with his father as being characterized by his father's neglect. He remembers his father always leaving or being too busy. He remembers other boys' fathers playing baseball games in the early evenings. He remembers wishing he had a father with whom to play ball. Several reported behavioral incidents of that nature lead us to hypothesize that as a boy our patient felt unaccepted and unloved by his father. We discover from other sources that the father was a traveling salesman. He left on Monday mornings and didn't return until late Friday night. Weekends he spent recuperating from his exhausting week. He was, in fact, a loving and kindly person and although he spent little time with his son, he gave as much as he could within the physical limitations imposed upon him by his job.

The fact was the patient had a loving father. The patient's perceptions were otherwise. The feelings that stem from his perceptions are what the patient retains throughout life (Korchin, 1976). Later, these feelings may change based on a more realistic appraisal of his father. In spite of a later change in feelings, however, the early feelings remain. Thus, a boy may, in his teens, look upon his father more realistically and see him for the hardworking, loving man he is. He feels kindly and understanding toward his father. He may say he loves him; yet, he cannot confide in him. It is these later perceptions and the feelings based on them that often confuse the patient and color his early memories. These later feelings can obscure the deeply held feelings of which the patient is unaware. It is the job of the Examiner to penetrate to the core of early acquired feelings not remembered by the patient.

Other than with the transference of psychoanalysis, and sometimes with hypnosis, the Examiner cannot uncover the feelings. He has to get data with which he can anthropomorphize about the feelings the child must have acquired. Sometimes these data emerge from the facts of the early environment. For instance, a boy has four older sisters in a household dominated by the mother. We may anthropomorphize that the boy early acquired the feelings that females are the source of succorance and power. If such anthropomorphizing fits the facts of the patient's current behavior toward females then we are apt to accept it as a tenable hypothesis. Unfortunately, the facts of the patient's early environment do not often lend themselves so easily to workable hypotheses. Most often we have to dig to get the data we need.

So, we begin with the environmental milieu into which the patient was born. At this point we would like to know about the mother's pregnancy and the facts of the patient's birth, but these are not available in data obtained from the patient except on rare occasions when the patient has been told of unusual events by a parent. (We will consider these data in a later section.) Having noted that there are data we cannot get, we proceed to ask the patient if he has been told of any difficulties he had as a baby. Most often we draw a blank. Sometimes we get useful information. For instance, one patient told me his mother said he cried a lot and had been a feeding problem. He had been bottle fed and no formula would do. Later, he developed asthma. Maternal deprivation? This might do as an hypothesis if other behaviors of the mother fit this notion. The Examiner has to be careful lest he seize upon such a notion and unwittingly let his bias guide his later data gathering.

We go on with the acquisition of factual data, being primarily concerned with the preschool years. Has the patient been told or does he remember illnesses and accidents in these early years? What about toilet training. Usually, we don't get much, but we need to ask in order to find out what data we do not have. But we never know. Not too long ago, I had an alcoholic tell me he was enuretic until the age of 13. Was it hostility against his mother? Well, his mother was an alcoholic and a swinger. She spent much time away from home, abandoning him to relatives. Many of the behavioral incidents he cited centered around his mother dropping him off at some relative's home and leaving him there for days at a time. We hypothesize he must have had much unexpressed hostility toward his mother. Currently we find that he has hostility toward his wife, unexpressed except when he gets drunk. We accept the hypothesis and make it the basis for part of our treatment program.

At the risk of being repetitive, again the Examiner must be warned against overeagerness in grasping at hypotheses (Campbell & Stanley, 1963; Garfield, 1974). The hypothesis, in order to be tenable, must explain current behavior.

Thus, a young adult female complains of inferiority feelings in the presence of her female peers. These feelings have a long history in her life. The young Examiner might say, "Aha, trouble with her mother!" Such a conception would not "fit" the data. Our patient gets along well with older women. Our patient has no difficulty in heterosexual relationships. We draw blanks when we inquire concerning behavioral incidents involving her mother and her father in the patient's childhood years. It is not until we obtain data about her early relationship with a sister two years older that we can formulate an hypothesis that fits the data of current behavior. The sister was abusive both verbally and physically. The young Examiner might be misled by the patient's statements (1) that now she has a good relationship with her older sister and (2) that the patient's mother seemed to favor her older sister. Only the data from cited behavioral incidents involving the older sister lead to a hypothesis that explains current behavior, and that is the hypothesis we accept as a basis for treatment. It makes a difference both in prognosis and treatment! We shall consider prognosis in Chapter 12.

As indicated, there is much you can surmise from factual data. So you go on obtaining an account of the patient's life as he remembers it. Try to get an orderly sequence, chronologically. Occasionally, you will need to prompt the patient. How did he get along in school? Did he have friends? Did he have fights? Did he mind reciting in class? You guide the patient through his school years with illnesses and accidents and familial events that occurred in the sequence of years. How about dating and sex in high school and college years? Smoking, alcohol, drugs? And so you go on through the years of his life, getting from him the kind of life he led. Most patients do not mind telling you the facts of their lives. Most tell the truth. Some patients are so uncommunicative that it becomes a tedious question and answer session. Some will tell you a pack of lies. Sometimes, these lies are detectable because what they tell you doesn't fit with what you know of current behavior. For instance, a man might tell you about what a fighter he was in his school years. That story just doesn't jibe with the scared rabbit of a man you see before you. True? Not necessarily! Other data may reveal a traumatic experience of crippling emotional impact.

We have approached the gathering of case history data in somewhat the same manner as we did cross-sectional data. First, we attempt to get the less sensitive data. Hopefully, in the process we are establishing rapport so that when we come to the area of feelings the patient will feel free to communicate.

Getting a patient to remember his experiences during his early years is sometimes a problem. Many patients will, at first, deny any early memories. With a little help they sometimes surprise themselves. Ask the patient to relax, close his eyes, take a deep breath, slowly exhale. Ask him to see himself as very small. Let his mind go back in time, to before he started school. Do any scenes from those early years come to mind? Sometimes you draw a blank but most often you get some remembered scene. The scenes reported are frequently insignificant; for example, moving from one house to another. Occasionally, the patient will recover a traumatic incident. The important consideration is that you have helped the patient to start recalling his very early years.

I usually go on to early memories of his mother. Those must be remembered specific events. To guard against culturally toned generalities, such as "Mother always had something for us to eat after school," you need to coach the patient. Where were you? What did she do? Then what did you do? The incident needs to be placed in time and situation and the stimulus-response sequence elicited.

An example might help. For instance, the patient reports that he remembers his mother taking care of him when he was sick. Can he remember one time? Yes? Good! About how old was he? What happened? He was in bed with the measles. He remembers being awakened. His mother was washing his face with a cool, wet cloth. Then she kissed him. End of behavioral incident.

Another example. Father used to take me hunting with him. Do you remember one such time? Yes? Good! When? He remembers it was just after he began in the first grade. What happened? They went deer hunting. He and father took their station. He wandered a bit. His father grabbed him, shook him, and scolded him for wandering from the station. This memory was elicited with much questioning from the Examiner in order to obtain the stimulus-response sequences. For instance: Where was father? What did you do? Then what happened? And so on.

The Examiner continues to obtain specific memories of the patient's experiences with important persons in his early life. These specific memories do not just flow from the patient. Very often much prompting is required with questions such as: Do you remember sitting on your father's lap? Do you remember a spanking? The Examiner continues to obtain these specific memories about important persons in the patient's early life until he is satisfied about the nature of the relationship, or until he is certain that no data can be obtained. The Examiner obtains these specific memories from the time of earliest recall to later prepubertal years.

For example, a patient reports early memories with his mother which indicate fear, compliance and unexpressed hostility in response to harsh, critical and demanding behavior by his mother. The father's behavior emerges as kindly and receptive but with few activities with the patient. Little data could be obtained about the early relationship with a brother four years younger. The data obtained "fitted" with the patient's current behavior, fear of his wife and repressed hostility, and an easy relationship with male peers and a male Examiner.

The behavioral incident technique does not ensure that the Examiner will obtain the truth about how the patient perceived the important figures of his early environment. It does help, however, to reveal to the Examiner those cases in which no reliable data can be obtained. The glib patient who is fabricating early memories will have difficulty with the specificity of the stimulus-response sequences. The patient also will report improbable inconsistencies. For instance, in one incident the father will appear as kindly and patient and in another as rejecting and punitive. The patient who is lying will also report memories that make no sense when we try to use them as the bases for hypotheses related to current behavior. We believe in the lawfulness of human behavior; that is, the discernible effects of early learning on later behavior. It follows, therefore, that what we discover about the patient's early environment has to "fit" a reasonable hypothesis related to current behavior. If the findings make no psychological sense in terms of current behavior they are in doubt.

We have found the behavioral incident technique to be nonthreatening to most patients. In telling of specific incidents the patient seems unaware of what he is revealing about his early life experiences. Patients who give a glowing account of early relationships with father, mother, and siblings will relate specific memories which indicate poor relationships. Instead of accepting the patient's opinion about the nature of the relationships, the Examiner is required to make his own judgments. This is an important point because beginning Examiners are often too prone to accept the patient's generalities at face value.

I have been at some length to suggest to the Examiner ways in which knowledge can be acquired about the nature of the patient's early life experiences. Over 35 years of clinical experience garnered through my own patients and those of my students has convinced me, beyond doubt, of the crucial importance of such knowledge in understanding the patient's current behavior. I am very aware that such a Freudian approach can lead to a glibness in diagnosis. For instance, a man who has difficulties with peer females is often relegated to a difficulty with mother category without any knowledge of early experiences with the mother. The trouble could have been with an older sister. It makes a difference in our understanding of the patient's behavior. It also makes a difference in prognosis. Also, overemphasis on early life experiences tends to obscure the effects of later experiences on current behavior, not to mention the importance of the current stimulus situation!

The foregoing was meant to reassure the reader that we are not about to neglect the effects of later experiences on behavior. The psychological effects of early life experiences remain in the patient and motivate later behavior. Those effects that result in maladaptive behavior lead to the acquisition of defenses, if the child is to survive. Thus a child, in frustration and anger, may display temper tantrums. This behavior begets rejection and punishment, maybe banishment and loss of a meal. The child might learn, through trial and error, that docile conformity gets him the acceptance that he needs. The anger and frustration are repressed only to emerge in some other behavior more acceptable such as poor school grades. Docile conforming, the appeasing behavior, is an example of a relatively adaptive defense mechanism. Withdrawal as a defense is an example of a maladaptive defense.

The point of the above discussion is that we need to know the defenses acquired by our patient through the years, if we are to understand him. To gain this understanding we need to inquire concerning the patient's life experiences and the nature of his responses to them. A good place to begin is the school experience. This is an important area because for most of us the school is the first truly demanding social experience. How did the patient adapt? As before, you need to obtain specific memories. Did the patient have trouble reciting in class? Did he get in trouble with his teachers, grades, and so on? What, if any, were his extracurricular activities? Did he get into any fights? Who were his friends? What did they do together? What was waiting for the patient when he returned home from school? What were the responses to behaviors of his mother, his father, his siblings? Try to obtain data about his reactions to stress situations. Did he withdraw; did he fight; did he become passive-aggressive? What, in short, were his patterns of adjustment in those later formative years? What deviant behaviors were exhibited?

Of particular importance at this stage of the Examiner's inquiry is the patient's behavior in the early adolescent, immediately postpubertal years. It is at this time in the patient's life that those inner hormonal surges meet society's demands. Prepubertal patterns of adjustment now emerge full-blown. Thus, if the patient continues this behavior in adolescence, a child who is somewhat shy and withdrawn will be more noticeable in contrast to peers. The child will be of concern to the parents and feel the exclusion by peers, starting a vicious cycle. A child who feels rejected by the parents may, after puberty, join a closely knit peer group and take on the mores of the group. In adolescence old defenses may become strengthened or new defenses may be acquired.

Often the patient's behavior in adolescence gives us a clearer insight into familial relations prior to puberty, particularly in those cases where the patient disclaims memories of earlier years. For instance, a patient who says he had "a good Christian" upbringing tells us that as a teenager he joined a delinquent peer group and displayed behaviors contrary to the morals of his parents. He rejects his parents. Why? In rebellion against a felt rejection by them? How long he stays with the peer group seems to be related to the intensity of the rejection he felt from his parents.

Let us see if I can clarify the reasoning that lies behind my discussion thus far. The young child, relatively helpless in the environment, reacts to experiences by acquiring attitudes and feelings about himself and the people in his environment. These feelings manifest themselves in behaviors toward those people. The child cannot intellectualize his behaviors. He just reacts. The experiential bases for these reactions are lost to conscious memory. The emotional reactions to people on some continuum of similarity to those people of the child's early environment remain. What the child does with these emotional reactions depends on later life experiences and the developing ability to control the environment. This ability takes a sharp rise in adolescence. The adult the child will become, comes into sharp focus. His defenses become apparent.

Let me cite an example that might clarify my thinking to you. The following is a case known to me throughout the patient's life. The father came to me about his son, age three. The boy would spend hours listening to classical records, seemingly oblivious to what was going on around him. The mother complained she couldn't relate to the boy. The father was a busy professional man. There were no other significant complaints. Alone with the boy in the playroom, I discovered that he would respond to me and even exhibit a sad little smile.

The mother had had an active and uneventful pregnancy. Delivery was normal. Shortly after the child's birth the mother was hospitalized with a psychotic break. The father, with the help of a housekeeper, took care of the child for the first two years of the boy's life. The father would come home at lunch time and spend his evenings with the boy. The mother returned. The father returned to his busy schedule working 12 hours a day. It was not long after the mother returned that the boy's peculiar, isolated behavior was noticed. With the help of playroom therapy and the father's close cooperation we were able to get the child to behave more "normally." The autistic-like behavior disappeared and he was generally more responsive to people. The mother stopped complaining about him. He was enrolled in preschool and did well. Thereafter, I maintained infrequent but regular contact with the boy.

Through his preadolescent years he seemed perfectly normal, did well in school, had friends, and so on. He took guitar lessons. In his early teens he joined a rock group that played at high school dances. He was a good-looking, popular youngster. There was one behavior that marked him as different from the other boys of his subculture. He did not date. All through high school and college he had not a single date. In the fourth year of college he became the patient of a female psychotherapist. Gradually, he became less avoidant of females and, finally, was able to establish close relationships with peer females. The psychotherapy was successful but to this day, at the age of 30, this young man is still unmarried.

Obviously, the foregoing case was oversimplified to make a point. The boy's avoidance of females did not manifest itself until adolescence. Although the difficulty with females could have been predicted from the early experiences of the child, the form the difficulty would take could not. He did not become homosexual. He did not seek in females the mothering he did not get from his mother. He did not vent his frustration on them. To get back to our thesis, the defenses covering the feelings acquired in early life begin to manifest themselves in adolescence. They may be modified and changed but they form the bases for the behavior pattern learned later in life.

What these behavior patterns become we learn by pursuing our patient's life to the present. What were his reactions to achievements and disappointments? How did people behave toward him? His reactions? What about his social behavior through the years? His intimate relations with his family, his close friends, if any? Here, if you have not already obtained the information in the course of your inquiry, you fill in the gaps of your knowledge of his sexual behavior from early masturbation to the present; similarly, with physical and mental illnesses.

By the time you finish with your study of the patient's history you should have a grasp of his dynamics and defenses. His current behavior should be comprehensible. Without knowledge of the patient's early life experiences and the feelings engendered by them, without knowledge of the development of defenses you cannot treat the patient in a definitive way (Lazarus & Davison, 1971). You cannot know even if you can help the patient. About this latter point we shall have more to say in Chapter 12, "Prognosis."

We have outlined a history to be taken from the patient. It includes the events and people the patient has experienced in the course of his life, from earliest memory to the present. It may seem exhaustive and time consuming; and it can be, especially for the beginner. The inexperienced Examiner is apt to fill the history with inconsequential trivia. Thus, he is apt to report that the patient moved from J Street to K Street when such data have no bearing on the dynamics of the case. The important thing for the worker to remember is that the history is not a social one but, rather, a history of the patient's psychological development. The life history data reported must contribute to understanding the patient's current behavior. This is the criterion for inclusion, or exclusion, in the history.

Let us summarize the interview for obtaining the life history.

1. Factual data
   a. The environmental milieu at birth—Composition of the family, mother's and father's vocations, siblings.
   b. Birth and early infancy—Prenatal complications, delivery, early infancy, breast-fed or bottle, feeding problems, illnesses, and so on. (If adult patient ask what has been told.)
   c. Preschool—Toilet training (enuresis?), family composition, special events.
   d. Early school—Difficulties, companions, after school hours. (Through grammar school.)
   e. High school—Activities, grades, companions, heterosexual behaviors—family events.
   f. College or first job—Same as (e).

2. Perceptual data
   a. Early memories of mother, father, and siblings, behavioral incidents, on up to puberty. Derive early attitudes about self and others.
   b. Postpuberty—Memories of family, friends, behavioral incidents. Derive emerging defenses.
   c. Adulthood—Patterns of behavior in response to environmental stimuli.

REFERENCES

Campbell, D. T., & Stanley, J. C. *Experimental and quasi-experimental designs for research.* Skokie, Ill.: Rand McNally, 1963.

Garfield, S. L. *Clinical psychology: The study of personality and behavior.* Hawthorne, N Y.: Aldine Publishing, 1974.

Korchin, S. J. *Modern clinical psychology.* New York: Basic Books, 1976.

Lazarus, A. A., & Davison, G. C. Clinical innovation in research and practice. In A. E. Bergin & S. L. Garfield (Eds.), *Handbook of psychotherapy and behavior change: An empirical analysis.* New York: John Wiley & Sons, 1971.

Pascal, G. R., & Jenkins, W. O. *Systematic observation of gross human behavior.* New York: Grune & Stratton, 1961.

10 | Interview of children

Usually the early development of the child is left in the hands of the pediatrician. It is only rarely that the pediatrician, as a last resort, will call in the mental health specialist, but it does happen. I remember the case of a one-year-old baby whom I saw in the office of a very concerned pediatrician. The baby was listless and unresponsive. I could elicit none of the expected behaviors for a child of that age (Gesell & Amatruda, 1962). The child's reactions were similar to those described by Margaret Ribble (1944). The pediatrician reported an uneventful pregnancy and delivery. The mother, an attractive young woman, was evidently distressed. She denied any implication that she might be neglecting the child. I later was able to establish through careful and, I might add, nonthreatening inquiry that the mother was away from home most of the day. The baby was left in the care of a teenage girl who left the baby in the crib all day, even for feeding, only occasionally picking up the baby to change its diaper. It was an obvious case of maternal deprivation. The pediatrician had been misled by the mother's deceptions.

The above case is cited to make several points about the examination of young children. The first and most obvious point is that the collaboration of a pediatrician is required. His knowledge of the child is a necessary base from which the examination proceeds. The second point is that the Examiner must have a secure knowledge of the expected behaviors of a child of any given age. This knowledge must encompass not only behaviors in response to stimuli but also spontaneous behaviors of the child. Third, the examination of the child must include the child's environment. It can be said safely that the younger and more helpless the child, the greater the impact of the environment.

Let us get some perspective on the diagnostic interview with children. Children are people. Within the limits of their capabilities, which must be known to the Examiner, they react to their environment as adults do. Much that is esoteric has been attributed to children's behavior disorders. When I was a beginner in this field the hue and cry was on cerebral disrhythmia. Today, it seems to have veered to chemical imbalance in the brain and minimal brain dysfunction. What beautifully convenient diagnoses! The parents are relieved of culpability and the treatment is easy. The child is dosed with drugs. Symptoms go away. The child's problem doesn't.

It seems to me that much of the confusion about children's disorders stems from a lack of knowledge of the physiological and psychological development of the child. The younger the child the less specific the response of the child to the environment. Thus, very young children react to frustration of their needs with their total bodies as did our one-year-old. As children get older and the cerebral cortex develops, their reactions to frustration may result in increased motor activity. These children are often called hyperactive or hyperkinetic and also are treated with drugs (Ross & Ross, 1978). Some children shut out the frustrating environment by becoming inwardly involved with repetitive motor movements. We are apt to call such children autistic (Rutter, 1978). To reiterate, outside of obvious physical factors such as nutrition, chemical imbalance, brain damage, or specific physical illnesses, children's behavior disorders have a common source, frustration of the needs for consistent loving behavior, and a lack of constant, unmanipulable firmness in handling the child.

Anyone reading the above would believe I disavow brain dysfunction in children. That is not the case! There are subtle indications of brain dysfunction, often missed in routine neurological examinations. The experienced Examiner is alert to subtle variations of behavior which may indicate brain dysfunction (Conners, 1975). What are these subtle cues? I am not sure I can be very specific. Sometimes I am not sure to what cues I respond. It may be a confusion of laterality; for example, the child cannot consistently tell left from right. It may be a hesitation in speech, where the child seems to be searching for a word. It may be a momentary blankness. It may be a variation in eye movement. These and other subtle variations in expected behavior, during the interview, may suggest to the Examiner the possibility of minimal brain dysfunction. In such a case the Examiner should refer the child for neuropsychological examination. I repeat, however, that the incidence of true brain dysfunction is rare in practice. The Examiner needs to be alert to the possibility, but not to let the possibility interfere with the search for the dynamic factors related to the child's behavior.

In the diagnosis of children's disorders, therefore, we ordinarily first interview the parents (R. Jenkins, 1966). We get a list of the child's symptoms as the parents describe them. We also get a history of the mother's experiences during pregnancy. We inquire about the actual delivery. Information is obtained about the mother's behavior toward the infant following delivery and the first year of life. Of particular interest is the child's response to feeding, breast or bottle. We go on to toilet training, walking, talking, eating habits, and activities of the child in the present. What we are interested in, of course, are early signs of psychopathology such as unusual difficulties in feeding, difficulties in the development of talking, walking, and toilet training, peculiarities of behavior, and always, the mother's reactions to the child (Greenspan & Greenspan, 1981; Katoff & Reuter, 1980).

While we are getting all this information from the mother we are also examining her. She is, usually, the most important stimulus in the child's environment. What was going on in her life while the child was developing? And here, it seems to me, is a good place to talk about the usages of psychological common sense. If a mother is reluctantly breast-feeding her child the chances are good that the child is going to be unhappy with its food. If a child is held only during feeding and never played with while it is in the crib, it's going to be unhappy in the crib. One mother I knew of held her baby so tightly while giving the baby the bottle the baby spent most of its feeding time crying. The baby is most sensitive to the nuances of the mother's behaviors. Mothers will protest that their love and care of the child never change. It is up to the Examiner to be aware that a mother responds to her environment and that her responses affect the baby. The father is important in two ways: (1) by his behavior toward the mother and (2) by his behavior toward the baby. I once had a graduate student who after five years of marriage became a father. Not long after the baby was born he went to bed, ill from he knew not what, nor could a physician diagnose his illness. Before the baby was born his wife had given him her undivided attention. After the birth of the baby she was completely engrossed in caring for it. The graduate student could not accept that he felt neglected. He just got sick! The mother got worried. The baby got upset. It was a very unhappy household until we took the father in hand. Yes, fathers can affect baby's adjustment through their behaviors toward the mother.

There are some enlightened fathers who participate in the care of the baby from birth onward. For the most part, however, fathers play an ancillary role in the baby's upbringing. Busy and successful fathers, particularly, are noteworthy by their absence. The majority of little boys we see in our clinic suffer from a lack of association with a father. This lack becomes most noticeable when the boy is thrust into the rough, tough world of little boys on the school playground.

Primarily, the above text is directed toward focusing your attention on the importance of thoroughly investigating the parents or surrogates.

I state it here, as a premise that barring accidents and untoward physical factors, the child is born into the world emotionally "clean." Given this premise it follows that whatever deviancies of behavior the child displays are a result of its experiences in the world. People, other than the parents, are also experienced by the child. Inquiry, therefore, must also be directed toward those others in immediate contact with the child, such as siblings, grand-parents, maids, and nurseries. It is not uncommon to find a child's deviant behavior stemming directly from its reaction to an older, competitive sibling, an indulgent grandmother, or an irresponsible maid or nursery school. If the Examiner cannot understand the child's behavior as a response to his environ-ment he can be sure in practically all cases that some significant aspect of the child's environment has been missed. In that case the Examiner needs to recheck the findings or institute further inquiry.

Suppose that after exhaustive study of the child's environment, we cannot explain the child's behavior as a reaction to the environment? This would be a rare event but it has happened. We would be forced to admit the possibility of an inherited predisposition to deviant behavior. I have discussed this factor at some length elsewhere (Pascal, 1959), and shall only mention it here. The inherited tendency toward deviant behavior most likely exists but it is en-countered rarely in clinical practice. I do not wish to emphasize it lest the mental health worker find it a convenience in support of his failure to uncover the environmental factors related to the child's behaviors. Neverthe-less, the Examiner should inquire concerning the incidence of mental illness in the child's family where psychosis in the child cannot be related to the child's environment, or where it is felt the child has overreacted to minimal stress; for example, his cat dies and the child becomes psychotic.

We come, now, to the direct examination of the child. How we proceed depends upon the age. The younger the child, the more we are dependent on the observations of the parents. The very young child has a limited repertoire of responses. Thus, in examining a one-year-old child, our expectations are limited. Psychometrically speaking, we have few test items. The reliability and validity of the examination leaves much to be desired. It is only in the ex-tremes of deviations from expected behaviors that we trust our diagnosis.

As I have indicated previously, in examining a very young child the close collaboration of a pediatrician is required. Suppose that the child is delivered to us physically "clean." We have the child, most often with its mother, in our consulting room. Firm in our knowledge of normative data we face the child with a set of expectancies. We try to engage the child. How does he respond to you as a person? We present various stimuli. We draw blanks and decide the child is deviant. To understand the child's behavior, we are com-pletely dependent on knowledge of the child's experiences since birth.

Contrast this situation with the one that prevails with a four-year-old child. We take the child into the playroom. The child seizes upon a papa doll and starts bashing it about, and the child talks! The point here, of course, is that the older the child the greater the range of responses and, psychometri-cally speaking, the more reliable and valid are interview data.

The examination of children requires a thorough knowledge of child development. A vague knowledge will not do. For instance, children have a rich imagination, sometimes peopling their world of fantasy with animals and persons who are quite real to them. When does this fantasy life become a concern? I remember a bright seven-year-old girl, oldest of three sibs. She was brought in by her parents, professional people, because they felt she was too shy and lacked friends. She was shy with me, responding to questions but offering nothing. In the playroom she built a castle and peopled it with a king and a princess and retainers, giving them all names. She even told me the life histories of her people. She became animated and communicative. The princess was her best friend. They talked to each other. She told me of the adventures they had had together. Would the child grow out of it? I did not think so. I felt the child was emotionally invested in her fantasy world. She was slipping into a "world of irreality" (Lewin, 1936, p. 196). I told the parents and took her for treatment.

The examination of children also requires that the Examiner treat the children as people. This statement may seem unnecessary and even absurd to the inexperienced clinician, yet it needs to be stated. I have observed too many students approach children as if they were of a different species. To repeat an old saw in our business, children and psychotics know how you feel, regardless of how you behave. The child, screaming in the waiting room, responds with surprising compliance to the confident Examiner who takes him by the hand and leads him into the playroom. If you do not like children, are uneasy with them or are afraid of them in the sense that their behavior is unpredictable, you should not attempt to examine them.

To repeat, children are people. The methods and observations discussed in previous chapters apply just as well to children. There are a few differences which we will consider. With children you previously obtain information about their experiential background before you see them. The younger the child the more you are dependent upon collaterals for this information. With a child, as with an adult, you approach with a set of expectancies. These expectancies for children are determined by chronological age, more so than with adults. Thus a two-year age difference is of relatively little moment in your expectations for adults but may make a vast difference in the expected behavior of a young child.

There is another difference between children and adults, too often overlooked. Children tend to generalize from previous life situations more easily than adults. Here, again, the age of the child makes a difference. Thus a traumatic experience in a one-year-old child may, on examination, elicit a negative reaction to all adults. This same experience in an older child might, on examination, elicit a response based on the sex of the Examiner. The young child's response is generalized to all adults. The older child's response is based on its ability to discriminate the sex of the original traumatic stimulus. The older the child the more the subtleties of this tendency to generalize manifest themselves. Thus, a child, who for one reason or another, has learned to resist demands made by the parents, will show the same resistance to demands made by the Examiner.

This discussion of the child's relative inability to discriminate stimuli is important because judgment of deviations from expectancy is tempered by such knowledge. For example, hostile reactions in an adult during the diagnostic interview could be considered a serious deviation from expectancy. This same reaction in a seven-year-old child would not have the same weight. The destructive adult might well be considered psychotic. The destructive child might be considered merely frustrated and angry. In connection with this tendency to generalize the sex of the Examiner becomes a consideration. Hostility toward his mother could be displayed by hostility toward a female Examiner. Thus, based on our knowledge of the child's experiential background, our expectations would vary with the sex of the Examiner.

Everyone tends to respond similarly to similar stimulus situations. The ability to differentiate between degrees of similarity varies with a number of variables, some of them not known. We do know, however, that this ability certainly varies with age, emotional adjustment and, most likely, with basic intelligence. Thus, the adult paranoid may fear and distrust all men, similarly the young child who has been previously frightened by a man. Given no other frightening experiences with men, when does this child learn to discriminate between men? The point is that I do not know the answer to that question. There are no norms. It depends on what happens to the child between the initial frightening experience and the time of the examination. Thus, although I do make allowance for the greater tendency to generalize in children, I cannot tell you when to stop making that allowance. A child at the age of one who was frightened by a man with a beard might still be frightened of all men at the age of two. This same child, still frightened of all men at the age of seven, would be considered deviant. It is a matter of clinical judgment and investigatory acumen. It depends on the experiential background of the child and the severity of the child's response. For instance, a two-year-old who has been repeatedly spanked by a harsh father might be expected strenuously to avoid being alone with a male Examiner. On the other hand, one would expect this same child at age seven to be able to discriminate between the Examiner and his (the child's) father and respond differently.

Let us go on with the direct examination of the child. If possible, see the child alone in your consulting room, not in the playroom. The purpose here is to obtain data about the child's reaction to another person, the Examiner. How does the child react, positively or negatively? Seeing the child in the playroom for the first contact is, I believe, a mistake. The child is apt to be distracted by the playroom material and thus the reaction to the Examiner is diluted.

The Examiner as a stimulus is a nonthreatening, receptive human. One way or another, the child will react, regardless of age. It is in this first contact that the effects of the child's previous experiences with other people will be manifest. It might be helpful to think of a dog being introduced into your consulting room. You would know, it seems to me, if the dog had learned to like or fear people. If he had learned fear he might bristle and growl or he might whimper and curl up in a far corner. If on the other hand his experiences with people had been good he would sniff, test the air, so to speak, and then with a positive indication from the Examiner, wag his tail and allow himself to be stroked.

Children are not dogs but the reactions to another human are similar in their basic movements. You would expect the child to "sniff the air," waiting for a reaction from you. If your reaction is positive as with a smile, a warm greeting, or a handshake, then you would expect a positive reaction to you. The deviations from this expectancy vary from a screaming, terrified avoidance to a glassy immobility. The in-between reactions, especially in older children, are more subtle but, nevertheless, are there to be observed by you (Lobitz & Johnson, 1975).

If possible, you then go on with the interview in your consulting room. You talk to the child, try to get him to respond to you. Will the child talk about what he likes, dislikes, a toy, a game, or whatever? You observe his speech, his mannerisms, the presence or absence of affect, alert for deviations from expectancy, just as you would with an adult. For very young children I bring out blocks and play with them encouraging the child to participate, using the play to facilitate the interaction between myself and the child.

At this point the Examiner decides whether or not introducing the child into the play room will add to the data already obtained. Generally speaking, with older, verbal children the playroom session is not necessary. With children who have difficulty communicating the playroom with its variety of play material is a less threatening situation and eases tension in the child. Very often children who were silent in the consulting room will, with the excitement of the playroom material, relax and talk to the Examiner. The severely withdrawn child, on the other hand, will not react. Some hyperactive children overreact, tossing toys about and generally messing up the playroom. Some children immediately involve themselves in play igoring the Examiner.

A well-equipped playroom should contain mother, father, and sibling dolls, games for various age levels, construction toys, aggressive toys such as soft bats. For most children it is an exciting place which they proceed to investigate. For the unresponsive child the Examiner may introduce various objects such as dolls, or playballs, in an attempt to involve the child. Other than that the playroom interview is unstructured, the child being allowed to react or not react. The Examiner should not begin play therapy. The purpose of the playroom interview is to observe the reactions of the child to the playroom as a stimulus situation. (A note of caution: if the child is known to be violently aggressive, potentially dangerous toys such as darts should be put out of reach.)

As I already have implied, the examination of children requires specialized knowledge. I do not feel that the mental health worker has been given that specialized knowledge in this chapter. I hope, rather, that I have presented some of the problems encountered in the examination of children and indicated where specialized knowledge is required. It occurs to me that I have not even spelled out who is a child. I know we can all agree on the extremes of chronological age; that is, that a 7-year-old is a child and a 21-year-old is not. It is at the older end of the age continuum that the definition gets hazy. Suppose we try the following definition: the more a person's behavior depends on relationship with parents (or surrogates) the more the person is a child. With this definition a 16-year-old could be treated as a child or an adult. But that definition doesn't help too much. We need information that is part of the examination in order to use it. For practical reasons I use the age 16 as a cutoff. With a child under that age I go through the usual procedure of obtaining a history from the parents before seeing the child. With persons over that age I just see them. Whether or not I see the parents depends on the wishes of the person interviewed.

One other point is to be made before ending this chapter on children. In my time I have had to examine many children in orphanages where information about the children's experiential background has been scanty or totally lacking. In such cases emphasis must be placed on extensive psychological testing including projective techniques. Data from psychological tests must be integrated with that obtained from the direct examination of the child. The clinician conducting an examination of a child without benefit of an interview with parents or collateral should be especially observant so that this information can be passed on to a person with specialized knowledge of children. The Examiner should not hesitate to request a second interview with the child if he feels the need.

REFERENCES

Conners, C. K. Minimal brain dysfunction and psychopathology in children. In A. Davids (Ed.), *Child personality and psychopathology* (Vol. 2) New York: John Wiley & Sons, 1975.

Gesell, A., & Amatruda, C. S. *Developmental diagnosis.* New York: Paul B. Hoeber, 1962.

Greenspan, S. I., & Greenspan, N. T. *Clinical interview of the child.* New York: McGraw-Hill, 1981.

Jenkins, R. Psychiatric syndromes in children and their relation to family background. *American Journal of Orthopsychiatry*, 1966, *36*, 450-457.

Katoff, L., & Reuter, J. Review of developmental screening test for infants. *Journal of Clinical Child Psychology*, 1980, *9*, 30-34.

Lewin, K. *Principles of topological psychology.* New York: McGraw-Hill, 1936.

Lobitz, G. K., & Johnson, S. M. Normal versus deviant children: a multimethod comparison. *Journal of Abnormal Child Psychology*, 1975, *3*, 353-374.

Pascal, G. R. The "P" factor. In *Behavioral change in the clinic—A systematic approach* (Chap. 6). New York: Grune & Stratton, 1959.

Ribble, M. A. Infantile experience in relation to personality development. In J. M. Hunt (Ed.), *Personality and the Behavior Disorders* (Chap. 20). New York: Ronald Press, 1944.

Ross, D. M., & Ross, S. A. *Hyperactivity: Research theory and action.* New York: John Wiley & Sons, 1978.

Rutter, M. Diagnosis and definition of childhood autism. *Journal of Autism and Childhood Schizophrenia,* 1978, *8,* 139-161.

11 | Interview of collaterals

It may seem to the mental health worker that the last chapter was primarily concerned with the interview of collaterals. True enough! The diagnostic examination of children has to be integrated with the interview of parents. The examination of adults, on the other hand, can stand alone. In this chapter we shall discuss those cases where interview of collaterals is necessary for an understanding of the adult patients' behaviors.

The first of these cases will be familiar to anyone who has worked in a mental hospital setting. We are referring to those obviously psychotic patients who come to us disoriented and confused or withdrawn and inarticulate. In such cases preliminary diagnosis of the patient is relatively easy but that part of the examination that has to do with an understanding of the patient's behavior becomes difficult and sometimes impossible.

In those cases where data from the patient is incomprehensible, investigation is pursued through collaterals. We question spouse, parents, siblings, close relatives, or whoever can tell us something about the patient's experiential background. Sometimes such an investigation requires that we go outside the clinical setting to the patient's home area. This need is rare, but however rare, I have yet to know of a resident in psychiatry or clinical psychology who has done so. I am reminded of the study (Rosenhan, 1973) in which graduate students and mental health professionals were sent to various mental hospitals pretending to be psychotic. They were admitted, diagnosed, retained, and treated as psychotics! Such a thing could not have happened had there been a careful investigation of the persons' experiential background.

Whether the patient be an inpatient or outpatient, the Examiner should consult collaterals when sufficient data cannot be obtained from the patient to set up a reasonable hypothesis about the patient's disorder. This need is particularly true when dealing with married patients. I remember the case of a young man who said he wanted to check with me before going ahead with his plan to divorce his wife. He wanted to marry his paramour of one year. His wife, he protested, was a fine woman. He could think of no complaints against her. After running him through the diagnostic interview, he came out a passive-aggressive personality. I decided to call his wife. With his permission, I told her that her husband was planning to divorce her. She was shocked! He had given her no indication that he was unhappy in their marriage. In interviewing her I discovered that she took her husband for granted, was very busy with volunteer work and social functions, and often not home to prepare his dinner. When I got them together, he admitted to feeling neglected and to his inability to communicate his feelings to her. She admitted to being careless of his needs. They ended by having a second honeymoon. There was no way I could have neglected the collateral in this case!

Whether or not you interview collaterals depends on the results of your examination of the patient. It depends on the nature of the patient's problem. Thus, if the patient's symptoms are related to intrafamilial stress then interview of collaterals is indicated. On the other hand, if a patient's current difficulties are related to long-standing problems in interpersonal relationships then interview of collaterals may not be indicated. In short-term, behaviorally oriented psychotherapy, where environmental stimuli are to be manipulated, interview of collaterals helps the Examiner to identify such stimuli. A hypochondriacal patient I had will illustrate this point.

The patient was a woman in her mid-40s, married, with two grown children. Her husband was a successful businessman. She had a long psychiatric history including hospitalization with shock treatment and eight years of psychoanalysis. Her symptoms were severe, almost delusionary but not quite. Prior to her analysis she had evidently been psychotic. This woman carried a deep and pervasive sense of guilt. She felt there was something very wrong with her as a person and as a woman. She was unable to function, constantly beset by physical symptoms, and spending most of her time besieging physicians.

She described her husband as a very busy man but one who, nevertheless, provided her with the best of care. I decided to see this long-suffering, paragon of a man. At my expressions of sympathy he shook his head sorrowfully. Yes, his wife suffered a great deal. They had tried everything without any luck. He personally felt fine, slept well, ate well, maybe a little too much smoking and drinking but nothing serious, you understand. What a lily! He was about half the size of his wife. She was a large, big bosomed woman. He was short and slight.

My investigation of this case would make a book in its own right. Suffice it to say that by successive interviews of the husband and wife, I was able to arrive at some notion of the precipitating stress for my patient.

The husband was a veritable leech. In bed he actually spent most of the time in sexual foreplay by suckling at his wife's breast. His wife, in 25 years of marriage, had never had a climax. The husband was impotent. He experienced ejaculation but only partial erection. For this sexual difficulty he blamed his wife, faulting her for not being responsive and telling her she was not much of a woman. When she demurred, he pouted and punished her by hostile silence. This treatment, because of her dynamics, was devastating to her, and she yielded to his demands. And thus the cycle went, year after year—his sexual behavior and criticism of her for being unresponsive, her demurring, his punishment, her distress, and consequent yielding, and then over and over again. Through the years she believed her husband and carried the burden for their difficulties. It was plain to see whose fault it was. After all wasn't she the one who got sick!

My approach was to put the husband into psychotherapy with another therapist. After a few sessions he quit, labeling all therapists quacks. He did not change but she did. It was the first time anyone had implied that there might be something wrong with her husband. Gradually, she was able to become more objective about her husband and was thereby relieved of the tremendous burden of guilt she had been carrying. She learned that her husband was emotionally very dependent on her and essentially afraid of her. She found the courage to put him down when he misbehaved and discovered that he, for awhile, behaved himself. She was relieved of her hypochondriacal symptoms. Was she cured? Not by a long shot! Alleviation of precipitating stress helped with the acute symptoms but did not get rid of the deep feelings of worthlessness rooted in her experiential background. Eight years of analysis could not do that and I could not. She needed regular reassurance that she had a right to be on this Earth like anyone else—and still does. But she functions!

The case exemplifies the need to interview a collateral. The patient's symptoms were acute. The Examiner reasoned there had to be precipitating stress. What this stress was did not emerge from interview of the patient. It was not until the husband was interviewed that the environmental stress came into focus. The first attempt to change the stress evoking stimulus, the husband, failed. The second attempt—to change her perception of her husband succeeded, at least partially, and her acute symptoms were relieved. The point, here, is that when interview of the patient indicates an unrealistic perception of the environment, interview of a collateral is indicated.

A short time ago a 50-year-old woman appeared in my consulting room. She complained of being persecuted by a college professor from whom she had taken a course two years previously. The town in which the professor lived and where she had taken the course was several hundred miles from her present residence. She said this professor had regular contact with her neighbors who were reporting her behavior to him. She had a daughter who was doing well but who was also under the influence of the professor. The patient's husband treated her well, but tended to minimize the influence of the professor. When I asked if she had any doubts that the professor was actually doing what she said he was doing she gave several "proofs" among which was a signal he used to indicate his presence. This signal was the flashing on of the neighbor's porch lights. Other than this persecution by the professor she denied any problems. In talking about the professor she mentioned casually that she had at first been attracted sexually to him. That was during the time two years previously when her husband had had an affair with another woman. Incidentally, she had had a lovely childhood!

Now I was quite sure I was dealing with a paranoid delusion which, from what I could gather, started about two years before. I was not at all sure, however, that I knew enough about the husband as a possible source of stress. When I asked the woman if I could see her husband, she refused me. My problem was could I treat this woman in any systematic way without the information I needed to understand her disorder? I told the woman that I could not help her in any efficient way unless she agreed to let me see her husband. We left it at that. She is to let me know.

What are the ethics of the situation? Should I have attempted to treat the woman? In all fairness to her and myself, I felt I could not. If she calls and still insists on seeing me without giving me permission to see her husband, I shall refer her to a therapist who uses drugs in treatment. Had she been a neurotic, I might have decided otherwise.

The point of this discussion is to bring home to the young Examiners that the diagnostic interview is an active investigatory process; that he should not be easily satisfied; that he should persist to the limits of his capability to obtain the information he needs. The dynamics hypothesized from the early experiential background should "fit" the patient's reaction to the current environment. Adherence to this principle would have helped the Examiners involved in Rosenhan's experiment (1973). Where information is lacking either about the experiential background or the current environment, the Examiner needs to pursue investigation with the help of collaterals.

REFERENCE

Rosenhan, D. L. On being sane in insane places. *Science,* January 1973, *179,* 250-258.

12 | Prognosis

We have studied our patient. We have completed our investigation. What comes next? Are we going to be satisfied with a diagnostic category? I hope not. Our job as diagnosticians is to recommend a course of treatment designed to be of help to a particular patient. In the light of our knowledge of the patient we predict the patient's reaction to the recommended treatment.

It seems to me that it ought to be obvious that diagnosis cannot stand apart from prognosis. Even the official diagnostic categories imply prognosis. Consider the differential prognosis implied by the terms *reactive depression* and *paranoid schizophrenia*. Within the diagnostic categories the prognosis varies from patient to patient. Consider two patients, both carrying the diagnosis paranoid schizophrenia, both having suffered a "nervous breakdown" as a result of excessive stress. They are two different people of differing experiential backgrounds and differing prognoses. But prognosis for what, nondirective therapy, psychoanalysis, behavioral therapy? And which should the therapist be, a male or a female, a quiet accepting person or an active interventionist? What are the goals for the therapy? Answers to these questions need to be in the mind of the Examiner as he completes his investigation and makes his recommendation.

I have often been asked if I recommend one approach to therapy over another. My response has always been that I am eclectic. It seems to me that any diagnostician who is worth his salt has to be eclectic. If diagnoses vary with prognoses and prognoses vary with goals, therapeutic techniques, and therapists, then the diagnostician has to be able to recommend which combination of these would be most helpful to the patient.

The upshot of this problem is that the diagnostician has to be sophisticated in the various approaches to psychotherapy. To help the clinician in this matter I will go over, briefly, what I have previously published in response to the needs of my students relative to psychotherapy (Pascal, 1959). In psychotherapy there are, essentially, three basic approaches: (1) change the environment, (2) change the patient's specific responses to the environment, and (3) change the patient's conception of himself. These approaches I have called Type I, Type II, and Type III, respectively.

Type I is used very often, particularly by people who are not mental health specialists. A disturbed child is placed in a foster home. Adult patients are sent to a hospital, not only because they cannot manage their affairs but to remove them from the stress of their environments. A fragile, emotionally disturbed woman is advised to divorce an abrasive husband. I have no statistics but I would guess that the Type I approach is the one most commonly used to help emotionally disturbed people. Friends and relatives recommend it. Couples contemplating divorce use it on each other. The Type I approach as you have surmised does not change the patient's perception of the environment or the conception of self. It merely removes the patient from the stress of the environment.

The Type II approach, on the other hand, is the one most commonly used by mental health specialists. This approach to psychotherapy includes a broad spectrum of techniques, mostly aimed at symptom alleviation. The variety of techniques available is such that the diagnostician can select one most suitable for the patient (Garfield, 1980; Kanfer & Goldstein, 1980). The diagnostician needs to have intimate knowledge of the various techniques. Thus, an approach that involves persuasion and reasoning in the attempt to elicit responses that can be reinforced requires more of the patient than an approach that only requires that the patient follow directions. To clarify this point, let me give you examples of two patients.

The first patient was a young man in his 20s. His presenting complaint was that he did not have the confidence to approach a girl and ask her for a date. He felt miserable about himself and inferior to other young men who seemed to get dates with ease. He had no other significant problems. He was successful in his work, healthy, had men friends, and had good relations with his mother, father, and sisters. He was the youngest of three siblings; the two older were girls. Yes, there had been sibling rivalry but he could not remember it as being severe. The mother was present and loving. The father was kindly and accepting but traveled, leaving most of his rearing to the mother. He grew up tall and strong, excelled in a minor sport which he continued through college. He hadn't felt any difficulty about girls until recently. Girls had sought him and he hadn't had to worry about them. When he got out of college, got a job, and lived alone the picture changed. Eager girls were no longer around. It was then that he began to be aware of his problem. This young man was put in a mixed group therapy situation. He was seen individually as well. He was persuaded and cajoled not to feel like a small boy responding to images of his sisters and his mother. Little by little, with much reinforcement, he learned he could respond to girls as if they were people. He became their peer and seemed to have no trouble with them thereafter.

The second patient was a woman in her mid-30s, married, a housewife, no children. Although she was panphobic her chief complaint, which brought her in for treatment, was that she was unable to go shopping. Her husband's complaints that he was tired of doing the shopping drove her to seek help. Her history was bad. She'd been a scared rabbit and a loner. She married right after graduation from high school to escape her home situation. Now, she only left the house in company with her husband. I decided to tackle the presenting complaint by using a method I call "crowding the threshold" (Bandura, 1971; Guthrie, 1938). I explained the methodology to her and she accepted. I drove her to a nearby supermarket. Before we got out of the car I told her that if she got the least bit anxious, she was to tell me. I took her by the arm and led her into the market. As we arrived in the center of the store she told me she was feeling nervous. I immediately took her outside. She felt all right. Thereafter, in several trials, she went into the market by herself, always leaving when she began to feel anxious, returning to the therapist who was waiting outside to reassure her. She learned to walk around inside the market without anxiety. Then she began taking cartons off of the shelf and pushing a cart around, always with the same admonishment, that she leave if she felt anxious. Once she got a cart full of groceries up to the cashier's stand and had to leave. To make a fairly short story shorter she learned to go shopping without anxiety. She and her husband were pleased that she could now do the family shopping while he was at work. There's more to her therapy but enough has been said to show the difference between the two cases.

Both patients were treated with Type II therapy. The treatment in both cases was aimed at changing the patient's responses to stress evoking stimuli. In both cases the treatment was designed for specific symptom alleviation. The techniques differed. Why? The answer lies in the experiential backgrounds of the two patients. On the one hand, we have a young man who's history indicated a successful adjustment to his environment. There was a flaw which did not emerge until a particular combination of circumstances elicited it. Also his degree of deviancy from expectancy was not severe. In my decision on the therapeutic approach I was guided by his experiential background and his reaction to current stress. If his history had shown early shyness in social situations and difficulty with girls, I might have decided differently. What the decision would have been, we will discuss in a later section. Let's get back to the comparison of the two cases.

With the female patient we have a very different combination of factors, a history of poor adjustment beginning early in life and a severe reaction to current stress. Implied but not stated explicitly was the fact that she felt unaccepted by both father and mother and was frightened by them. It seemed apparent to me that an approach based primarily on a relationship with the therapist would not work. She was already scared to death of men! Therefore, I decided on an approach involving minimal personal relationship—with much reassurance that it would work if she followed directions. Suggestion? Sure! There is no way the effect of one person on another can be avoided in the dyadic relationship. The point here is that the approach was well structured and only required that the patient follow instructions.

The Type II approach is widely applicable to severe and mild reactions. Which Type II approach depends on the severity of the reaction and experiential background. A general rule might be that the more severe the reaction the more objective the therapeutic approach. This rule can be extended to mean that in very severe reactions the ultimate objectivity, the administration of drugs or other physical treatment, is indicated. Another rule might be that the more the alienation from people, the more the approach should minimize the relationship with the therapist. Whether to use extinction, counterconditioning, hypnosis, psychodrama, group therapy (just to mention a few!) seems to depend on these two rules. Thus a paranoid person might reject hypnosis or any close personal relationship, but be able to tolerate a group therapy situation. You would hardly expect a contentious obsessive to respond to persuasion and response elicitation but he might be able to respond to a behavioral schedule.

However much we try to minimize the relationship between therapist and patient it always seems to be a factor. Lander (1978) reported that the doctor-patient relationship makes a difference even in placebo effects. Those patients whose doctors seemed interested and sympathetic responded better to placebos than did the patients whose doctors were uncaring and aloof.

In prescribing treatment a constant concern for the Examiner has to be with the therapist who will carry out the treatment. Too many treatment plans go awry because not enough attention is paid to the personal characteristics of the therapist. Better a warm, comfortable mental health worker with horse sense than a trained professional who can only be nondirective, or one who talks too much! This matter of therapist-patient has been of concern to researchers (Gomes-Schwartz, Hadley, & Strupp, 1978; Lambert, De Julio, & Stein, 1978) and results have been inconclusive. There are too many confounding variables. I take the simpleminded approach that it is easier for a student (patient) to learn from a teacher he likes than one he doesn't.

Maybe enough has been written about the Type II approaches. They are all aimed at symptom alleviation and that is first-order business! And very often that is all that is required! The Examiner should, however, be aware that Type II approaches are not always effective. Unfortunately, there are many people with long-standing personality disorders who do not respond to Type II therapies. The following case is an example.

The patient was a man in his mid-40s, a successful professional man, the father of two children. He had been urged into treatment by his wife who was also a patient. He exhibited several deviancies that interfered with the marital relationship. He drank too much at parties, so much so that his wife had to drive home. In any disagreement about disciplining the children he always sided with them against his wife. Whenever his wife raised her voice, he would withdraw and be noncommunicative for days. When seen he was a nice looking, affable man, seemingly at ease. He readily admitted to his wife's complaints. He became a willing patient. As you might suspect he had a history of a close relationship with his mother. He avoided his father and was afraid of him. He grew up a docile boy, pleasing to his mother. He was a good student, went to college, was an officer in the service and saw action in Korea. After that he got married, became very busy in his profession. He had two children. He admitted that he had little to do with the children. Occasionally, he felt his wife was too rigid but often did not dare to voice his opinion for fear of her reaction. He had no close male friends. He admitted he only felt at ease at a party after he had had a few drinks. He felt well most of the time, the exceptions being when his wife "got after him." He readily accepted that his problem was that women, especially his wife, were "10 feet tall" for him. He had a good talking relationship with the young therapist to whom he had been assigned. Various behavioral approaches were tried. He was put in mixed group therapy. The patient said all of these helped but after several months there were no changes in his reactions to his wife. He still drank to feel at ease. He was referred to me.

I put him on the couch and kept quiet. The patient's "professional good guy" defenses did not work. He became ill at ease, nervous, and anxious. His fear of his father, his feelings of rejection by his father emerged full blown. He graduallly learned to feel himself an acceptable and worthy male person. His need for acceptance and reassurance by his wife diminished. He reacted to her as if she were a person, not a symbol of mother. He no longer needed alcohol to feel at ease at parties. All these changes took place during more than 200 psychotherapy sessions. It was a Type III approach. It involved the stripping of defenses, the consistent acceptance of the patient, psychologically naked as he was, with all his childish emotions. It was a process that took place over time, time in which the patient learned to change his conception of self. It has been variously called long-term, intensive psychotherapy, psychoanalysis, and has been given other names, but whatever it is called, the essentials of the process are the same. Its purpose is to undermine maladaptive defenses by changing early acquired feelings that underlie these defenses. Ideally, the patient becomes a person who feels acceptable and worthy, a person in whom reality is not obscured by repressed feelings acquired in childhood. The ideal is seldom reached but quite often closely approached, enough so that behavioral change is obvious.

Type III therapy is not for all therapists; nor is it for all patients. Besides special training the therapist needs to have himself emotionally well in hand. This latter usually requires that the therapist experience Type III therapy as a patient. Where a Type II therapy does not work and the diagnostician recommends Type III he has to concern himself with the patient's status. Does the patient have supportive environmental satisfactions? Does the patient have sufficient cognitive control to withstand the stress of Type III, or are his behaviors primarily based on his emotions; that is, does he have impulse control? Sometimes a patient who is beset by environmental stresses has to be treated by a Type II therapy until such time as he is ready for Type III. The Type III approach even when it is indicated is often not feasible. It is too expensive for community-supported mental health clinics and too expensive for most people who seek private practitioners. Before recommending Type III, therefore, the diagnostician has to consider the practical aspects of such a recommendation. The diagnostician will see many patients whom he knows require Type III to do them any lasting good but will, nevertheless, have to recommend a Type II approach for practical reasons.

We have been at some length to give the Examiner a perspective of the tools available for the treatment of emotionally disturbed persons. This perspective is necessary if the Examiner is to make a prognosis. Diagnosis to be meaningful has to include prognosis. Take any diagnostic category such as paranoid schizophrenia. This is one of the most frequent diagnoses for hospitalized patients. I am not downgrading the value of diagnostic categories but merely wish to point out that each person so diagnosed represents a unique individual with a unique prognosis which depends on experiential background, symptoms, method and goals of treatment, and the therapist. Take two patients both hospitalized, both diagnosed paranoid schizophrenia. The first is a businessman, married, had a "nervous breakdown" in which he became delusionary. The second is a single man who suddenly took to sniping at people from a rooftop. The first patient had a history of being a shy person but one in which he had a social life, progressed uneventfully through school, entered business, married, and raised a family. The second had a history of being a withdrawn person, always a little bit "peculiar." He was docile and overconforming, no friends, a loner. He was a high school dropout, a night watchman. Both were attached to mother. In the first, a father was present but had little time for the boy. In the second, a father was absent from an early age. With just that amount of information the prognoses for these two patients differ. Basing our judgment on experiential background and symptoms, we can predict that the first person has a fair to good prognosis for psychotherapy to help him to regain the level of adjustment he had prior to his nervous breakdown. The second a poor prognosis. Why?

In considering the prognosis for a given patient there are some commonsense principles which guide us. Take, for instance, a child who very early in life reacts to its environment by withdrawal. Such a reaction deprives the child of the learning experience necessary for the acquisition of social skills. The earlier the development of the withdrawal reaction the greater the chances that it will lead to irreversible deficit in adulthood. Such an observation makes psychological common sense. In this case, it also is in accord with the findings in a study by Wittman and Steinberg (1944) who found that withdrawal as a defense when acquired early in life was particularly resistant to psychiatric treatment. So it is with all deviancies of behavior, the earlier their manifestation the more resistant to change. Thus, with patients who have a lifelong pattern of relatively minor deviancies of behavior (usually diagnosed as personality disorders) the prognosis for behavioral change is guarded. Type II therapies only produce superficial changes in such patients. Consider, for example, a paranoid personality. His essential problems are an estrangement and distrust of people which interfere with job success. He might be taught more ingratiating social manners and thus become "socially improved" but the essentials of his personality remain, awaiting the right eliciting stimulus situation for behavioral emergence. Whether or not such a person can be helped by Type III therapy depends on whether he ever has had a trusting relationship with anyone. If he did, providing the patient stays in therapy, the therapist can reach that deeply buried complex of emotions and teach the patient to feel himself an acceptable member of the human race. If he did not, then Type III therapy will fail. The only way the Examiner has to predict the outcome is by the history he obtains. Sometimes the history is not clear in that respect. In such a case the Examiner's choice should be a recommendation for a Type II approach with limited goals.

At this point an example is appropriate. The patient is a young woman in her late 20s. She was referred because of obsessive suicidal thoughts and one previous suicidal attempt. She was able to work but outside of her job she kept to her apartment. She was cajoled, persuaded, and rewarded for attempts at socialization. The details are immaterial for the point I am trying to make. Suffice it to say she lost her obsessive thoughts as she began to socialize more. It developed, however, that she only felt "good" when she had a boyfriend. She clung to them, demanding affection. No sex. Consequently, she lost them. Each time she lost one there was a period of depression. She said she didn't trust men, only wanted their attention and affection. Type II attempts to correct this problem failed. It was decided to put her in Type III therapy. The decision was based on her history. Prior to school age she had had a warm and loving relationship with her father. Mother and father were in conflict and the mother objected to the attention lavished on the patient by her father. The father dropped her. From then on her history was marked by superficial compliance and deep hostility toward her mother and avoidance of her father. The male therapist felt he could cut through the patient's defenses and "redo" the early relationship with father. The fair-to-good prognosis attached to the Type III approach in this case was based on this early relationship with the father. It worked and the patient achieved a "normal" relationship with men. Had the early relationship with her father not been there Type III for the male therapist would not have been recommended. How it would have turned out with a female therapist I don't know. The sex of the therapist is a problem that we will consider in a later section.

Early deprivation is always a factor to be considered in the prognosis for psychotherapy. If a child grows up with criticism, rejection, and other forms of psychological abuse from both parents, then it stands to reason that the child will feel alienated from the human race. What happens to the child depends on the defenses acquired. They may be more or less adaptable. Whatever the defenses, the prognosis for Type III therapy is poor when the person as a child has never experienced an accepting relationship with another human being. If the defenses acquired enable the person to adapt to his environment with reasonable success and result in neurotic symptomatology Type II is always feasible. Severely maladaptive behavior throughout life, on the other hand, argues for a poor prognosis for any kind of psychotherapy. Drugs may provide some amelioration of symptoms.

The nature of defenses acquired seems to depend on the nuances of the environment experienced by the child. One child learns it will not be punished if it withdraws. Another learns that its needs can be satisfied with a temper tantrum, and so on. The adaptability of the defenses may be a result of happenstance. It does not seem to be related to native intelligence, except in the extremes. It may be related to an innate factor. This innate factor has to be considered, especially in those cases where the deviant behavior cannot logically be related to experiential data. Behavioral genetics has a long history with a considerable upsurge of publications in recent years (De Fries & Plomin, 1978). I cannot believe ill-defined disorders portrayed in diagnostic categories are inherited. I can believe, however, in the inheritance of a faulty nervous system, some defect in circuitry, which results in a failure to adapt to stress. I discussed this matter years ago (Pascal, 1959). I even gave it a name, "psychophylaxis," the P factor, but neither the name nor the discussion ever caught on. Perhaps it was because of faulty reasoning and perhaps it was that the matter had little impact for the practicing clinician. Yet, every clinician when considering the prognosis for a given case pays attention to the familial background of the patient. A history of maladaption in the patient, his relatives, and his forebears is a consideration that is thrust upon the clinician. When I was a graduate student we called such patients triple Ps (piss poor protoplasm). Their prognosis for psychotherapy was poor then, and is now. Perhaps one reason the genetic factor is not often considered is because in ordinary clinical practice it seems to be of infrequent occurrence. Even if the clinician suspects an inherited tendency toward deviant behavior he has to cope with it. Nevertheless, he needs to be aware of the possibility that he may be dealing with a patient in whom there exists a genetic flaw. It makes a difference in prognosis for psychotherapy.

There are other factors of general application related to prognosis. One of these is the balance between precipitating stress and the patient's reaction.

Severe stress induces severe reaction and minimal stress, minimal reaction. Imbalance between stress and reaction is of prognostic significance. Thus, for a man whose wife and children are killed in an accident, the expected reaction is depression. If he had a reasonable adjustment prior to the accident, the prognosis is good for a return to the previous state of adjustment regardless of the treatment method. On the other hand, an elderly lady who regressed into psychosis after the death of her cat represents an imbalance between stress and reaction. Based on the imbalance above the prognosis for treatment would be poor.

Another factor of general application in prognosis concerns the time element in the deviancy of behavior. This factor is usually referred to as acute versus insidious onset. In acute onset of symptoms the prognosis is that the symptoms will subside and the patient return to a previous state of adjustment. With insidious onset the prognosis is that the symptoms will persist and be resistant to change. These aspects of prognosis, of course, are related to other prognostic indicators. They cannot stand alone and are mentioned here merely in passing.

One aspect of the prognosis for psychotherapy has been of interest to me through the years, the sex of the therapist. Certain considerations in connection with this prognostic factor make good psychological sense. For example, take the case of a 10-year-old girl who looks and acts like a boy. She refuses to wear girls' clothing. She has no mother, has been reared by a loving father. She is brought into the clinic because she is being made fun of by her peers, feels rejected, and has withdrawn from peer activities. Now, it seems clear to me that such a child needs a female therapist to help her achieve self-acceptance as a female. One could argue, psychotherapeutically speaking, that a male therapist could teach the girl to wear girls' clothing and could teach the girl to "get along" with her female peers. I doubt, however, that the male therapist could make the girl feel a full-fledged member of the subspecies female with all the feelings appertaining thereto. In my practice I have had more than one case in which the adult female's presenting problem has been shyness and feeling of being unattractive to men. I have been successful in changing their feelings and behaviors toward men. In those cases, however, in which there was a history of poor relations with mother and a superficial relationship with female peers, I have not succeeded in helping them feel truly comfortable with females. Such female patients seem to derive their feelings of self-worth and acceptability from males. If, for some reason, their relationship with males is shattered they go into a deep depression, at least until another male picks them up. In retrospect it seems to me that there was a time in their therapy when they should have been referred to a female therapist.

With children the sex of the therapist is an even more significant prognostic indicator. We had a case, a girl of 11, who seemed to have a school phobia. We went through our usual behavioral procedures without success. It wasn't until the male therapist, to whom she had been assigned, won her trust that she was able to reveal paranoid delusions about her female teachers and her mother. She still, however, did not return to school. She was transferred to a female therapist. From her she learned to overcome her fears of females and was able to go back to school.

Briefly, just one more case to drive home my point about the sex of the therapist. This case is about a six-year-old boy in the first grade. He was brought in because he was having difficulties with his male peers. He preferred to play with girls. At home he played with dolls. He wanted to dress in little girls' clothing. History revealed that this boy had been cared for since the age of two by his grandmother during the working hours of his parents. Grandmother dressed him like a girl, gave him dolls to play with, and treated him as if he were a girl. Are there any questions about the sex of the therapist for this boy? Lambert et al. (1978) conclude as I do: "At this point, relatively little is known about the variable of gender and implications for psychotherapy process research" (p. 483). In the meantime we do have psychological horse sense.

Here and there, throughout this book I have mentioned the gender of the Examiner or the therapist as a consideration. Research data are meager, inconclusive, and of little practical use. Nevertheless, I am convinced that the sex of the Examiner or therapist has a bearing on the results of the diagnostic interview and on psychotherapy. Several years ago one of my students conducted research that showed a profound effect on data obtained in an interview. This research is reported in Chapter 2 (Baugh, Pascal, & Cottrell, 1970).

The clinician, of course, is not in a position to do much about the sex of the Examiner in the diagnostic interview. He can, however, be aware of the sex of the psychotherapist as a consideration in recommending psychotherapy; that is, if his horse sense is functioning.

Writing about prognosis makes me think of my brother who was functioning as a meteorologist in the Air Force during World War II. In the preflight briefing he would go over all the variables which were affecting the weather. After he got all through with the rather elaborate meteorological report he gave an educated guess. It seems to me that that is where we are in prognosis for psychotherapy. Excepting the extremes, in the absence of research data we are left with an educated guess.

REFERENCES

Bandura, A. Psychotherapy based on modelling principles. In A. E. Bergin & S. L. Garfield (Eds.), *Handbook of psychotherapy and behavior change.* New York: John Wiley & Sons, 1971.

Baugh, J. R., Pascal, G. R., & Cottrell, T. E. The relationship of reported memories of early experiences with parent on interview behavior. *Journal of Consulting and Clinical Psychology*, 1970, *35*, 23-29.

De Fries, J. C., & Plomin, R. Behavioral genetics. *Annual Review of Psychology*, 1978, *29*, 473-515.

Garfield, S. L. *Psychotherapy.* New York: John Wiley & Sons, 1980.

Gomes-Schwartz, B., Hadley, S. W., & Strupp, H. H. Individual psychotherapy and behavior therapy. *Annual Review of Psychology*, 1978, *29*, 435-471.

Guthrie, E. R. *The psychology of human conflict.* New York: Harper & Row, 1938.

Kanfer, F. H., & Goldstein, A. P. (Ed.). *Helping people change.* (2d ed.) New York: Pergamon Press, 1980.

Lambert, M. J., De Julio, S. S., & Stein, D. M. Therapist interpersonal skills: Process, outcome, methodological considerations, and recommendations for future research. *Psychological Bulletin*, 1978, *85*, 467-489.

Lander, L. Why some people seek revenge against doctors. *Psychology Today*, 1978, *88*, 12.

Pascal, G. R. *Behavioral change in the clinic.* New York: Grune & Stratton, 1959.

Wittman, P., & Steinberg, D. Follow-up on objective evaluation of prognosis in dementia praecox and manic-depressive psychoses. *Elgin State Hospital Papers*, 1944, *5*, 216-227.

13 | Summary

The diagnostic interview is an examination conducted systematically, analogous to a physical examination. In the physical all systems are checked; for example, gastrointestinal and nervous. In the interview all areas of functioning are checked also. Just as in the physical, the Examiner looks for deviations from expectancy and, just as in the physical, he looks for the bases of found deviations.

In the diagnostic interview we examine the person who is subjecting himself to our scrutiny. What he has done and what he is manifest themselves in his appearance and his behaviors. These are measured by us on a subjective scale of expectancies and the deviancies noted. This measurement takes place as the verbal part of the interview is conducted. This and this only is all we know first hand. The rest is hearsay.

We begin with the patients' presenting complaints. These, sometimes vague, are pinned down with the behavioral incident technique so that they can be stated in stimulus-response terms. We go on to the cross-sectional study of the patients, their physical health, their "operant" behaviors such as sleeping. We proceed to people and things in the patients' environments and their responses until we have a clear view as to how the patients are functioning in their worlds. Deviancies noted are combined with those observed in direct observation. At this point in the examination we should have enough information to make a tentative diagnosis and to take emergency measures if necessary.

We should have well in mind the patients' deviant behaviors, the dependent variables. From the strictly behavioral treatment point of view we should at this stage in the interview know of independent variables; for example, high places beget an avoidance response, demanding females trigger an anxiety reaction, and so on. In order to understand the patient's deviant "operant" responding and his perception of the environment we have to dig deeper. This "digging deeper" involves getting data about the patient's early environment with the BI technique. Information obtained from the patient or collaterals should give us a good grasp of the patient's experiential background.

I cannot overemphasize the importance of early experiential data. The responses, feelings, attitudes learned early in life are still part of the adult patient, *no matter what we see currently.* Thus, a child who has learned fear of his father will experience fear of threatening males throughout life. The case is no different when a child experiences severe trauma in connection with water. Somehow, people find it easier to accept the adult's fear of water as a result of early trauma than they do fear of threatening males as a result of early trauma. I suppose that is so because a fear of threatening males is so often well concealed by defenses. You say, what difference does it make if the fear is well compensated? I can only say that no defense against such a fear is perfect. The man may become a boxer and yet the fear will be there and partially govern his behavior. I once knew a man, a good combat pilot, who chose the air force over the infantry because of his fear of angry males. In his relationship with his male peers this person was what we call "a professional good guy."

Fear of a father is, of course, just an example of the responses and feelings a child can learn. To get a handle on the feelings we have to "anthropomorphize." We have to say to ourselves, if the child experienced thus and so then the child must have acquired such and such feelings. We have to learn to believe the powerful, lifelong impact of early experiences on later behavior.

Lest you think that the above statement is merely theoretical, let me show you how practical it is by an example. The patient is a 22-year-old young woman, a recent college graduate. She is attractive, verbal, oriented. She lives with her mother, peacefully, no father. She has recently gotten a job. According to her account the job is practically perfect. She works for a kindly man in his 60s. The trouble is that she can't sleep, has nightmares, and feels "nervous" all the time. Now, I had had this girl as a patient previously, while she was still a student. At that time she complained of sleeplessness, nightmares, fear of the dark, fear of being left alone in a house. She was terrified of a younger brother, a rather large, hostile person. In college she only dated boys whom she could manipulate easily. For our purpose the important life history datum was that she had had a father, now dead, who spent most of his life in prison. As a child she had seen him brutalize her mother. Fear of her father was something she remembered very vividly. For practical reasons, distance to travel was one, she was treated with short-term psychotherapy with good result. Satisfied, she terminated herself with the knowledge that her fear of her father was still in her and might arise at some later date to plague her.

In the two years since I had last seen her she had done well in school, had dated regularly, had felt well, and had been pleased with herself. In her present situation she could not see any source of stress and could not understand why she should be emotionally upset. From her early history, I knew that fear of her father and fear of men somehow similar to him was in her. In her environment there was only one man she could not manipulate, her boss. And sure enough it turned out that she spent much of her time on the job appeasing her boss, trying to anticipate his wants. She lived in dread that if she did not he would turn on her in his wrath. Once she understood that she was distorting reality in her perception of her boss she was obviously relieved. She was encouraged to try other ways of responding to him and reinforced when she did. Her symptoms were alleviated and she terminated herself again! Knowledge of the patient's early environment helps the diagnostician to understand how the patient perceives the environment and to what aspect of the environment the patient is responding.

The diagnostic interview as I have suggested in the previous chapters may seem to the student a long and tedious process. I assure you it is not. Most of the time the experienced interviewer can obtain all the data needed to formulate the case in a 50-minute session. The worker needs to keep in mind what information he wants to obtain from the patient and how to get it. What are the problems that led the patient to seek help? How do these problems affect the patient's current behaviors? The transition is easily made to a cross-sectional study. Questions about physical health, eating, sleeping, and so on are not threatening. From these questions the patient is led to speak of important events and people in his life. From a question such as "Are your parents alive?" the transition leads naturally to early life material. All the while, of course, the patient is observed for nonverbal behavior.

To show you how rapidly the diagnostic examination can be conducted, I will try to give you the flavor of a recent examination. The patient was a man in his late 20s, slightly above medium height, brown hair, brown eyes, hair neatly brushed back from his forehead. He was meticulously dressed in sport coat and matching trousers, white shirt, a subdued necktie. His voice was of medium pitch. His words were well articulated. When he spoke he looked directly at me. His hands had a tendency to flutter. There was diffidence in his manner. His speech was logical. From the intake sheet filled out by the receptionist I saw that he was an architect, married, no children.

He complained that he couldn't sleep. He was nervous all the time. He felt "just miserable." When I asked if he were so miserable he wanted to die, he said no, no, it wasn't that; it was his wife. He wanted to divorce her. When I asked what the trouble was, I got a long list of complaints. His wife liked sex. He didn't. He did it just to please her and he couldn't do it any longer. She was "messy." Every morning he had to clean up her bathroom. He kept the home tidy. He did all the cooking, because he liked to cook. No, she did not wash the dishes because he couldn't trust her to do it properly. They had tried that but he found he had to go into the kitchen after she finished because she was not neat. He couldn't stand it any longer. They had been married four years.

When I asked about his wife, he said she was a beautiful girl—a lovely person. I discovered she worked part-time as a salesperson. Each evening when he came home, she would be either reading or watching TV. She did not complain. She was glad to go out with him. She was happy to be there and just do whatever he wanted. Through BIs I got the picture of a passive and compliant young lady, content in her role as wife. She had no idea he was unhappy in their life together. He could not tell her. He felt guilty.

He loved his work, was well paid. Although he worked for an architectural firm, he was relatively autonomous. He liked working with people. He said he had many friends, both male and female. Through BIs I judged he had no close friends, no one with whom he could speak freely. He was in good health. His last visit to a physician was several months ago when he had the flu. He slept poorly, had trouble going to sleep. He could remember no dreams. Occasionally, he got a headache, from stress he supposed. He could not stand any medication, not even aspirin.

He was an only child. His father died several years ago. His mother was alive and lived in a nearby town. His contacts with her were infrequent and casual. He could not remember any early experiences with his mother or father because he spent the early years with his grandmother. When he spoke of her his face lit up. Until the grandmother died during his last year in high school, his life was spent with her.

During second grade, his folks took him back to live with them, but every day after school he went to his grandmother's house and stayed there until bedtime. He spent the weekends with her. He went on vacations with her. When he was old enough to drive, he was her chauffeur. He remembered how much he admired his grandmother and how much he wanted to be like her. His father tried to take him hunting and fishing. He hated it and couldn't wait to get home to his grandmother. He could remember no peer relationships. He only felt comfortable with his grandmother.

In the seventh grade he tried suicide by cutting his wrist. The occasion was in connection with a physical education requirement, one in which he had to dress in gym clothes. He could not stand the thought of having to undress before the other boys. At that time his grandmother was in the hospital. He felt alone and desperate, to the point of wanting to die. He was excused from physical training from then on.

During his college career he had two homosexual experiences. Both were forced upon him, both widely separated in time. He was threatened and afraid to resist the advances of men he had thought were his friends. He said it was disgusting to him and felt he could never be a homosexual. After college he married a girl he had known in high school because they had been friends and because it was expected of him. He had never liked being married.

He wanted to live alone and not have a wife to take care of. He said he felt so nervous that if something weren't done very soon he would lose control. There was no one he could talk to. His mother would only try to persuade him to stay married. He didn't want to hurt his wife. He looked at me intently, leaned forward, poised as if ready to jump. I leaned toward him, told him to get back into his chair, close his eyes, and take a deep breath. He did. I told him I would try to help him.

Admittedly, this was an easy patient from whom to get data. He talked a steady stream. If I had any problem with him, it was to divert him from one area to another. For instance, he kept coming back to his grandmother over and over again long after I had sufficient information about her. At those times I would simply interrupt him by asking about his father or his mother or whatever area I was pursuing at the time. I had only 50 minutes for the interview. In that time I wanted a well-rounded picture of current behavior and experiential background, at least enough information to make a working diagnosis for immediate guidance. Before the session was over I decided he was an obsessive-compulsive neurotic. He was definitely identified with his grandmother. He was not an overt homosexual but the dynamics were all there. He was not dangerous to others, but potentially dangerous to himself. I told him I would see him and his wife together and explain his problem to her. This offer seemed to relieve him. I then took him to an adjoining room and had him lie down and listen to a hypnoidal relaxation tape.

A few days later I saw him and his wife together. She wept but was not surprised. She accepted separation and seemed to understand that her husband was the type who would be the charming, perennial bachelor. Thereafter, I saw the patient a few more times. He lived alone, had an active social life. In his environment there was a young man to whom he could be "grandmother." Also, he had a number of older ladies who were grandmothers to him. He seemed to be getting along quite well. I put him on a monthly basis. I felt that for some time he would need approval from a man that it was all right to be what he was. I did not consider Type III therapy. There was no relationship with a man in his history that would give me a purchase to form the relationship required for the Type III approach. He would form such a relationship with a female therapist, but that would only drive him deeper into femininity. I therefore decided to leave him with his present adjustment, one in which his neurotic needs were satisfied. He was, of course, completely dependent on his environment for his emotional needs. There would be times when these needs were frustrated but he could now easily seek professional help at those times.

The book is finished. It occurs to me that the reader will take from it what he needs to become his own diagnostician. I only hope I have conveyed a systematic approach to the diagnostic interview, one that yields identifiable dependent variables and manipulable independent variables.

Appendix I

The deprivation scale as it was used in the Veterans Administration Studies

SCORE _____   DATE _____

                                  EXAMINER _____

NAME _____ AGE _____ EDUC. _____ RACE _____

ADDRESS _____ PHONE _____

OCCUPATION _____ MARITAL STATUS _____ CHILDREN _____

SUBJECT'S STATUS (State whether patient or non-patient; if patient, state whether in-patient or out-patient; if in-patient, state where hospitalized; if out-patient, give name of patient's physician. In all cases, if patient, give diagnosis and indicate intractability.)

_____

_____

INDICATION FOR SURGERY (obstruction, hemorrhage, etc.) _____

DURATION OF ILLNESS (Give approximate dates) _____

CURRENT TREATMENT _____

108

APPRAISAL OF PHYSICAL WELL-BEING (In each item below rate poor, fair or good and note essential findings.)

Ingestion. Give a rating of poor if the subject reports poor appetite, lack of enjoyment of food or drink, frequent regurgitation, etc.

Sleep. Give a rating of poor if the subject sleeps less than six hours on the average or reports frequent nightmares, restless sleep, etc.

Elimination. Give a rating of poor if the patient reports difficulty with elimination.

Motility. Give a rating of poor if the subject suffers a marked diminution of gross bodily movements for a person of his age.

OVERALL JUDGMENT OF PHYSICAL WELL-BEING (Circle one.) Poor Fair Good.

TO THE EXAMINER: The scale is to be used in conjunction with an interview of the subject concerning his status *prior* to hospitalization. The Examiner's task is to obtain sufficient information from the patient to rate with confidence. In each case, *specific instances of behavior* should be obtained as a basis for judgment. Do not confuse the subject's opinion with your rating of his actual behavior.

The scale is two-point, forced-choice, the subject being judged either poor or good on each item. If the judgment is poor, the score is one (1). If the judgment is good, the score is zero (0). Write in either a zero (0) or one (1). Enter the total score on the face sheet in the space provided.

DO NOT USE THIS SCALE BEFORE READING THE MANUAL

_____ 1. *Employment.* Give a rating of poor (1) if the subject is unemployed or employed less than half time.

_____ 2. *Income.* Give a rating of poor (1) if the subject's annual income is less than $2500.

_____ 3. *Debts.* Give a rating of poor (1) if the subject complains of a number of debts which he is unable to meet.

_____ 4. *Job participation.* Give a rating of poor (1) if the subject shows little interest in his job other than as a means of earning a living, etc. If the subject is completely unemployed, give a rating of poor (1).

_____ 5. *Job status.* Give a rating of poor (1) if the subject feels his position is lowly in relation to his peers, and/or feels unnecessary on his job. Do not confuse this item with Job Participation. If the subject is completely unemployed, give a rating of poor (1).

_____ 6. *Status—Other.* Give a rating of poor (1) if the subject has no status outside of church, job and organizations.

_____ 7. *Education.* Give a rating of poor (1) if the subject has less than an eighth-grade education.

_____ 8. *Residence.* Give a rating of poor (1) if the subject has no pride in his house, grounds, or neighborhood; if he feels he is living "on the wrong side of the tracks" relative to his peers, etc.

_____ 9. *Church.* Give a rating of poor (1) if the subject attends church (or Sunday School) less than once a month.

_____ 10. *Other organizations.* Give a rating of poor (1) if the subject does not belong to any clubs, church groups, or other organizations.

_____ 11. *Friends.* Give a rating of poor (1) if the subject is essentially an isolate, if he has no intimate friends outside his family; if he has no one outside his family who he feels is concerned about him, etc.

_____ 12. *Relatives.* Give a rating of poor (1) if the subject expresses a strong negative relationship with his relatives, other than immediate family.

_____ 13. *Parents.* Give a rating of poor (1) if the subject's relationship with mother and/or father (or parental surrogates) is such as to imply a lack of affection and interest on his or her part. Give a rating of poor (1) if both parents are dead.

_____ 14. *Wife.* Give a rating of poor (1) if the wife behaves in such a manner to imply a general disinterest and lack of affection for the subject. Give a rating of poor (1) if the subject is adult, unmarried or divorced or separated, and gives no evidence of a satisfying relationship with a contemporary female.

_____ 15. *Children.* Give a rating of poor (1) if the subject expresses little interest in his children. If there are no children score the item poor (1).

_____ 16. *Fear.* Give a rating of poor (1) if the subject expresses anxiety about his job, apprehension about himself and his capacity to meet the demands of his environment.

Displays of affection from mother in early life of patient. Insofar as possible rate on the basis of remembered incidents of mother's behavior toward the patient. *Consult the Manual for a description of this variable.*

Circle one:

3—Behavior within normal expectancy limits.

2—Intermediate.

1—Behavior markedly deviant.

ND—Unable to obtain sufficient data to rate.

Appendix II

An adaptation of the deprivation scale

ADJUSTMENT INTERVIEW GUIDE

NO. _____   DATE _____

INTERVIEWED _____

NAME _____ AGE _____ SEX _____ RACE _____ RELIGION _____

ADDRESS _____ EDUCATION _____ VOCATION _____

MARITAL STATUS _____ NO. SIBS _____ NO. CHILDREN _____

FATHER LIVING? _____ DATE DIED _____

MOTHER LIVING? _____ DATE DIED _____

(To the interviewer: Ask for behavioral incidents whenever feasible. Check below during interview.)

SCALE A—MENTAL STATUS
_____ 1. Appearance: Height, weight, physical defects, dress, etc.
_____ 2. Motor behavior: Mannerisms, tics, speed of movement, eye contact, gait.
_____ 3. Verbal behavior: Stammers, intelligible, loud, appropriate.
_____ 4. Verbal content: Logical, confused, evasive, confabulatory.
_____ 5. Reactive behavior: Cooperative, suspicious, cautious, appropriate.

_____ 6. Alertness: Follows topic, preoccupied, perseverates.

_____ 7. Somatic concern: Preoccupied with health, realistic, delusionary.

SCALE B—OPERANT BEHAVIOR

_____ 1. Illnesses and accidents: Visits to physician, dentist, how often, why, accidents at home, in car, menses in women, difficulties.

_____ 2. Sleeping: Hours, dreams, sleeping aids, pajamas, conditions.

_____ 3. Eating: Typical foods, aversions, aftereffects, aids, smoking.

_____ 4. Drinking: Milk, coffee, soft drinks, alcohol, amounts, time.

_____ 5. Eliminations: How often, conditions, difficulties, aids.

_____ 6. Cleanliness: Bath, shower, how often, hands, face, teeth, food.

_____ 7. Motility: Physical activities, sports, exercises, leisure activities.

SCALE C—ENVIRONMENTAL SATISFACTIONS

_____ 1. Vocational training: Job, salary, percent time worked, promotions, superiors, another job, etc.

_____ 2. Avocational: Leisure activities, hobbies, solitary activities.

_____ 3. Religious: Church attendance, participation.

_____ 4. Other organizations: Clubs, service groups, participation.

_____ 5. Residence: Own home, cost, neighborhood, grounds, maintenance, same for room or apartment.

_____ 6. Friends: Other than family, contacts, closeness, number.

_____ 7. Relatives: Sibs, grandparents, cousins, etc., contacts, closeness, communication.

_____ 8. Parents: Condition of parents, frequency of contact, dependability.

_____ 9. Spouse: Contacts, quarrels, activities together, providing behavior, if no spouse, then spouse surrogate.

_____ 10. Children: Interaction with, discipline, pleasing behaviors.

_____ 11. Apprehensions: Debts, future plans, confidence in self.

We shall first consider Scale A, Mental Status Examination.

1. Appearance. The subject's appearance should be described, his height and weight obtained. It should be noted whether or not he is obese. Grossly noticeable physical defects such as limb missing, eye missing, deaf, or blind should be described. Thus, noticeable effects of a previous illness such as polio should be noted. Also, in this section a person's dress should be noted. Is the subject's dress appropriate for a person of his status? Does the subject look clean? Consideration should be given to the circumstances of the first contact. If a housewife is in the midst of cleaning, then the appropriateness of her dress hinges upon this fact. This description of the subject is based solely on appearances and should not be confused with manners and motor movement which will be discussed below. Insofar as possible, the interviewer should describe the person's appearance objectively.

2. Motor behavior. We are looking for unusual mannerisms and posturing. Does the subject have a tic? Does he go through some sort of ritualistic posturing? Does he constantly pat the floor or swing his leg? Does he bite his nails? Does he pick his nose constantly? Does he constantly look away from the interviewer? Are the subject's movements extremely slow? Is there a pronounced tremor? Do not give an opinion of the subject's behavior, but rather, describe it objectively.

3. Verbal behavior. This rubric is somewhat similar to the one above but focuses on verbal behavior. Does the subject stammer or lisp? Is the subject's speech intelligible? Does he speak very loudly or very softly? Is his flow of speech very fast or very slow? Is the subject's intonation appropriate for the words he is saying? Does he, for instance, tell you about something serious, such as his mother's death in a matter-of-fact voice? Is the speech flat or dull regardless of what he is saying? Is the voice raised or used in a manner that is inappropriate to what the subject is saying? There is a whole gamut of behavior to be noted. The subject's voice can be flat or monotonous. It can be loud or soft. It can vary in loudness and pitch. All of these verbal behaviors can either be appropriate or inappropriate to what is being said. They also can be consistent one way or another regardless of what the subject is saying. The interviewer should note these aspects of verbal behavior and report them as accurately as possible.

4. Verbal content. This category has to do with *what* the subject says. Particularly, it has to do with the logicalness of what he says. Do his thoughts progress reasonably from one topic to another? An extreme example of what we mean is often given by people with a manic-depressive psychosis, which is called word salad. There is no relation between one thought and the other. Another example is one displayed by schizophrenics from which "tangential thinking" is inferred. In this type of verbal content non sequiturs occur within the sentences. Here is an example: "In regard to your inquiry we can make a test item of wood for your department although there seems to be a barrage of delays and evasions based on the tax situation." This sentence was written by a hospitalized schizophrenic who was making a simple box for the addressee. It is the kind of speech where you have to do a double take to realize that the sentence doesn't hang together. Verbal content can be confused, unusual and odd. It can be fanciful. It can be confabulatory. It can be meager.

5. Reactive behavior. In this category we are interested in the subject's responses to the interviewer. Is the subject cooperative? Is it appropriate? Some subjects will respond aggressively. This aggressiveness may be warranted by the interviewer's behavior but, hopefully, with a kindly and accepting interviewer, it will be unwarranted. Aggressive behavior toward a person who has done you no harm is inappropriate. The subject may be responding to the interviewer as if he were someone else, perhaps a symbol of someone else. This sort of behavior implies that the subject cannot discriminate between the interviewer and the symbol that the interviewer may represent. This inability to discriminate between people is very often a characteristic of a disturbed individual. Is the subject unduly suspicious of the interviewer? Does the person question the interviewer's motives? Does the subject imply that the interviewer has some personal gain which will be derived from the interview? Is the subject overly cautious about giving even simple kinds of personal information? Ordinarily, we would expect that a person who agrees to the interview will be courteous, cooperative, and fairly frank with the interviewer. The interviewer, for this category, describes the subject's reactions to him as a person and with particular reference to the different parts of the interview.

6. Alertness. In this section we are interested in the flexibility of the subject as the interview proceeds. Does the subject respond to changes in the questions of the interview? Does he follow the interviewer from topic to topic? Does the subject, instead, permeate the interview with statements of guilt which crop up and interfere with the flow of the interview? Is he continually depressed so that despondent statements interfere with the interview? We would expect the subject to follow the interview with a reasonable amount of alertness to changes in topics. If, however, the subject perseverates so that it is difficult to get him off a topic, this behavior should be reported. Report if the subject is preoccupied. Is the subject "with you" or does he seem removed and distant so that he has to be brought back to the interview?

7. Somatic concern. This category is related to one in Scale B, "Illnesses and Accidents," but differs from it in that we are interested here in the subject's concern with health. When some subjects are given the opportunity to talk about their health, they will go on and on, seemingly preoccupied with it. They will relate, in minute detail, every little ache and pain that they have had. The subject's account of his health may have little relation to the actual number of visits to a physician or number of diagnosed illnesses or described accidents. We are interested in the degree to which physical health is felt to be a problem by the subject, whether the complaints have a real basis or not. In its extreme this concern can become a somatic delusion. The degree of somatic concern is to be described in terms of the number of words devoted to it, whether or not it is realistic, and how difficult it is to get the subject off the topic.

Now let us consider Scale B, Operant Behavior.

In this section we are interested in the subject's personal habits as they are reported to the interviewer. Insofar as possible, obtain factual data of behavior, not opinions. It is important, here, that the interviewer obtain behavioral data about what happens from day to day. Enough information should be obtained to satisfy the interviewer that the data are representative of the subject's daily behavior.

1. Illnesses and accidents. This category is distinguished from "Somatic Concern" in that we are interested in the actual number of visits to a physician or dentist. We want to know the number of accidents of all sorts the subject has had over the past couple of years. When was the last time the subject visited a physician or dentist in the past two years? Has the person seen a psychotherapist? Has he been hospitalized and what for? What accidents around the house, on the street, or in an automobile has the subject had over the past two years? Describe these accidents and their effects.

2. Sleeping behavior. How many hours did the subject sleep last night? The night before? Get a good estimate of the number of hours the subject sleeps per night. Does he take naps and when? Does he wake up feeling rested? Does he dream, have nightmares? Does he use a sleeping aid? Does he sleep alone? Where? Does he wear pajamas; sleep in the nude? Does the subject have any peculiarities about going to bed such as the need to read himself to sleep; have music on? For instance, does the subject always have to have a bowel movement before going to bed?

3. Eating. Obtain enough information in order to determine whether or not the subject has peculiarities in eating behavior such as, aversions for particular types of food. Ask what the subject ate for breakfast, lunch, and dinner. Does the subject eat between meals, what and when? Find out the aftereffects of eating. Is the subject nauseated, and so on? Is it necessary for the subject to take antacids such as Alka-Seltzer? Where does the subject eat meals? Under what conditions and with whom? In this section also find out about the smoking habits of the subject. How much does the subject smoke and what?

4. Drinking. Obtain information about all liquid intake such as milk, coffee, soft drinks, and alcohol. Get enough information so that the data will be representative of week-to-week behavior. Pay particular attention to alcoholic intake. What does the subject drink, how much, and under what conditions? What are the aftereffects of drinking? Has any time been lost from work? If the subject is a regular consumer of alcoholic beverages, obtain enough information to determine whether or not the subject is a problem drinker or an alcoholic. The following items will help us in making this decision.

Amount consumed per week.

Variety of alcohol: for example, beer, wine, whiskey.

Rate of drinking in any given session: for example, drinks per hour.

Time between drinking periods, every day, once a week, and so on.

Behavior changes with drinking such as excessive talking, increased sexual behavior, avoidance.

Conditions of drinking—does the subject drink alone, in company, before breakfast, only at parties, and so on?

Aftereffects of drinking—does the subject pass out, get amnesia, nauseated?

Long-range consequences of drinking—has the subject ever been arrested, hospitalized, lost a job, and so on?

5. Elimination. How often does the subject urinate, defecate? Does the subject have trouble with elimination? Are there any peculiarities about his stool such as being dark, fluid? Diarrhea? Constipation? What are the conditions under which the subject defecates and when? For instance, does the subject read while defecating? Can he only defecate at home? Does he have hemorrhoids?

6. Cleanliness. How often does the subject bathe or shower? At what times of the day? How often does he wash his hands and face? Under what conditions? How often does he brush his teeth? How does the subject feel about his living quarters? Does it bother the subject if the room in which he lives is "messed up?" Does he worry about whether or not what he eats is clean? For instance, when the subject eats at a restaurant does he always wipe off the knife, fork, and spoon with a napkin?

7. Motility. In this section information is obtained about the activity level of the subject. Does the subject exercise in any other way than what is required in his vocation? Does he engage in any form of sports? When he is not working, does the subject just sit? Does he work in the garden? Is the housewife concerned about her exercise? Is the subject a moving person or a sedentary one? In this section we want information about the gross motor activity of the subject, as reported. Thus, a 25-year-old young man who spends all of his leisure away from his job as a bank clerk sitting, might indicate an important deviancy. Contrariwise, a person who spends all of his time in constant motor activity might also be considered deviant. A certain amount of gross motor activity is normal for a healthy individual. The amount required depends on the status of the individual and his vocation.

Lastly, let us consider Scale C, Environmental Satisfactions.

In this section we are entirely dependent on the subject's report of his behavior. The information to be obtained can sometimes arouse emotional reaction in the subject. The subjects are prone to have attitudes and opinions about their friends, relatives, spouses, and other people in their environment. We are interested in the reported behavior which characterizes the interaction between the subject and other people. The precautions mentioned previously about the nature of the interview are particularly pertinent here.

1. Vocational satisfaction. What we are looking for is information about the subject's vocation which will contribute to a judgment about the emotional support the subject receives from a job. What is the subject's job? What hours does he work? What percent of the time has the subject worked during the past year? What has been his income over the past year? Who is the subject's superior? When was the last time he had contact with his superior? What happened? Obtain further accounts of the interaction between the subject and superior. Who are his peers? What do they do? Has he had contact with them recently? What happened? Does the job the subject have require training? How does the subject's education compare with the education of his peers? Is the subject training for advancement in his job? Does he work beyond the number of hours required? Would the subject leave his present job for a different job at the same rate of pay? Does the subject see a future for himself in this job? Is the job merely a means of making a living or is the subject emotionally involved in it? The data to be obtained from a housewife will, of course, differ from data obtained from the head of the family. Nevertheless, data must be obtained from the housewife which can form the basis for a judgment as to whether or not her role is emotionally satisfying to her. Does she, for instance, prepare all of the meals? How much time does she devote to her housework? How much time does she devote to decorating the interior of the house? What aspirations does she have for the house? Are there any children? What does the subject do for them and with them? How many activities does she have that would take her away from her housework? Does she have a job away from home? Is it satisfying to her? Does it interfere with her duties as a housewife? Is it necessary? If the subject could afford a full-time maid what duties would she delegate to the maid and what would she retain for herself?

If the interviewee is a student, the data gathering proceeds in the manner indicated above. The interviewer should obtain data about grades reported by the student, extracurricular activities, aspirations for the future, and so on.

2. Avocational satisfactions. The purpose of this category is to obtain information from the subject about what he does with his leisure. Does the subject have a hobby? What is it and how much time is spent with it? We are interested in such things as does the subject take pride in repairing the lawn mower or other mechanical things around the house? Does the subject help the neighbors with their mechanical problems? Is there something he does beside his job in which he takes interest and in which he has pride? Is the subject a sportsman? Is he an avid baseball or football fan? Is he pursuing a course of study for cultural purposes? Does he have within himself resources so that solitary behavior is emotionally satisfying? Does the subject read? What? Does he spend a good bit of time watching television? Find out what the subject does in his spare time from day to day and on weekends. Obtain enough data so that it will be representative.

3. Religious activities. Does the subject attend church? Where? How often? Does he participate in church activities? Has he within the past two years talked to a minister about any problem? If so, what was it? Does the subject read the Bible daily? Does he say Grace at mealtimes?

4. Other organizations. Does the subject belong to any community clubs, civic organizations, lodges, and so on? How often has the subject attended meetings during the past year? Is he on any committee or does he hold office? How much time is devoted to these activities? What does he do?

5. Residence. Where does the subject live? Does he own his own home? Does he rent? Describe the house in which he lives? How many people live in it? When was it last painted? Is the house comparable with other houses in the neighborhood? What is its value? What is the mortgage? What are the payments? What about the grounds? Are they well cared for? How much time is spent in caring for the grounds? If the subject lives in a rented house or apartment, what is its condition? How does it compare with others in the neighborhood? What is the rent? Does the subject aspire to move from the house or apartment to something better?

6. Friends. Does the subject have contact with people other than immediate family and relatives? When was the last time the subject called on someone not a relative, or was called on? What happened? What activities does the subject engage in with other people outside the family? Who are these people? What do they do together? How often do they engage in an activity together? Is there any particular person or persons outside the family with whom the subject spends a considerable amount of time? Does the subject have a person with whom he can frankly discuss personal problems? Does the subject know people from whom he can borrow money in case of need?

7. Relatives. This category has to do with brothers, sisters, in-laws, and other close relatives. This excludes spouse, children, and parents. Does the subject have brothers and sisters? Where do they live? How far away is it? When did the subject last see any of them? What happened? How frequently does the subject see them? On what occasions? Does the subject feel free to call on close relatives in case of need? Has subject ever called on them for assistance of any sort? What happened? Is there communication between the subject and relatives on birthdays and holidays? How often do they write or telephone?

8. Parents. Are the subject's parents alive? If not, when did they die? If they are alive, when was the last time the subject saw his parents? What happened? How did they greet each other after an absence, verbal greeting, handshake, hug? How often are parents seen? What is the frequency of communication? Are parents financially dependent? Have parents loaned the subject money? What happened the last time the subject was ill? Did parents call or telephone? What activities are engaged in with parents? How frequently?

9. Spouse. Is the subject married? Have him or her describe the spouse. What happens when the subject leaves for work? How often do they display affection toward each other? What happened the last time one of them was ill in terms of supportive behavior? Do they sleep in the same bed? What activities do they engage in together? When was the last time they quarreled? What was it about? Obtain other incidents of quarrelsome behavior. Do they have mutual friends whom they see together? Do they have friends in for dinner or go out to dinner with friends? Are they concerned about each others' well-being? Would the subject like to be unmarried if it were feasible? How much time does the spouse spend at home? What do husband and wife talk about?

10. Children. If the subject has children, how many, what sex and age? What do they do? Obtain incidents of interaction between subject and his children? How often are the children disciplined? On what occasions? When was the last time the subject did something with the children? What was it? How often does the subject engage in activities with the children? What are they? If the subject has children who live away from home how often do they visit? What happened? How do the children greet him on first contact? What are the displays of affection between the parents and children? What have the children done that displeases the parents? What have they done that pleases them?

11. Apprehensions. What are the subject's debts? Is he paying on them? What are the subject's plans for the future? Does he express confidence in his ability to meet environmental demands now and in the future? Does the subject have family problems that seem unsolvable? What are the subject's solution to problems now, and those that he anticipates in the future?

Appendix III

Suggestions for further study

Axline, V. M. *Play therapy.* New York: Ballantine Books, Inc., 1969. A good book to get the flavor of what goes on in the playroom.

Christie, M. J., & Mellett, P. (Eds.). *Foundations of psychosomatics.* New York: John Wiley & Sons, 1981. Thorough, solid coverage of the area.

Freud, S. *A general introduction to psychoanalysis* (J. Riviere, trans.). New York: Doubleday, 1938. This important work is available in a pocket-book edition. It needs to be read to appreciate its value to the interviewer.

Greenspan, S. I. & Greenspan, N. T. *Clinical interview of the child.* New York: McGraw-Hill, 1981. A good place to start for the diagnostic interview of children.

Harper, R. G., Wiens, A. N., & Matarazzo, J. D. *Nonverbal communication.* New York: John Wiley & Sons, 1978. Covers research in the area but also has a practical section for the interviewer.

MacKinnon, R. A., & Michels, R. *The psychiatric interview in clinical practice.* Philadelphia: W. B. Saunders, 1971. A more advanced work which considers the interview of people in various diagnostic categories.

Piaget, J. *The child's conception of the world* (1926). (J. Tomlinson & A. Tomlinson, trans.). New York: Humanities Press, 1960. An important work to get a grasp of the child's thinking. Necessary if you're going to work with children.

Powell, B. J. *A layman's guide to mental health problems and treatments.* Springfield, Ill.: Charles C Thomas, 1981. A good place to begin for an overview of the mental health area.

Pryser, P. W. *The psychological examination.* New York: International Universities Press, 1979. An academic book which carefully covers the areas about which interview data are needed for a diagnosis.

Reik, T. *Listening with the third ear.* New York: Arena Books, 1972. This is a pocketbook edition. The book was first published in 1948. A delightful text which is most helpful.

Robins, L. N., Helzer, J. E., Croughan, J. R., & Ratcliff, K. S. National Institute of Mental Health diagnostic interview schedule: Its history, characteristics and validity. *Archives of General Psychiatry*, 1981, *38*, 381-389. This article is especially slanted so that so-called lay interviewers can make a diagnosis according to DSM III criteria.

Author index